Technical English

Vocabulary and Grammar

Nick Brieger

Alison Pohl

Summertown
Publishing

**Technical English
Vocabulary and Grammar**

ISBN: 1902741765

Published by:
Summertown Publishing Limited, 29 Grove Street, Summertown,
Oxford, OX2 7JT. England.
Tel: 00 44 (0) 1865 454130, Fax: 00 44 (0) 1865 454131
Email: info@summertown.co.uk
www.summertown.co.uk

Editor: Yvonne de Henseler
Authors: Nick Brieger – Alison Pohl

Page design and setting: Oxford Designers and Illustrators

Cover design: Richard Morris, Stonesfield Design
© Summertown Publishing Limited 2002

Acknowledgements

The authors would like to thank Steve Flinders of York Associates and
Yvonne de Henseler for their comments and advice.

Nick Brieger is a partner at York Associates which produces innovative
materials for and delivers training in the areas of specialist language,
communications skills and intercultural communication. For more
information, contact: www.york-associates.co.uk

The publisher would like to thank and acknowledge the following
sources for diagrams, copyright material and trademarks reproduced
on the following pages:

Constructware ®: 34 (graphic courtesy of Constructware ®, © 2002,
all rights reserved); Clifford F. Grimes of www.accel-team.com: 6
(Conceptual Productivity Model – The Productivity Tree); HLCC: 64
(registered as trade marks in most European countries, owned by
GINETEX); Malcolm Hubbert of www.calibre.co.nz: 54; Chris Madden
of Chris Madden Cartoons: 10; Ohio State University Extension: 22;
Pauleys of www.pauleys.co.uk: 56 (Training Department); The
Commonwealth Department of Health and Ageing: 30 (Australia's
Pharmaceutical Benefits Scheme).

Although every effort has been made to trace and contact copyright
holders before publication, this has not been possible in some cases. We
apologise for any apparent infringement of copyright and if notified,
the publisher will be pleased to rectify any errors or omissions at the
earliest opportunity.

Illustrations by Oxford Designers & Illustrators.

Contents

Introduction

What is *Technical English: Vocabulary and Grammar* **and who is it for?**
Technical English: Vocabulary and Grammar will help you increase your knowledge of technical English and develop your vocabulary and grammar. By working through the materials you will become more accurate and more appropriate in a range of key technical contexts. You can use it on your own (self-access) or in class (as part of a course).

What is in *Technical English: Vocabulary and Grammar?*
There are 50 topic areas divided into vocabulary (30) and grammar (20):

- 1–9 Vocabulary: Professional activities
- 10–30 Vocabulary: Company profiles
- 31–50 Grammar uses

In addition to the topic areas there is:
- an answer key
- a grammar glossary explaining key grammatical terms
- a vocabulary glossary of 1500 vocabulary items, based around the technical themes covered in the topics 1–30. **A multilingual glossary is available on our website at www.summertown.co.uk**

Each topic consists of input on the left-hand page, and exercises and tasks on the right-hand page. The left-hand page presents language through:
A sample sentences to show the language forms in use
B an explanation and extension of the language forms
C examples and descriptions of the uses of these forms

The right-hand page presents exercises and tasks to:
1 familiarize you with the language forms
2 provide a controlled task to check that you can apply the language
3 help you practise using the language in a practical context

Using the material

The book may be used either in class or for self-study. For classroom use, teachers should choose topic areas to supplement the language areas covered by the English course book being followed, either to consolidate the presentation of language forms or to provide additional exercises. For self-study use, students should choose topics according to their own interests or to problems they or their teachers have identified. For both teachers and students, the contents at the front of the book and the detailed index at the end will help to locate appropriate units.

Having chosen a topic area, we recommend you work through the language presentation on the left-hand page:
A read through the sample sentences and note the use of the language forms
B study the language forms presented
C study the use of these forms
The glossary will help you to understand any words and phrases that you don't know.

Next you can move on to the practice exercises and tasks on the right-hand page. Before you start an exercise:

- make sure you clearly understand the task
- look at any examples that have been given
- refer back to the language forms and uses on the left-hand page, if necessary

After you have finished an exercise:

- check your answer with the key at the back of the book
- if your answers to an exercise are wrong, look again at the left-hand page. If you are not sure, then ask your teacher.

An introduction to the topic, with examples of the vocabulary or grammar in context

Unit number

The words in **bold** are defined in the glossary

The first exercise aims to familiarize you with the language forms

The second exercise provides a controlled task to check that you can apply the language

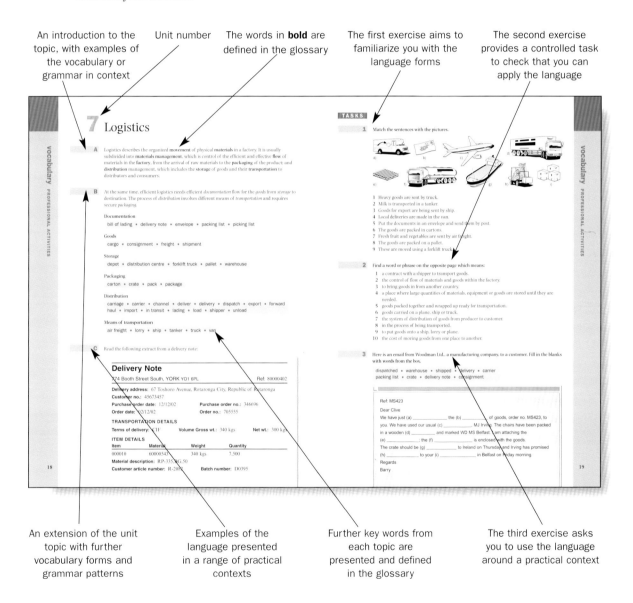

An extension of the unit topic with further vocabulary forms and grammar patterns

Examples of the language presented in a range of practical contexts

Further key words from each topic are presented and defined in the glossary

The third exercise asks you to use the language around a practical context

1 Production 1

A

Production management is concerned with **planning** and **controlling** industrial **processes** which **produce** and **distribute** products and services. Techniques of production management are also used in service industries; here they are called **operations** management. During production processes, **inputs** are **converted** into **outputs**. These processes take many forms: from basic agriculture to large-scale **manufacturing**. Much manufacturing takes place in **factories**, where **assembly lines** allow a steady **flow** of **raw materials** (inputs) and **finished products** (outputs).

People in production focus on **efficiency** and **effectiveness** of processes in order to maximize **productivity**. To achieve overall success, it is important to **measure**, **analyse** and **evaluate** these processes. However, other activities also contribute to success: **purchasing**, **inventory** control, **quality** control, **storage**, **logistics**.

B

Production varies according to the inputs, *processes* and outputs. Other important factors are the *place* of production and the *resources*. In addition, *stock*, a major cost, needs to be carefully controlled, and the equipment must be regularly *maintained* to remain productive and prevent breakdowns.

Production place

factory • layout • plant • site • unit • workshop

Process

assemble • batch • component • convert • effectiveness efficiency • line • lot • maximize • optimize

Resources

equipment • fixtures • machinery • materials handling • raw materials

Stock

inventory • stock • store

Maintenance

breakdown • failure • fault • maintain • repair

C

Study the *Productivity Conceptual Model* below:

A simple way of looking at productivity in a business organization is to think of it in terms of the productivity model. The *Productivity Conceptual Model* below takes the form of a 'productivity tree'. The roots denote the inputs to the system, the trunk the conversion process and the leaves and fruit the system outputs.

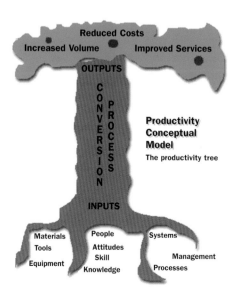

Productivity
Conceptual
Model
The productivity tree

1 Match the words that go together and then complete the sentences below.

quality	material
finished	manager
industrial	lines
production	process
large-scale	levels
assembly	control
raw	products
productivity	manufacturing

1 Improved _____ _____ has led to higher efficiency in production.

2 The manufacture of paper is an _____ _____.

3 Crude oil is the basic _____ _____ for the plastics industry.

4 Increased _____ _____ have reduced the number of manufacturing workers.

5 The large warehouse is used to store _____ _____ waiting for delivery.

6 Large car manufacturers use _____ _____ in production.

7 The company began in a single room but has now developed into _____ _____.

8 The manufacturing process is the responsibility of the _____ _____.

2 Complete the sentences below. The first letter of the missing word has been given.

1 A quantity of goods prepared at the same time is known as a b_ _ _ _.

2 To put parts together to produce the final product is to a _ _ _ _ _ _ _.

3 Production processes convert inputs to o _ _ _ _ _ _.

4 The process of buying inputs is known as p _ _ _ _ _ _ _ _ _.

5 A part which is used in the final product is called a c _ _ _ _ _ _ _ _.

6 To get the best possible level of production is to o _ _ _ _ _ _ _.

3 Here is part of a memo from a company director to the production manager. Complete it with words from the box.

faulty • equipment • repair • site • workshops • factory • stock
breakdowns • layout • maintain • fixtures • machinery

MEMO

From Robert George   **To** Sarah Bridge   **Re** Premises

We are making good progress with the new (a) _____ development. A new (b) _____ close to the river has been acquired. Designers are currently working on the (c) _____ of the area and exact location of the factory building. All (d) _____ and fittings will be carried out by Alan Shores Ltd. The new manufacturing (e) _____ has been ordered and we hope to be able to install it ahead of schedule. New (f) _____ will be purchased for the engineering (g) _____ once they have been completed.

The present machinery is old and several (h) _____ recently have caused production backlogs. We will continue to (i) _____ and (j) _____ these machines until the new ones are up and running.
I would ask you to carry out a full (k) _____ inventory as soon as possible. Any (l) _____ goods should be removed from store and disposed of.

2 Production 2

A A production planning system is essential to ensure that a company's processes, **machinery**, equipment, labour skills and **material** are organized efficiently for better profitability. There are many factors that need to be considered in the planning system. For example, a firm may require a large number of different **components**. Also **demand** can vary daily in this ever-changing world. New sales orders come in. Some get cancelled; there may be **breakdowns** in the **workshop**; **backlogs** build up; there may be late or early **delivery** from suppliers. It is difficult to keep track of all these changes manually. To handle these situations, many companies keep safety **stock**. However, if a company has an effective production planning system there is no need to keep high safety stock. The money blocked in the excessive safety stock can be released. At the same time, opportunity costs due to **stock-outs** can be minimized.

B All areas of management require careful *planning* and *organizing*. Planning and organizing production is essential for efficient operations.

Planning

> aggregate • backlog • back order • bottleneck • capacity • cycle • downtime
> flow • forecast • idle • lead time • make-to-order • make-to-stock
> optimization • output • productivity • prototype • requirement • run • satisfy
> schedule • sequence • set up • set-up time • slack • throughput • uncertainty
> update • work in progress

Work organization

> lot • overtime • shift • workforce • workload

C Study the *Market Needs Analysis Model* below:

There are two principal aims of the *Market Needs Analysis Model* opposite:

- to identify market needs for your product
- to analyse the market potential for new products or services

The product performance specifications detail the operational features of the product.

At the product design stage, designers and product managers will redefine how the product is to work and how it is to be made.

At the production system specifications stage, we focus on the manufacturing requirements.

Investment decision methods focus on the alternative methods for financing the investment needed.

The objective of production system design is to standardize both the methods of production system design and the machine units for production system construction.

A production cost model calculates production costs and capacity factors.

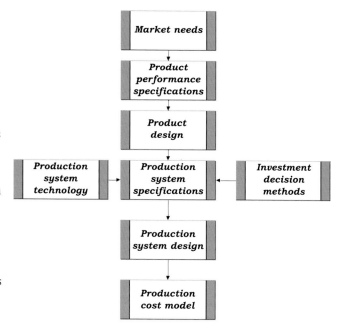

TASKS

1 **Choose the correct answer in the following.**

1 Recent faults with machines have cost the company a great deal of _____.
   a) maintenance   b) slack time   c) downtime
2 Once the mock-up of the new design has been tested, we can build the _____.
   a) prototype   b) update   c) set up
3 It's unprofitable to manufacture small quantities because of the machine _____.
   a) lead time   b) set-up time   c) sequence
4 The production manager has to produce a production _____ for the next four weeks.
   a) set up   b) schedule   c) output
5 Once the order has been agreed and production begun, the designer is still responsible for the _____.
   a) work in progress   b) workload   c) back order
6 These items are produced together as one _____.
   a) cycle   b) delivery   c) lot

2 **Match the correct word with each definition.**

workload   the movement of materials through a production system

workforce   an order from an earlier time which hasn't been produced yet

back order   the volume of goods which are produced

material flow   something that is needed for a particular process

throughput   the series of activities following one another to produce a product

output   the amount of work that has to be done

cycle   the volume of goods that can be dealt with in a certain period of time

requirement   all the people who work in a particular company

3 **The works manager is showing a group around the factory. The letters of the missing words are mixed up. Complete the dialogue with the missing words.**

We're not particularly busy at the moment. Believe it or not, the (a) _____ (manedd) for furniture is seasonal.

So, do you (b) _____ (kaem-ot-osckt)?

Well, all our units are made- (c) _____ (ot-reord). However, we make components-to-stock.

When are your busy times?

Normally from September to May but there is always a great deal of (d) _____ (cerunintyta) and it's difficult to (e) _____ (recatfos) sales trends.

So does the (f) _____ (adel mite) vary?

No, not really. Our (g) _____ (adel mite) is usually 8 to 10 weeks. When we are very busy, the workforce usually do (h) _____ (mitevero) to try to avoid a (i) _____ (lockbag) of orders. If necessary we introduce a (j) _____ (fisht) system when we're working at full capacity to avoid (k) _____ (beckslotten) at key machines.

During a busy period do you have (l) _____ (toskc-tous)?

Seldom. We use the time when work is (m) _____ (lacks) to build up stock of components. We don't like machines or workers to be (n) _____ (lide)!

3 Research and development 1

A

Research and development (R and D) is the **search** for new and **improved** products and industrial processes. Both industrial firms and governments **carry out** R and D. **Innovations** in products or processes normally follow a path from **laboratory** (lab) idea, through **pilot** or **prototype** production and manufacturing start-up, to full-scale production and market introduction. There are two main types of research. **Pure** or **basic research** aims to clarify **scientific** principles without a specific end product in view; **applied research** uses the **findings** of pure research in order to achieve a particular commercial objective. **Development** describes the improvement of a product or process by **scientists** in conjunction with **engineers**. Industry spends vast sums to **develop** new products and the means to produce them cheaply, efficiently, and safely.

B

Research is important in many disciplines and there are different *types of research* with different *research professionals*. The type of research reflects the environment and the objectives. In addition, many research words have entered the general language.

Types of research

academic research • applied research • clinical research
development and evaluation research • experimental development • experimentation
innovation   practical application • product development • pure basic research
pure research   strategic basic research

Research professionals

analyst • engineer • lab technician • research assistant • scientist • technician

General terms

breakthrough • carry out • feasible • feasibility • me-too product
patent • file* a patent • pipeline • pilot • prototype • register* a patent
technical know-how (TKH)

file/register a patent

C

Notice the stress in the word families below often changes:

verb	noun (process)	noun (person)	adjective
'analyse	an'alysis	'analyst	ana'lytical
'innovate	inno'vation	'innovator	inn'ovative
de'velop	de'velopment	de'veloper	develop'mental
ex'periment	experimen'tation	ex'perimenter	experi'mental
in'vent	in'vention	in'ventor	in'ventive

'What a breakthrough – we've bred the first germ we can attack with everyday household objects!'

1   Match the term with the correct definition.

applied research	the study of pure scientific principles
clinical research	the study of the parts and their relationship to one another
pilot study	changing and improving a product to achieve the best possible result
experimentation	looking at how scientific theory can be used in practice
pure basic research	looking at the effects of drugs or treatment on patients
product development	a new technique or idea
innovation	the process of tests and trials to see what happens under different conditions
analysis	small-scale experiment

2   Use the word in brackets to form a word which fits in the sentence.

1   The scientists have presented a detailed _____ of the results. (analyse)

2   They have brought in a food _____ to help in the research. (analyse)

3   All process materials are tested using highly developed _____ techniques. (analyse)

4   The researchers have come up with an _____ idea for the use of recycled plastics. (innovate)

5   Charles Dyson is the _____ of a vacuum cleaner which works on a new principle. (invent)

6   The advent of the ballpoint pen was a wonderful _____ . (invent)

7   They employ a large team of software _____. (develop)

8   A report has been prepared on the _____ tests that have been carried out. (develop)

9   Increasing numbers of people can now work from home thanks to _____ in telecommunications. (develop)

10   These methods of production are still at an _____ stage. (experiment)

11   The _____ is continuing work on the new drug. (experiment)

12   Many people are against animal _____. (experiment)

3   The following email has been received by the R and D department. Complete it using words from the list.

breakthrough • prototype • developmental • engineers
design • patent • innovative • experiment

Dear Frank

I had a preliminary meeting with Maria Altefors regarding her (a) _____ for a new children's pushchair. It's a simple but (b) _____ invention which will allow two children of different ages to be transported in a single unit. She has already registered a (c) _____ and I'd like us to develop a (d) _____. Could you arrange a meeting with the (e) _____ to discuss this? We will have to carry out (f) _____ tests to assess safety features and (g) _____ with different weight loads.

This could be a real (h) _____ in pushchair design!

Regards

Ruth

4 Research and development 2

A If you want to get **feedback** on a product or service, you can use **qualitative research**. Qualitative **research** uses open-ended **interviewing** to **explore** and **understand** the attitudes, opinions, feelings and behaviour of individuals or a group of individuals. Qualitative research has many common uses, including:

- **investigating** current product/service/brand positioning
- **identifying** strengths and weaknesses
- **exploring** alternative communication messages
- understanding why customers buy and use a product or service
- **evaluating** the impact of advertising or public relations campaigns

B Research is based around a wide range of *activities* – from detailed analysis to product improvement. Results from research activities need to be scientifically *measured* and then *reported*.

Research activities

analyse • assess • compile • determine • develop • discover • evaluate experiment • explore • find • identify • improve • innovate • investigate modify • record • search for • study • survey • test • trial

Measuring the results

constant • correlation • deviation • distribution • frequency • mean measurement scale • median • mode • norm • random • reliability sampling • standard • statistics • validity • variable • variance

Reporting the results

feedback • report • response

C The following words can be used as both nouns and verbs:

study • test • trial • experiment

We plan to conduct a *study* of consumer attitudes.
We are going to *study* consumer attitudes.
We intend to *test* the reactions to our new advertising campaign.
We will carry out the *tests* in order to get feedback on our advertising campaigns.
The *trials* produced some very interesting results.
We aim to *trial* our new products over the coming months.
We have evaluated the reliability of the *experiments*.
It is important to *experiment* with new processes.

Notice the following verb and noun patterns

Form	noun ending	Noun
compile	-ation	compilation
standardize		standardization
evaluate		evaluation
identify	-ication	identification
modify		modification
assess	-ment	assessment
develop		development
improve		improvement

12

TASKS

1 Choose the correct word from the box to complete the following.

> distribution • random • scale • sampling • statistics
> mean • frequency • median • mode

The collecting, classifying and analysing of information shown in numbers is known as (a) _____.

The middle value of a set of numbers is known as the (b) _____.

The average value is also known as the (c) _____.

The value which occurs most often is the (d) _____.

1,480 ball bearings were measured as part of quality control. The results are shown in a histogram. The histogram shows frequency (e) _____. The figures are based on a (f) _____ of 2,000 ball bearings. They were chosen at (g) _____ ; in no particular order, time or pattern. The measurement (h) _____ is in millimetres. The (i) _____ of 14.96mm is two.

Answer the following questions from the graph below.

The median is (j) _____. The mode of distribution is (k) _____. The mean is (l) _____.

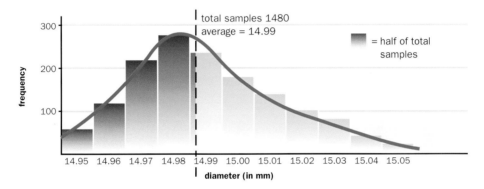

2 Complete the following sentences with an appropriate verb from *Research Activities* on the page opposite. You will have to put the verb in the correct form.

1 They _____ a report on future energy requirements.

2 The temperature was measured every hour and carefully _____.

3 Following the accident, fire experts have to _____ the cause of the fire.

4 These clothes have not worn well so we will have to try and _____ the quality.

5 Scientists continue to _____ for a cure for cancer.

6 They are trying to _____ a solution to the problem of friction.

3 Put the following sentences in the correct order to describe the steps in the process of developing a new drug.

a After hospital specialists have evaluated the drug, information gathered from clinical trials is analysed.

b Data is subsequently sent to the Committee on Safety of Medicines.

c Then an application is made to the government for a clinical licence.

d Tests are then carried out on volunteers.

e They are monitored closely for any other unwanted effects which were not identified earlier.

f A decision is made by the committee and a licence issued before the new product is introduced.

g Any side effects or toxicity are identified at this early stage.

h First of all, a new substance is tested in the laboratories.

5 Information technology 1

A

Information systems **collect**, **organize**, **store**, **process**, **retrieve** and **display** information in different formats (text, video, and voice). Information technology allows very fast, automated manipulation of **digital** data and their transformation from and to **analogue**.

Two basic technologies have been responsible for the development of the necessary **hardware**: **integrated circuits** and **digital communications**. Parallel advances have been made in **software**, particularly easy-to-use software products to **create**, **maintain**, **manipulate**, and **query files** and **records**. Many of these **software programs** are designed for use both by computer professionals and enthusiastic amateurs. Another important factor is the development of **computer networks** (➽ 6).

B

As technology develops, new *models* and *types* of computer appear. At the heart of all computers is the *hardware*. However, without *software*, computers are just dumb boxes, unable to perform any calculations or operations.

Models and types of computer

desktop • laptop • mainframe • notebook • server • terminal • workstation

Computer hardware

CPU (central processing unit) • dot matrix printer • expansion card • inkjet printer
keyboard • laser printer • monitor • mouse • RAM (random access memory)
scanner • screen • storage devices

Software

applet • application software • browser • database software • email software
graphics software • operating system • search engine • spreadsheet
word processing

C

Many words in the field of IT come from American English. So you may see the following spellings:

British English	American English
programme	program
analogue	analog

The area of IT is developing very quickly; and the language to describe hardware, software and applications is also evolving at a high speed. As a result new noun + noun combinations often change to single nouns

noun + noun	single noun
lap top	laptop
note book	notebook
work station	workstation
desk top	desktop

TASKS

1 Label the diagram.

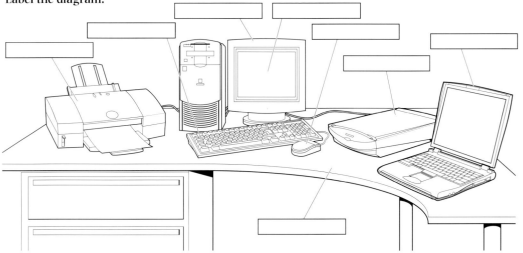

2 Combine one word from A and one word from B and match it with the appropriate definition in C.

A	B	C
create	products	a monitor will do this on a computer screen
central	information	this describes the format of 0 and 1 in which information is stored
software	processing unit	these enable a computer to perform word processing, to create databases, and to manipulate numerical data
display	card	when two or more components are combined and then incorporated into a single package
digital	files	to make new programs, utilities or documents
expansion	network	a group of electronic machines connected by cables or other means which can exchange information and share equipment (such as printers and disk drives)
integrated	data	the principal microchip that the computer is built around
computer	circuits	you plug this into a slot to add features such as video, sound, modem and networking

3 Complete each gap in the following text with a phrase from the table above.

1 The computer monitor will _____ _____ so you can see it on screen.

2 Information is stored on a computer as _____ _____.

3 Spreadsheet and graphic software are examples of _____ _____.

4 Digital communications and _____ _____ have allowed developments in hardware to be made.

5 In order to organise data you should _____ _____ where you can store data.

6 When several computers are linked together you have a _____ _____.

7 The part of the computer which interprets and carries out instructions is the _____ _____.

8 An _____ _____ can be inserted in your computer to give your computer extra capabilities.

6 Information technology 2

A A **network** includes:
- – **techniques**
- – **physical connections**
- – computer programs

used to **link** two or more computers.
Network users can:
- – **share files**, printers and other resources
- – send **electronic messages**
- – **run** programs on other computers

Each network operates according to a set of computer programs called network **protocols** for computers to talk to one another. Computer networks can now be **interconnected** efficiently through **gateways**. The biggest network is the **World Wide Web**. It consists of a large number of smaller interconnected networks called **internets**. These internets may **connect** tens, hundreds, or thousands of computers. They can share information with each other, such as **databases** of information. The internet allows people all over the world to **communicate** with each other effectively and inexpensively.

B Before a network can operate, it needs physical *connections* so that signals can be transmitted. After the network has been connected, it is ready for *operation*.

Network connections

> bandwidth • baud • bits per second (bps) • optical fibre • packet
> receive • signal • transmit • transmission speed • twisted pair

Network operation

> configure • download • hack • hub • install • internet service provider (ISP)
> local area network (LAN) • switch • transmit • upload • web page • website
> wide area network (WAN) • wireless

C A prefix comes at the beginning of a word and usually has a specific meaning, for example inter = between.

Look at the following prefixes and their use in the above IT words/phrases:

prefix	meaning of prefix	example of use
inter-	between	internet, interconnect, interactive, international
intra-	within	intranet, e.g. company intranet
trans-	across	transmit, transfer, transaction
co-/com-/con-	with	combine, compatible, connect, configure
up-	up (to internet)	upload
down-	down (from internet)	download, downtime, i.e. when the network is down (not working)

1 Choose the correct word in each of the following.

1 The speed with which a modem can process data is measured in _____.
   a) bandwidth   **b)** bits per second (bps)   **c)** signal
2 Cables consisting of several copper wires each with a shield are known as _____ cables.
   a) twisted pair   **b)** optical fibre   **c)** power cables
3 Computers that are connected together within one building form a _____.
   a) WAN   **b)** ISP   **c)** LAN
4 If you transfer a file from a remote computer to your computer, you _____.
   a) download   **b)** upload   **c)** run
5 To send out information is to _____.
   a) signal   **b)** packet   **c)** transmit
6 A document containing information and graphics that can be accessed on the internet is
   _____.
   a) a website   **b)** a web page   **c)** the World Wide Web

2 Complete the words in the following sentences by adding the prefix *inter-, intra-, trans-, com-, con-, up-* or *down-*.

1 Last month computer _____time cost the company over €10,000 in lost production.
2 The computers in the production department have now been successfully _____connected with those in the planning department.
3 Once you have completed payment details the data will be _____mitted via a secure link.
4 We cannot network these computers because the systems are not _____patible.
5 Many companies distribute internal documents on their own _____net.
6 Once the home page has been completed, we'll be ready to _____load the site.
7 Cables are being laid throughout the building as the network requires physical _____nections.
8 Using the network he was able to _____bine the data from different reports.

3 Here is a list of instructions for someone wanting to set up a small network. Put the instructions in the correct order.

a Make wiring and layout plans for your network.
b Hook up the network cables by connecting everything to the hub.
c Check that each computer has an IP address and give it a name.
d If you're installing a small network, twisted pair will be adequate. However, in order to span greater distances and to minimize magnetic and electrical interference use fibre optic cable.
e Decide on the type of network you want to install. To enable you to transfer large amounts of data, choose Fast Ethernet (100BaseT).
f Install network adapters in the computers.
g Add an internet gateway to your network to set up a shared internet connection.
h Install driver software for the adapter driver and install client software to share printers and files.
i Check which protocols are installed and add any other protocols you require.
j Get the hardware you need: an Ethernet adapter card for each computer that doesn't have an Ethernet port, a hub if you've got more than two computers, cables and wall jacks.

7 Logistics

A Logistics describes the organized **movement** of physical **materials** in a factory. It is usually subdivided into **materials management**, which is control of the efficient and effective **flow** of materials in the **factory**, from the arrival of raw materials to the **packaging** of the product; and **distribution** management, which includes the **storage** of goods and their **transportation** to distributors and consumers.

B At the same time, efficient logistics needs efficient *documentation* flow for the *goods* from *storage* to destination. The process of *distribution* involves different means of *transportation* and requires secure *packaging*.

Documentation

bill of lading • delivery note • envelope • packing list • picking list

Goods

cargo • consignment • freight • shipment

Storage

depot • distribution centre • forklift truck • pallet • warehouse

Packaging

carton • crate • pack • package

Distribution

carriage • carrier • channel • deliver • delivery • dispatch • export • forward haul • import • in transit • lading • load • shipper • unload

Means of transportation

air freight • lorry • ship • tanker • truck • van

C Read the following extract from a delivery note:

Delivery Note

774 Booth Street South, YORK YO1 6PL   Ref: 80000402

Delivery address: 67 Toshoro Avenue, Rotaronga City, Republic of Rotaronga
Customer no.: 45673457
Purchase order date: 12/12/02   **Purchase order no.:** 346696
Order date: 02/12/02   **Order no.:** 705555

TRANSPORTATION DETAILS
Terms of delivery: CIF   **Volume Gross wt.:** 340 kgs   **Net wt.:** 300 kgs

ITEM DETAILS

Item	Material	Weight	Quantity
000010	60000543	340 kgs	7,500

Material description: RP-335,BG,50
Customer article number: R-2082   **Batch number:** D0395

TASKS

1 Match the sentences with the pictures.

a)   b)   c)   d)

e)   f)   g)   h)   i)

1 Heavy goods are sent by truck.
2 Milk is transported in a tanker.
3 Goods for export are being sent by ship.
4 Local deliveries are made in the van.
5 Put the documents in an envelope and send them by post.
6 The goods are packed in cartons.
7 Fresh fruit and vegetables are sent by air freight.
8 The goods are packed on a pallet.
9 These are moved using a forklift truck.

2 Find a word or phrase on the opposite page which means:

1 a contract with a shipper to transport goods.
2 the control of flow of materials and goods within the factory.
3 to bring goods in from another country.
4 a place where large quantities of materials, equipment or goods are stored until they are needed.
5 goods packed together and wrapped up ready for transportation.
6 goods carried on a plane, ship or truck.
7 the system of distribution of goods from producer to customer.
8 in the process of being transported.
9 to put goods onto a ship, lorry or plane.
10 the cost of moving goods from one place to another.

3 Here is an email from Woodman Ltd., a manufacturing company, to a customer. Fill in the blanks with words from the box.

dispatched • warehouse • shipped • delivery • carrier
packing list • crate • delivery note • consignment

Ref: MS423

Dear Clive

We have just (a) _____ the (b) _____ of goods, order no. MS423, to

you. We have used our usual (c) _____, MJ Irving. The chairs have been packed

in a wooden (d) _____ and marked WD MS Belfast. I am attaching the

(e) _____; the (f) _____ is enclosed with the goods.

The crate should be (g) _____ to Ireland on Thursday and Irving has promised

(h) _____ to your (i) _____ in Belfast on Friday morning.

Regards

Barry

8 Quality

A Quality means **meeting** the minimum set of **requirements** in a product's **specification** and then being **delighted** that the customer's **expectations** have been met and **exceeded**. Therefore, the goal of a business should be to find out **customer needs** and then fine tune the **process** to ensure that they are met.

Quality **improvement** concepts have developed over several decades. They began simply as a method for **detecting defective** products by **inspection** at the end of the production line. In recent years the emphasis has changed from inspection to **prevention**. Today **sampling** methods **monitor** processes and keep them under control. The ultimate aim, of course, is **zero defects**.

B In recent years different approaches to quality improvement have been developed. The overall aim is to prevent *defects* through:

continuous process improvement
customer focus

Defect prevention

> error • failure • inspect • prevent
> process control • repair • rework • scrap

Continuous process improvement

> add value • analysis • cause/effect analysis • check • commitment
> control • define • facilitate • monitor • prioritize
> inventory control • system failure analysis • variability

Customer focus

> accurate • comply with • needs • rectify

C Below are three examples of useful quality summary charts:

A **Pareto chart** is a type of bar chart typically used to improve quality, process capability, or to conserve materials and energy.

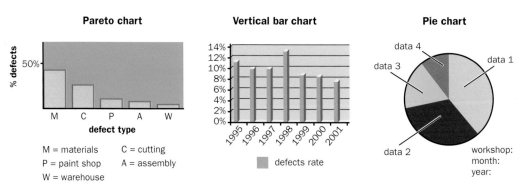

Pareto chart

% defects
50%

M C P A W
defect type

M = materials   C = cutting
P = paint shop   A = assembly
W = warehouse

Vertical bar chart

14%
12%
10%
8%
6%
4%
2%
0%

1995 1996 1997 1998 1999 2000 2001

☐ defects rate

Pie chart

data 4
data 3
data 1
data 2

workshop:
month:
year:

A **bar graph** uses either horizontal or vertical bars to show comparisons among categories.

A **pie chart** helps you to visualize the relative importance of several categories of a variable.

TASKS

1 Choose the correct word in the following sentences.

1 We must **check/control** the temperature regularly to make sure it doesn't rise.
2 To compare the number of defects over the last ten years, it would be best to use a **Pareto/bar** chart.
3 We try to **detect/define** faulty products before they are sent to our customers.
4 But it's a better idea to **protect/prevent** faulty products in the first place.
5 Making sure that materials are stored correctly is part of **process/inventory** control.
6 We're sending our engineer who will **repair/remake** the faulty motor.
7 We have had problems with the electronic equipment due to power **errors/failures**.
8 This process is very inefficient because of the volume of **scrap/error** left over.
9 Here is a list of things we could do to improve quality, and now we must **define/prioritize** them.
10 Improving the design quality of these cars will add **value/variability**.

2 Choose the correct ending from B to complete each of the following sentences in A and then produce a short article about Japanese cars.

A	B
Let us consider what happened when Japanese cars	as often as British or American cars.
Local manufacturers thought they were cheap	which exceeded their expectations.
But soon people noticed that they didn't break down	they provided value for money.
At the same time, Japanese manufacturers started trying to	were first imported into the UK and America.
Customers were delighted with the new cars	and of low quality.
The cars did more than simply satisfy customers' requirements,	meet customer needs in terms of style and design.

3 Here is a memo from the head of quality control to the managing director. Complete it with words from the box.

improvement • sampling • defects • zero • prevent • analysis • monitor
continuous • cause/effect • defective • Pareto

MEMO

From Sue Braun   **To** Alois Vicent   **Re** Quality control

As you know we recently carried out a (a) _____ analysis of the bottle manufacturing plant. Our aim was quality (b) _____ and to reduce the number of (c) _____ products. As you can see from the attached (d) _____ chart, raw materials and system failures are the areas we must improve on.

We will introduce new systems to change our (e) _____ methods and (f) _____ raw materials more carefully. We carried out a system failure (g) _____ and we are now repairing the moulding machine. This will (h) _____ future failures and reduce (i) _____. With (j) _____ process improvement, our aim is (k) _____ defects.

9 Health and safety

A The average person finds it difficult to assess **risks**. For this reason, work practices need to be **regulated**. Examples of **dangerous** activities are:

- welding or grinding without **goggles**
- working on a construction site work without a **hard hat**
- working in **noisy** factories, cabs, on airport tarmacs and with outdoor machinery without ear **protection**
- working in chemical areas without **protective** clothing
- **smoking** near hazardous **substances**

Without regulation some employees will take risks.
Health and safety is a part of employment (labour) law. It covers general matters such as:

- **occupational health**
- **accident** prevention regulations
- special regulations for hazardous occupations such as mining and building
- provisions for risks such as **poisons**, **dangerous machinery**, **dust**, **noise**, **vibration**, and **radiation**
- the full range of dangers arising from modern industrial processes, for example the widespread use of chemicals

B The key concerns for health and safety are to assess the *risks and hazards* by identifying and quantifying the *effects* so that appropriate *protective measures* can be taken.

Risks and hazards

> combustion • contamination • drains • dust • explosion
> flammable • friction • fumes • fumigation • gas
> harmful • shock • spraying • toxic • vapour

Effects

> adverse effects • birth defect • burn • cancer • dizziness
> drowsiness • genetic damage • impair fertility • irreversible effect • vomiting

Protective measures

> avoid contact with • dispose of • dry • handle • keep
> precautionary • protect • recycle • rinse • seal
> tightly • wash • well-ventilated

C The following health and safety notices show some protective measures that can be taken:

Hat
Goggles
Protective clothing
Gloves
Boots

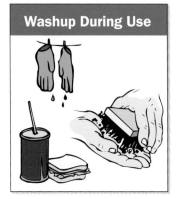

Washup During Use

Washup After Use

1 Choose the correct word in each sentence.

1 Store containers in a **well-ventilated/good-ventilated** place

2 Wipe up any spillages immediately and **wash/rinse** with soapy water.

3 Process cooling water can be **returned/recycled**.

4 This chemical is **toxic/intoxicating** if swallowed.

5 Leftover chemicals should be **disproved/disposed** of safely.

6 Please wear protective gloves when **fingering/handling** this material.

7 Remember that asbestos fibres can cause **cancer/coma**.

8 Pregnant women should not take this medicine as it may cause birth **defects/effects**.

9 Increased levels of radiation may lead to **compared/impaired** fertility.

10 Do not empty chemical paint products into the **drains/grains**.

11 **Protect/Avoid** contact with skin and eyes.

12 Do not use with other products as it may release dangerous **fumes/fumigation**.

2 Complete the following sentences with a form of the word in brackets.

1 When working in this area, please wear _____ clothing (protect).

2 Don't pour used chemicals into the drains as they will cause _____
(contaminate).

3 Heating this liquid may cause an _____ (explode).

4 These chemicals must be kept in a locked cupboard because they are _____ (harm).

5 While they repair the roof, we will close this department as a _____ measure
(precaution).

6 _____ health is one part of Health and Safety (occupation).

7 Working in a noisy factory without ear protectors is a _____ activity (danger).

8 Petrol and oil are _____ chemicals (flame).

9 Make sure the containers are closed _____ (tight).

10 Make sure you are wearing breathing equipment before starting _____ (fume).

3 The manager in charge of health and safety is explaining things to some new employees.
Complete what he says by filling the blanks with the correct word from the box.

noise • protection • drowsiness • dust • accidents • smoke
poisonous • fumes • risks • burns • goggles

MANAGER: New government regulations mean that we are all required to be more aware of
(a) _____ in the workplace. As your employer, we will provide you with the
necessary safety equipment. You must wear (b) _____ to protect your eyes when
working on this machinery. You should also wear ear (c) _____ because the
(d) _____ from the machines is high enough to cause damage to your hearing.
And of course, there is a lot of (e) _____ in the air, so please wear masks to stop
you breathing it in. But, you too are responsible for your safety and for preventing
(f) _____ happening.

EMPLOYEE: Are we looking at fire risks?

MANAGER: Yes, of course. Remember that it is very dangerous to (g) _____ near the
chemical store. In fact, we have a no smoking policy throughout the company. Chemicals
themselves are, of course, (h) _____ so they should never enter your mouth.
They could cause (i) _____ if you get them on your skin. If you leave them
without a lid, (j) _____ may escape and cause headaches,
(k) _____ or dizziness.

10 Engineering

A Engineering is based principally on **physics**, **chemistry**, and **mathematics**, and their extensions into materials science, solid and fluid **mechanics**, **thermodynamics**, **transfer** and **rate processes**, and **systems analysis**.

Engineering as a profession involves different tasks. It can refer specifically to the manufacture or assembly of **engines**, **machine tools** and **machine parts**. It is also used more generally to describe the creative application of scientific principles to **design**, **develop**, **construct** and forecast the behaviour of **structures**, **apparatus**, machines, **manufacturing processes** and works.

The function of scientists is to know, while that of **engineers** is to do: they must solve specific problems.

See also: Chemical (12), Civil (20, 21), Electrical (16), Electronic (17, 18), Mining (22), Petroleum (23, 24), Production (1, 2), Construction (15).

B Different *branches of engineering* require different *equipment* and are based on different *processes*.

Branches of engineering
The following words/phrases are all followed by 'engineering'

chemical • civil • electrical • electronic • highway • hydraulic • industrial
mechanical • mining • petroleum production • production • structural

Equipment in engineering

boiler • crane • gas engine • machine tool • pump • turbine

Processes in treating metals

anneal • anodize • electroplate • forge • found • galvanize • grind
harden • mint • plate • roll • soften • temper • tinplate

C Notice the following adjective endings:

-al • chemical • mechanical • physical • structural
-ial • industrial
-ic • electronic • hydraulic

Notice the following verb endings:

-en • harden • soften
-ize • anodize • galvanize

Notice the following nouns which are a plural form but are normally used with a singular verb

mathematics • mechanics • physics • thermodynamics

1 Match the following verbs with the correct definition.

anneal	to melt metal and then pour it into a form, e.g. iron components
anodize	to make thin sheets of metal by passing it between large rollers, e.g. steel
electroplate	to shape metals by heating and then hammering, e.g. horse shoes
forge	to make materials tough by cooling them slowly, e.g. glass
found	to make something softer, e.g. fibres
galvanize	to heat and then cool metals to obtain the required hardness and elasticity, e.g. steel
grind	to cover with a thin layer of metal using electrolysis, e.g. car components
roll	to protect from rusting by coating in zinc, e.g. food cans
plate	to give a metal a protective coat by using it as an anode in electrolysis, e.g. car components
soften	to polish or sharpen by rubbing on a rough surface, e.g. stone
temper	to cover one metal with a thin layer of another, e.g. silver plate

2 Complete the following sentences with a form of the word in brackets.

1 In the _____ industry, _____ develop processes for producing plastics, fibres, medicines, etc. from simple chemicals. (chemistry)

2 Producing steel using the Bessemer process is one of the best-known _____ processes. (industry)

3 Most _____ devices need oil as a lubricant. (mechanics)

4 Following the earthquake, every building had to be inspected to see whether it had suffered any _____ damage. (structure)

5 Certain chemicals are added to glue to _____ it. (hard)

6 Excavators and power shovels are two types of _____ equipment used by _____ when they are removing rocks from the ground. (mine)

3 Here is an extract from a speech made by a careers advisor to a group of students choosing their future courses of study at university. Complete the speech by choosing one of the words from the box.

machines • highway • mechanical • chemical • civil • physics
electrical • develop • production • electronic

Engineering students should have an understanding of maths, (a) _____ and chemistry. Working with pharmaceuticals, food, mineral processing and chemical manufacturing, a (b) _____ engineer is trained to understand, design, control, and investigate material flows. If you enjoy problem solving and find projects such as the Channel Tunnel and the Three Gorges Dam interesting, (c) _____ engineering may be for you. You will produce creative designs at an economical price while paying due concern to the environment. If your interest is in road building then you may decide to follow a specialized course in (d) _____ engineering. By studying (e) _____ and (f) _____ engineering you learn about the design of complete systems, such as computers, controllers, power and transport systems. (g) _____ engineers plan, design and (h) _____ a wide range of things: washing machines, cars and spacecraft. (i) _____ engineers work very closely with mechanical engineers, to make new products at the right price, on time and in the correct quantity. As well as designing and selecting (j) _____ and materials, they also organize people and finance.

11 Automotive

A Building a car takes a long time – from **research**, through **design** to final **development**. First, researchers need to determine what consumers want, and then suggest what kind of **automobile** to make. During the design phase, new ideas are converted into tangible **parts** or products. At the same time engineers modify existing parts and **features** for the new **model** and draft new plans for the **prototype** (a working example of a new design). Then manufacturers begin to **construct** a few prototypes. These are extensively **tested** in **wind tunnels** and **dust tunnels**, factory **tracks**, **water-proofing** bays, **desert heat**, **Arctic cold**, and **crashes**. At the next stage a plant is **set up** to build the new model and the necessary **components**. Product planners monitor the process to ensure that the new car programme finishes on time and within budget. Managers must also coordinate different activities, including producing the cars, purchasing materials, and training the workers.

Marketing teams must then sell the car. Every year the major car manufacturers launch their new models, but a single car design can take several years from the **drawing board** to the **showroom** floor. A typical company will therefore have several new designs in various stages of development at any given time.

B Automobiles have developed over the years, both in terms of mechanics and design. Today's *automobile system* is more efficient and safer, and the range of *models* more varied. A central part of car manufacture is the workshop where car bodies are *shaped and painted* (the bodyshop).

Models

> bus • executive • 4 x 4 • jeep • lorry • luxury • medium • mini
> multi-purpose vehicle (MPV) • people carrier • pickup • small family
> sports • supermini • truck • van

Body shaping and painting

> body panel • cast • cut • fibreglass • forge • machine operator
> mould • paint shop • press shop • spray gun • stamp • steel

Automobile system

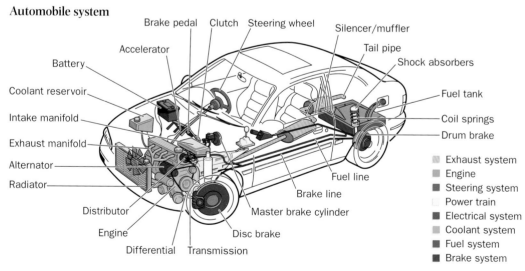

C Advertising plays an important role in promoting the features of cars. Read the following:

> advanced braking system (ABS) • air conditioning • airbag • alarm
> alloy wheels • central locking • climate control • electric windows
> immobilizer • power assisted steering (PAS) • sunroof

1 There are several steps in the process of developing a car. Put the following steps in the correct order.

a A plant is set up to build the new model.

b Marketing teams work to promote the new model and the new car is launched.

c Researchers analyse the answers and suggest the type of car to be built.

d Engineers work to modify existing parts for the new model.

e Customers are asked questions about the sorts of features they would like in a car.

f Product planners make sure that the new car is ready on time.

g Tests are carried out in different conditions.

h A prototype is built.

i Designers work to design a new car based on these suggestions.

2 Match the part of the car with its function.

steering wheel	holds brake fluid
exhaust manifold	provides the power
radiator	stores electricity
fuel tank	ensures that the rear wheels turn at a different speed to each other when a car corners
brake line	produces electricity
silencer/muffler	sends an electric current to the spark plugs
battery	carries waste gases to the exhaust pipe
clutch	makes the car go faster when it is pressed
differential	used by the driver to turn the car
engine	holds fuel
brake cylinder	cools water from the engine
accelerator	connects the brake cylinder to the brakes
distributor	reduces the exhaust noise
alternator	disconnects the engine from the gearbox while the gears are changed

3 Here is a newspaper article reviewing a new small family car. Fill in the blanks with words from the page opposite. The first letter is given to help you.

Launched soon after their competitor's failure, the new LOTE A1 is the perfect car for Mum, Dad and two kids. Just back from its (a) t_____ in the heat of the (b) d_____ and the cold of the Arctic, the LOTE is the perfect small (c) f_____ car. The interior is classy and comfortable with surprisingly good leg room in the back. The (d) a_____ c_____ is highly efficient for the heat of summer, but if you prefer the carefree image, you can open the (e) s_____. There should be no arguments about how far to open the windows as the driver has full control of the (f) e_____ windows in the back, and of course, (g) c_____ l_____ saves telling the kids to lock their doors.

Driving this little beauty is a real pleasure. (h) P_____ a_____ s_____ makes those corners easy and the (i) a_____ b_____ s_____ will stop you comfortably in those tight moments. Safety is also high on the agenda here with fitted (j) a_____ for the front passenger as well as the driver. A car (k) a_____ is fitted as standard and an (l) i_____ will prevent someone starting the car without your permission.

It's a great-looking vehicle, bigger than the (m) m_____, less roomy than the (n) p_____ c_____ but faster than a (o) v_____! With aluminium (p) a_____ w_____ and a price that's less than anything else in this range, it's one that's hard to beat.

12 Chemical

A The chemical industry covers the business that uses chemical **reactions** to turn raw materials, such as **coal**, **oil**, and **salt**, into different products. Technological advances in the chemical industry have dramatically altered the world's economy. Chemical **processes** have created **pesticides** and **fertilizers** for farmers, **pharmaceuticals** for the health care industry, **synthetic dyes** and **fibres** for the textile industry, **soaps** and **beauty aids** for the cosmetics industry, synthetic **sweeteners** and **flavours** for the food industry, **plastics** for the packaging industry, **chemicals** and **celluloid** for the motion picture industry, and **artificial rubber** for the automotive industry. The chemical industry includes makers of more than 70,000 different chemicals, with global sales worth more than €1.1 trillion.

B Chemicals can be broken down into:

- *basic and intermediate chemicals*
- *petrochemicals*
- *paints and coatings*
- *agricultural chemicals*
- *plastics and fibres*
- *specialty chemicals*

Some basic and intermediate chemicals

acids • alcohols • alkalis • aromatics • benzene • carbonates
chlorides • ethylene • fluorides • industrial gases • methanol
nitrates • olefins • oxides • polyethylene • polypropylene

Agricultural chemicals

fungicide • herbicide • insecticide • nutrient management
pest management • pesticide • soil management • sustainable production systems

Features of plastics and fibres

easy flow • flame resistant • flame-retardant
heat resistant • stiff • tough • transparent

Use of petrochemicals

agriculture • aircraft • automobile • explosives • plastics • synthetic fibres

Paint finishes

baked • crack resistant • fast drying • glossy • hard • matt

C Notice the following endings and their meanings:

ending	meaning	example of use	meaning
-cide	something that kills	herbicide	a chemical that kills weeds
-ide	group of related chemical compounds	oxide	any of various oxides
-anol	denotes alcohol	methanol	colourless, toxic, flammable liquid used as an antifreeze, a general solvent, and a fuel
-ate	a derivative of a specified chemical compound or element	carbonate	a derivative of carbon
-ene	organic compound, especially one containing a double bond between carbon atoms	propylene	a flammable gas derived from petroleum hydrocarbon cracking and used in organic synthesis
-fin	making	olefin	oil forming gas

1   Match the chemical with the correct description

benzene	an alcohol with the formula CH_3OH
aromatics	compound of oxygen and another element
ethylene	compounds that react with acids to give off carbon dioxide
olefins	contains six carbon atoms in a ring
fluorides	made from propene and often used for kitchen tools for example
carbonates	the simplest olefin, it is a sweet-smelling gas that is used to make plastics
chlorides	a group of compounds made by cracking alkanes and used to make plastics and antifreeze
methanol	chemicals that contain the benzene ring
nitrates	compounds containing chlorine and another element
oxides	inorganic compounds of fluorine that are added to toothpastes
polypropylene	contain NO_3 and a metal cation

2   Fill in the blanks with a word from the opposite page.

1 Farmers use this to kill insects: _____

2 These fibres are made from chemicals: _____

3 Farmers use these to make plants grow: _____

4 This describes a paint which dries quickly: _____

5 This describes a paint that doesn't have a shiny appearance: _____

6 This industry makes soaps and beauty aids: _____

7 These give food a good taste: _____

8 This describes a plastic that doesn't bend: _____

3   Here is the first part of a speech about the chemical industry. The letters of the missing words in brackets are mixed up. Complete the text with the missing words.

Huge quantities of chemicals are used today. Products of the chemical industry include (a) _____ (sposa), fibres and explosives. The starting point in the manufacture of chemical products is (b) _____ (bicsa) chemicals and these include (c) _____ (adics), for example sulphuric acid, and (d) _____ (akillsa), for example sodium hydroxide. Sulphuric acid is one of the best-known acids and is used to make (e) _____ (fizterriles), plastics, (f) _____ (ptaisn), dyes, detergents and many other chemicals. Alkali mixtures containing sodium and potassium are used to manufacture (g) _____ (gslas), soap and textiles and are also used in refining crude (h) _____ (lio). (i) _____ (lmeditterane) chemicals such as synthetic resins are made from these basic chemicals, and then used in further chemical (j) _____ (peecorsss).

The modern chemical industry began towards the end of the 19th century. William Perkin discovered (k) _____ (dsey) from coal. These were soon being used by the (l) _____ (tlextie) industry. Shortly after, Alfred Nobel invented dynamite which was the start of the (m) _____ (epsolxevis) industry. The discovery of celluloid by Hyatt and bakelite by Baekeland led to the creation of the (n) _____ (piltascs) industry. The (o) _____ (pchemlacetori) industry grew rapidly after 1950 when petroleum became very important in the production of organic chemicals.

Plastics have different properties: strong and (p) _____ (tugho), (q) _____ (tpentrasrn) or heat (r) _____ (ritessant).

13 Pharmaceutical 1

A A pharmaceutical is any substance or mixture of **substances** for use in the **diagnosis**, **detection**, **treatment**, **cure**, **mitigation**, or prevention of **disease** – abnormal physical states, e.g. **chronic depression** in man or animals.

The pharmaceutical industry produces **medicinal drugs** used for the above purposes.

The sale of new drugs is controlled by strict legislation. When a new drug is discovered, a rigorous testing programme is initiated,

- first on small animals, such as mice
- then on larger animals, such as monkeys and dogs
- next on **healthy** volunteers
- finally on **patients suffering** from the **illness** or **affliction**

B After testing drugs in a range of *clinical processes*, the next stage is to seek approval. The *regulatory process* is carried out by the relevant local authority, e.g. the Food and Drug Administration (FDA) in the US or the Medicines Control Authority (MCA) in the UK. Finally, the drug is ready for *production*.

The clinical process

double-blind technique • evaluate • hospital • investigate • laboratory
observe • placebo • stringent conditions • therapeutic practice • validate

Regulatory process

approve • certificate • exemption • factory inspection • harmful • inspect • licence
product labelling • purity standards • safety risk • safety standards • seize • test

Producing pharmaceuticals

aerobic • biological product • boiling point • chemical purity • concentrate
crude drug • cultivate • density • distil • extract • ferment • harvest
inorganic elements and compounds • melting point • odour • organic compound
particle size • plant • preservative • solubility • viscosity

C The following chart shows the evolution of a Pharmaceutical Benefit (in Australia):

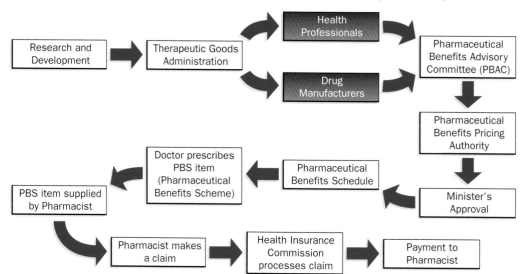

TASKS

1 Complete the sentences below. Some of the letters of the missing word have been given.

1 Measuring the presence of certain substances in the blood may lead to the early
<u>d e</u> _ _ _ <u>t</u> _ _ <u>n</u> of disease.

2 Clinical trials are often carried out in <u>h o s</u> _ _ _ _ _ where doctors and nurses can <u>o b</u> _ _ _ _ _
patients.

3 Any illegal drugs will be <u>s e</u> _ _ _ <u>d</u> by the authorities.

4 There are regular factory <u>i n s</u> _ _ _ _ _ _ <u>n s</u> to check that standards are being met.

5 One important factor in packaging and selling a drug is product <u>l</u> _ <u>b</u> _ _ _ <u>i n</u> g.

6 Doctors may disagree about good <u>t h e</u> _ _ _ _ _ <u>t i</u> _ practice.

7 X-rays are of great importance in the <u>d i a</u> _ _ _ _ _ _ of a medical condition.

8 Laboratories carrying out tests on animals must have a <u>l i</u> _ _ _ <u>c e</u> to do so.

2 Find a more accurate word under *producing pharmaceuticals* on the opposite page to replace the word or words in bold.

1 Heating the liquid will decrease its **thickness**.

2 Liquids with a low temperature at which they boil are more volatile than those with a high **temperature at which they boil.**

3 Our bodies and the bodies of animals obtain oxygen through **using air for** respiration.

4 To obtain pure water from sea-water you have to **condense the vapour after evaporating** it .

5 In wine and beer making as well as in the manufacture of bread, yeast is used to **change** the glucose from sugar to carbon dioxide, ethanol and energy.

6 Water, H_2O, and sodium chloride, NaCl, are **not containing carbon atoms** compounds.

7 Toiletries are products which have been developed to remove or disguise body **smell**.

8 The food industry uses **substances to inhibit the action of enzymes** in order to keep food fresh for a longer period of time.

9 Saponaria is a plant **substance that has been obtained from a plant**.

3 Here is the beginning of a talk to a group of volunteers. Fill in the blanks with words from the box.

approved • placebo • stringent • suffering • regulatory • evaluate • patients
safety • laboratories • treatment • harmful • healthy • disease

I'd like to thank you all for coming along today and for agreeing to take part in these drug tests. This drug is to be used in the (a) _____ of a specific illness. The drug was developed in our (b) _____ under (c) _____ conditions, and has already been tested on small and larger animals. We are now at the stage of testing on (d) _____ volunteers which is why you are here. Once we have analysed the results of these tests we will be able to test the drug on
(e) _____ who are (f) _____ from the (g) _____.
The drug can only be sold once the local (h) _____ authority has
(i)_____ it and a licence has been obtained. The authority is concerned about any (j) _____ effects of the drug as well as (k) _____ standards.

In our tests, half of you will be given the drug while the others will receive a
(l) _____. You won't know which you have received. Afterwards we will be able to compare the two groups and (m) _____ the results.

14 Pharmaceutical 2

A A disease is an **impairment** of the normal condition or functioning of the body or any of its parts. Some diseases are **acute**, causing **severe symptoms** that last only for a short time, e.g., pneumonia; others are **chronic disorders**, e.g., arthritis, and last a long time; and still others return periodically and are termed **recurrent**, e.g., malaria.

Diseases may result from:

- **infectious** agents which can be transmitted by humans, animals and insects, and infected objects and substances
- chemical and physical agents such as **drugs**, **poisons**, and **radiation**
- internal causes including **hereditary abnormalities**, **congenital** diseases and **allergies**
- natural **ageing** of the body tissues
- emotional disturbances, such as **psychoses** and **neuroses**

B There are many *diseases* which can be treated with pharmaceuticals. Appropriate treatment depends on the correct drug and the correct *dosage*. Help with these areas is available from a range of *carers* and *treaters*.

Some diseases

> AIDS • allergy • arthritis • asthma • bronchitis • cancer • diabetes epilepsy • heart attack • haemorrhage • influenza • malaria multiple sclerosis • pneumonia • stroke • tuberculosis • tumour • ulcer

Some carers and treaters

> anaesthetist • dentist • midwife • nurse • nutritionist • obstetrician occupational therapist • orthodontist • orthopaedist • osteopath • paediatrician paramedic • pharmacist • physiotherapist • radiographer • radiologist • surgeon

Dosage forms

> dispersion • pill • radioactive dosage form • solid dosage form solution • sterile medicament • tablet

C The language of pharmaceuticals and medicine is generally based on many Latin and Greek forms. Study the forms and their use in the terms in B above: (US spellings are given in brackets)

Form	Meaning	Origin
arthr-	joint	Greek
haemo- (hemo-)	blood	Greek
sclero-	hard	Greek
pneu-	air, wind; breathing	Greek
dent-/dont-	teeth	Latin
ortho-	straight, right, upright, regular	Greek
nutri-	food	Latin
obstet-	relating to midwifery or the delivery of women in childbirth	Latin
therap-	heal, cure, treatment; service done to the sick	Greek
paedia- (pedia-)	children and infants	Greek
physio-	nature	Greek

TASKS

1 **One word is wrong in the following sentences. Underline it and correct it.**

1 Patients normally recover fairly quickly from an acute condition.

2 A patient suffering from a recurrent disease is unlikely to get it again.

3 Neuroses is an infectious illness.

4 The tropical disease which is transmitted by mosquitoes is known as asthma.

5 Someone suffering from bronchitis will have difficulties walking.

6 Multiple sclerosis is a disease of the digestive system.

7 A person whose body cannot regulate salt in the blood is known as a diabetic.

8 A physiotherapist is someone who is qualified to prepare and dispense medication.

2 **Which medical specialist will be able to help the following people? Choose from *Carers and treaters* on the opposite page.**

1 A woman who is pregnant and expecting her baby in the next few days.

2 Someone who has cancer and requires radiotherapy.

3 Someone who is about to have an operation and must first go into a deep sleep.

4 Someone who has discovered that they are allergic to wheat products and who wants to know what they can eat.

5 Someone who has just been injured in a car crash and must get emergency help.

6 Someone who has been recovering from severe injuries following an accident and who now wants to go home and possibly to work.

7 Someone who has toothache.

8 Someone who had a broken leg and who now needs exercises to help them get mobility back.

9 A baby who is very unwell.

10 Someone who should have an X-ray taken to help make a diagnosis.

3 **Complete the following article about aspirin using the words from the box.**

side effect • chronic • doses • stroke • tablet • heart attack • arthritis • cancer

The drug known as aspirin is over one hundred years old. It was patented in 1899 by the German pharmaceutical company, Bayer. However, it was not until 1971 that Professor Vane discovered exactly how aspirin worked. People who have had a (a) _____ are advised to take a low dose of 75mg (b) _____ a day to reduce the risk of another attack. For the majority of people it is known to reduce the risk of a (c) _____ but for a very small number of people this risk is in fact a dangerous (d) _____. Scientific tests have also shown that aspirin taken twice a week reduces the risk of bowel (e) _____. At high (f) _____, aspirin reduces pain in people suffering from the (g) _____ disorder, rheumatoid (h) _____.

15 Construction

A Construction means the **erection** or **assembly** of large structures, primarily those which provide **shelter**, such as commercial and residential buildings. It also includes major works such as ships, aircraft, and public works such as roads, dams, and bridges.

The major elements of a building include:

- the **foundation**, which **supports** the building and gives it **stability**
- the **structure**, which supports all the imposed loads and transmits them to the foundation
- the **exterior walls**, which may or may not be part of the primary supporting structure
- the **interior partitions**, which also may or may not be part of the primary structure
- the **environmental-control** systems, including the **heating**, **ventilating**, **air conditioning**, **lighting**, and **acoustical** systems
- the **power**, **water supply**, and **waste disposal** systems

B *Jobs in construction* are many and varied, ranging from architects to painters. However, every building needs a solid *foundation* on which the *structure* can be erected, paying special attention to the *exterior walls* which will need to withstand the elements.

Jobs in construction

architect • carpenter • electrician • mason • painter
plasterer • plumber • quantity surveyor • roofer

The foundations

caisson • deep • mat • pile
reinforced concrete • shallow • spread footing

The structure

beam • bracing connection • column • floor • girder
rigid connection • roof • truss • wall

The exterior walls

curtain wall • exterior skin • load-bearing wall • nonload-bearing wall
roofing felt • sound-deadening material • vapour barrier

C Constructware is a US company which provides collaboration solutions to construction companies to help them achieve business success by increasing productivity, improving risk management and reducing costs. Look at the diagram opposite which shows their areas of activity:

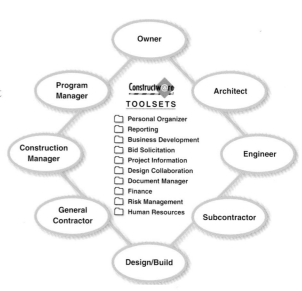

TASKS

1 Choose the correct word in the following sentences.

1 A flat roof is usually covered in roofing **felt/skin** for protection against the weather.

2 Rooms in a building are divided by interior **supports/partitions**.

3 To prevent water entering the cavity of the wall, moisture barriers are used on the external surface and **vapour/insulating** barriers are used on the internal face.

4 The **assembly/structure** of a building transfers all the loads acting on the building to the ground.

5 The **ventilating/acoustical** system provides fresh air.

6 Sound-**deadening/-barrier** material is used to reduce sound passing from one room to another.

7 The foundations for a skyscraper building must be **deep/shallow**.

8 A **spread footing/caisson piers** is/are used when the soil is weak.

2 Label the following diagrams using words from the opposite page.

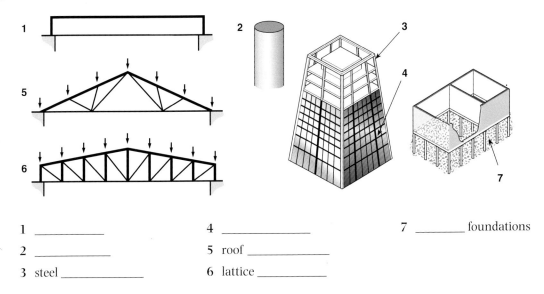

1 _____   4 _____   7 _____ foundations

2 _____   5 roof _____

3 steel _____   6 lattice _____

3 Here is part of a text about house building. Complete the text with words from the opposite page.

There are two main methods of building houses. In one, solid walls known as (a) _____ walls are constructed. They support the floors and the roof of the building. In the other, a framework of steel, timber or concrete is constructed. The frame can be covered or filled in with lightweight material.

When building a house, the (b) _____ first of all examines the site and makes a plan of the size and shape of the plot of land. Next, an (c) _____ makes a detailed drawing of the building, and gives information about the materials which are to be used. A (d) _____ calculates exactly how much of these materials will be needed for the building. Then, the ground is dug out and the (e) _____ laid. During building, (f) _____ make the wooden structures, (g) _____ cut and place stone, (h) _____ construct the roof and (i) _____ cover walls and ceilings with plaster. Once the building has been completed, (j) _____ lay meters of electrical cable, and (k) _____ install pipes for heating and water. Finally (l) _____ paint the walls and ceilings of the building.

16 Electrical

A   Electrical engineering deals with the practical application of the theory of electricity to the construction and manufacture of **systems**, **devices** and **assemblies** that use electric **power** and **signals**.

Electrical engineering can be divided into four main branches:

| electric power and **machinery** | **communications** and control | electronics (➤ 17&18) | computers (➤ 5&6) |

Electrical applications are used in many industrial areas including:

- electric power and machinery
- **electronic circuits**
- **control systems**
- **computer** design
- **superconductors**
- **solid-state electronics**
- medical imaging systems
- **robotics**
- lasers
- radar
- consumer electronics
- **fibre optics**

In recent years, the electronic computer has emerged as the largest application of electrical engineering. However, another very large field is concerned with electric **light** and power and their applications. Specialities within the field include the design, manufacture, and use of **turbines**, **generators**, **transmission lines**, **transformers**, **motors**, **lighting systems**, and **appliances**.

B   *Electrical problems* can be avoided by always using the right *devices* and taking appropriate measures for *electrical protection*.

Electrical problems

> ground fault • overcurrent • overload • short circuit

Electrical protection

> dustproof • explosionproof • rainproof • raintight • watertight • weatherproof

Electrical devices

> branch circuit • (circuit) breaker • cable • circuit • feeder
> fixture • fuse • ground • junction (electrical) box • panelboard
> service panel • switch • switchboard

Circuit breaker operation

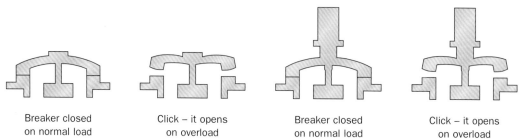

| Breaker closed on normal load | Click – it opens on overload | Breaker closed on normal load | Click – it opens on overload |

C   Compounds are short ways of giving information. They are used to express complex ideas economically:

- noun + noun, e.g. panel board (or panelboard) = a board consisting of a number of panels
- noun + adjective, e.g. explosionproof = material which cannot be damaged by explosions
- adverb + noun, e.g. overload = current which is greater than the load for which the system or mechanism was intended

1 Express each of these ideas as a compound.

1 a board consisting of a number of panels

2 material that does not allow water to get into it

3 material that doesn't allow rain to get into it

4 a board consisting of a number of electrical switches

5 conductors which are perfect, conducting a current without a battery

6 material that will not be damaged in an explosion

7 current which is greater than the load for which the system or mechanism was intended

8 material that does not allow dust to get into it

2 What is being described? Find a word or phrase from the page opposite.

1 It produces a narrow beam of light and can be used to read barcodes in a supermarket, play compact discs, etc.

2 A word to describe any piece of equipment made for a specific purpose.

3 A pulse of light, current or sound that is used to convey information.

4 A device that uses electromagnetic waves to calculate the distance of an object.

5 Glass fibres that are used for data transmission.

6 The study of how robots are made and used.

7 A circuit where the current has a choice of paths.

8 A situation where the electrical current takes an easier path than the one intended.

9 A piece of equipment that stops an electrical current if it becomes dangerous.

10 A connection point where several cables are connected.

3 Complete the text below with words from the page opposite. The first letter of the missing words has been given.

In power stations, high pressure steam, gas, water or wind is used to drive
(a) t_____ which turn huge (b) g_____. Large power stations generate
electricity at 25,000 volts. This is then stepped up to 275,000 or 400,000 volts using
(c) t_____ before being fed into a network of (d) c_____ known as the
Grid. Electrical (e) p_____ is then carried across the country by overhead
(f) t_____ _____. The Grid voltage is reduced by stepping down
(g) t_____ at substations before it is used in homes and factories. Some
industrial plants take electrical energy from the Grid system at 33,000 or 11,000 volts,
but for use in homes and offices it is stepped down to a lower level.

In the home, supply from the mains (h) c_____ passes through a main
(i) f_____ and then to a fuse box. The fuse box is a distribution point for the
electricity supply to the house. Most houses have two or three ring main
(j) c_____ connecting electric sockets. There are also two or three
(k) l_____ circuits and separate circuits for (l) a_____ such as cookers
and hot water heaters.

17 Electronics 1

A Electronics is a branch of engineering and physics. It deals with the **emission**, behaviour, and effects of **electrons** for the **generation**, **transmission**, **reception**, and **storage** of information. This information can be **audio signals** in a radio, **images** (**video signals**) on a television screen, or numbers and other data in a computer. **Electronic systems** are important in communication, **entertainment**, and **control** systems.

Electronic circuits consist of interconnections of electronic components, at the heart of which are **semiconductors**. **Transistors**, which are made of **silicon** or **germanium**, are made from semiconductors. Commercial products range from **cellular radiotelephone systems** and video cassette recorders to high-performance **supercomputers** and sophisticated **weapons systems**. In industry, electronic devices have led to dramatic improvements in productivity and quality. For example, **computer-aided design** tools facilitate the design of complex parts, such as aircraft wings, or intricate structures, such as **integrated circuits**.

B The development of microelectronics has had a major *impact* on the electronics industry. *Electronic components* are expected to deliver ever higher performance, while electronic circuits continue to benefit from miniaturization.

Function of electronic circuits

amplification • demodulation • electronic processing • generation
information extraction • modulation • radio wave • recovery (of audio signal)

Electronic components

absorb • active • battery • capacitor • diode • energy • generator • inductor
passive • resistor • transducer • transistor • vacuum tube (AmE) • valve (BrE)

Impacts

device size • digitization • fidelity • high speed • increased reliability
manufacturing cost • storage capacity • storage system • ultrahigh image definition

C One way of increasing your vocabulary is to learn the associated words from a key word. Look at the word table below, which shows words related to the key words presented above:

Noun	Verb	Adjective
activation	activate	active
amplification	amplify	amplified
emission	emit	emitted
entertainment	entertain	entertaining
extraction	extract	extracted
generation	generate	generative
integration	integrate	integrated/integrative
reception	receive	receptive
recovery	recover	recovered
reliability	rely	reliable
storage	store	stored
transmission	transmit	transmittable/transmissible

1 Choose the correct word in the following sentences.

1 **Transistors/inductors** are the key component in electronics.

2 They consist of three layers of silicon **semiconductor/superconductor**.

3 All **electronic/electrical** systems consist of input, a processor and output, and usually memory.

4 The input **receives/resists** and converts information while the output converts and supplies electronically processed information.

5 The memory may not be present in simple systems, but its function is the **storage/transmission** of information for the processor.

6 Continual developments in electronics give us increased **reliability/recovery** in electronic devices.

7 Electronic equipment controls **microprocessors/microwaves** in, for example, weapons systems, cellular radiotelephone systems and domestic appliances.

8 Electronic devices have improved our lives by providing high quality **communication/combination** and entertainment.

2 Use the word in brackets to form a word which fits in the sentence.

1 The weak audio signal entering a radio is _____ by the _____ thus making it audible. (amplify)

2 Computer games are just one example of electronic systems being used for _____. (entertain)

3 Due to developments in mobile telecommunications systems, a new _____ of mobile phone is now available. (generate)

4 IC stands for _____ circuit. (integrate)

5 Computer software is _____ if it does what the manual says it should. (rely)

6 One area of electronics is concerned with the _____ of information. (store)

7 The _____ of signals to satellites is made by microwaves. (transmit)

8 A computer chip is capable of holding vast amounts of _____ information. (store)

9 _____ of speech was first carried out through _____ of the amplitude of a radio signal. (transmit, modulate)

10 In a laser, energy is released in the form of _____ light. (emit)

3 Complete the text about electronics by choosing a word from the box.

> diodes • semiconductor • electrons • devices • germanium • transistors
> circuits • capacitors • silicon • integrated • resistors

Electronic circuits are built from basic components. (a) _____ are the most important components. They can be used to amplify the strength of a signal by converting a weak signal into a stronger one or to switch other circuits on or off. (b) _____ reduce the flow of (c) _____ through the circuit, adding resistance to that circuit. (d) _____ function as electronic valves allowing current to flow in only one direction. (e) _____ store electricity in order to smooth the flow. They can be charged and discharged. The two most common capacitors are ceramic and electrolytic.

Most electronic devices use (f) _____ _____ (IC) or microchips. Inside an IC is a very small piece of (g) _____ with circuits built in. Today, semiconductors are usually made of (h) _____ which is cheaper and easier to manufacture than (i) _____.

Researchers are constantly trying to reduce the size of transistors in order to reduce the size of (j) _____.

18 Electronics 2

A The electronics industry creates, designs, produces, and sells **devices** such as **radios**, **televisions**, **stereos**, **video games**, and **computers**, and components such as semiconductors, transistors, and integrated circuits. In the second half of the 20th century, this industry had two major influences. Firstly it transformed our lives in factories, offices, and homes; secondly it emerged as a key economic sector. Specific advances include:

- the development of **space technology** and **satellite communications**
- the revolution in the computer industry that led to the personal computer
- the introduction of computer-guided **robots** in factories
- systems for **storing** and **transmitting** data electronically
- radio systems to automobiles, ships, and other vehicles
- **navigation** aids for aircraft, automatic pilots, altimeters, and **radar** for traffic control

B The *applications of electronic engineering* cover almost every aspect of modern life; the industry involves a wide range of *tasks*.

Applications of electronic engineering

aerospace • automotive • consumer goods • chemical
defence • energy/power • environmental • imaging equipment
industrial automation • medical instrumentation • oil and gas • pharmaceutical
pulp and paper • semiconductor • telecommunications • transportation

Tasks in electronic engineering

design • develop • diagnose • evaluate
manufacture • repair • test

C Electronic engineers are highly sought after, well rewarded and can be found in practically every branch of industry and commerce. Here is an extract from a job description for an electronic engineer:

Scope and responsibilities

Senior Electronics Design Engineer

The **Senior Electronics Design Engineer** will be responsible for enhancing and supporting the entire electronic design process, including, but not limited to:
- electronic product development from design to production release
- electronic design, analysis and testing of new products from product specification, producing electronic prototypes and preparation of all necessary design documentation
- firmware design for electronic devices
- electronic circuit design and board layout for very small devices and instruments
- accurate project and design documentation

- interfacing closely with marketing to create and develop products according to customer needs
- interacting with contract engineers that support product development
- developing and maintaining vendor selection and involvement to ensure the highest quality products
- obtaining necessary product approvals and communicating progress throughout the design process
- providing technical support for new and existing products in manufacturing and in the field
- producing design schedules
- staffing and operating an electronics lab

TASKS

1 Put these words and phrases into one of the three categories below.

> develop solutions • transportation systems • robot • automotive industry
> transmit data • diagnose problems • radio • pharmaceutical industry
> evaluate results • television • provide support • chemical industry
> altimeter • defence • computer

devices	functions	applications

2 Choose one word from A with one word from B to complete the sentences below.

A	B
space	computer
computer-guided	goods
satellite	robots
consumer	technology
navigation	communications
personal	aids

1 _____ _____ has enabled people to survive in space.

2 Communications systems for aircraft and ships are dependent on _____ _____.

3 Many people today have their own _____ _____ at home.

4 Industrial processes have been made more efficient through the use of _____ _____.

5 Ships and aircraft require _____ _____ to find their way.

6 _____ _____ such as washing machines and dishwashers contain electronic circuits.

3 Here are two extracts from advertisements for jobs in electronics. Complete them with words from the box.

> architecture • repair • examined • technicians • instrumentation • medical

(a) _____ **Electronics Technician**

The Biomedical Engineering Department provides electronic and mechanical engineering as well as ITU support to different specialities within the hospital. We are looking for (b) _____ to join our team of engineers. You will be involved in the management, (c) _____ and maintenance of the hospital's highly sophisticated medical electronic (d) _____. You will be required to work unsupervised in maintaining complex systems and equipment.

There have been great changes in crime and in its detection over the past ten years as a result of technological advances. Computers and mobile phones have become more common and, as a result, criminal activity involving them has also risen. Computers and SIM cards are (e) _____ in our department to recover data that is required in criminal investigations.

You will have knowledge of electronic (f) _____ of computers, PDAs or mobile phones and possibly an understanding of computer operating systems.

19 Energy

A   The UK's energy system has changed dramatically over the last century.

In the first half of the twentieth century:

- **coal** was the dominant **fuel** in industry and electricity **power plants**, and in houses and businesses
- **town-gas** networks existed in larger towns, with the **gas** derived from coal

In the second half of the 20th century:

- coal continued to be of central importance for electricity **generation**, although its importance elsewhere fell substantially
- **nuclear power plants** began to be **commissioned** from the mid-1950s
- the electricity industry was combined into state-owned monopolies, during the 1950s
- the **high voltage** electricity **transmission network** was created in order to transport electricity over long distances from big power plants
- electricity **distribution networks** shrank in importance and activity
- during the 1960s and 1970s there was a move to an extensive **natural gas** network for **heating** (industry, commerce and domestic)
- demand for **transport fuel** increased dramatically
- **gas-fired central heating** largely replaced **open coal fires** in homes
- the use of **electrical appliances** in commerce and the domestic sector increased hugely

B   Today we are seeing increasing interest in those renewable *sources of energy* which can deliver clean and cheap *types of energy*, using environmentally-friendly processes and *equipment*.

Sources of energy

renewable	non-renewable
sun • water	fossil fuels: coal, oil, natural gas, petroleum
wave • wind	biofuel • plutonium • uranium

Types of energy

electrical energy • fire • fossil fuels • gas power • geothermal energy
greenhouse effect • hydraulic power • hydroelectric energy • kinetic energy
magnetic energy • nuclear energy • solar energy • steam power • tidal power
water power • wave power • wind power

Equipment to produce energy

atomic energy plant • gas station • gasworks • generating station • generator
heat exchanger • hydroelectric scheme • motor • nuclear plant • power station
powerhouse • solar cell • solar panel • tidal barrage • tide mill • turbine
waterfall • waterworks • wind farm • windmill

C   **Study the sentences below.**

In 1950, the energy system for both industry and domestic demand was fuelled by coal. Today domestic natural gas is the UK's largest source of energy.
Developments in technology are gradually lowering the costs of generating electricity from alternative and renewable sources. The increasing and fluctuating prices of natural gas are contributing to making biomass and wind energy competitive.

TASKS

1 Rearrange the letters to name six sources of energy.

1 uns   2 fbielou   3 dwni   4 piumutoln   5 weva   6 peumroetl

2 Complete the crossword with words from the opposite page.

Across

1 When a nuclear plant is put into action it is _____.

3 The flow of electrons produces this type of energy.

7 This heat comes from the earth itself.

9 This is where gas was made from coal in the past.

10 Almost all the energy we use comes from this.

12 The reactor in nuclear power stations contains a nuclear fuel such as _____.

13 These turn the energy in sunlight into electricity.

14 This kind of energy is in things that are moving, e.g. a moving turbine.

15 This is a hydroelectric power station together with its dam and reservoir.

16 This is made from plant or animal matter.

Down

2 The main way of heating homes in the UK before central heating.

4 This energy is associated with electric current.

5 Exhaust gases from vehicles and power stations, methane from oil and gas rigs and CFCs in refrigerators all contribute to this effect.

6 This type of fuel is used to power all sorts of vehicles.

8 This power comes from the pressure or movement of a liquid.

11 Another word for oil.

15 This type of energy comes from the sun.

3 Complete the following text about power using the words from the box.

barrage • gas • non-renewable • produce • water • wave • fossil fuels
power stations • generators • renewable • tidal • coal • turbines

Most large power stations burn (a) _____ which were formed from the remains of plants and animals that lived on the earth millions of years ago. The first type of fossil fuel to be used in large quantities was (b) _____. Today, it is increasingly expensive to mine, however, many (c) _____ still burn it to (d) _____ electricity. Oil and natural (e) _____ have now largely replaced coal. These fuels are all (f) _____ and will eventually run out. Wood is used by 2 billion people in the developing world and unlike fossil fuels, it is a (g) _____ energy source. Alternative energy sources include (h) _____ power technology. In hydro schemes, water from a reservoir or from a river powers (i) _____ which drive (j) _____.
(k) _____ power systems use the energy from wind and sea or take mechanical energy from wave movement. The UK offers a good position to exploit wave energy. The movement of the sun, moon and earth combine to produce (l) _____ power. Electricity can be generated when tidal water passes through turbines positioned in a (m) _____.

20 Civil engineering 1

A The term civil engineering describes engineering work performed by civilians for non-military purposes. In general it describes the profession of designing and executing **structural works** for the general public and the **communal environment**. Civil engineering covers different areas of engineering, including the design and construction of large buildings, **roads**, **bridges**, **canals**, **railway lines**, **airports**, **water-supply systems**, **dams**, **irrigation**, **harbours**, **docks**, **aqueducts**, and **tunnels**.

The civil engineer needs a thorough knowledge of **surveying**, of the properties and mechanics of construction materials, of the **mechanics** of **structures** and **soils**, and of **hydraulics** and **fluid mechanics**. Today civil engineering includes the production and distribution of **energy**, the development of **aircraft** and airports, the construction of **chemical process plants** and **nuclear power stations**, and **water desalination**.

B A range of *civil engineering tools and equipment* is used in the construction of *roads*, *bridges* and *waterways*.

Roads

camber • crown • culvert • kerb/curb • macadam
main • manhole • metal • pavement • pedestrian crossing
pothole • sewer • soft shoulder • tarmac • underdrain

Bridges

arch • bascule • cable • cantilever • clapper • crossover • lift
footbridge • span • suspender • suspension • swing • viaduct

Canals, rivers and other waterways

aqueduct • barrage • dam • dike • drainage
flume • lock • paddle • pier • sluice
watercourse • water main • weir • well

Civil engineering tools and equipment

bulldozer • dredger • earthmover • excavator
plate girder • pylon • road roller • shovel

C Here are the vital statistics of the famous *Golden Gate Bridge* in San Francisco:

Total length of bridge	2,737 m	Length of suspension span	1,966 m
Length of main span	1,280 m	Length of one side span	343 m
Width of bridge	27 m	Width of road between curbs	19 m
Width of pavement		3 m	
Clearance above mean higher high water		67 m	
Deepest foundation below mean low water		34 m	
Total weight of bridge, anchorages and north and south approaches (1994)			887,000 tons

1 Name the bridges opposite. Choose from the following.

masonry arch
cantilever
swing
suspension
clapper
bascule

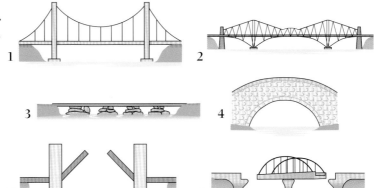

2 What is being described? Choose from the words on the opposite page.

1 This structure is built across a river to hold back the water to produce power, improve navigation or control flooding.

2 This structure is built along the banks of a river or along the coast to hold back water and prevent flooding.

3 This carries a road or railway across water.

4 This carries water (canal or river) across land, usually over a valley.

5 The section of a canal where the water level changes to raise boats from one level to the next.

6 These allow water to flow in or out in order to change the water level in a canal.

7 A deep hole in the ground where people can get water.

8 These are dug underground for roads and railways.

9 This is the process of removing salt from sea water.

10 This large powerful vehicle uses a large blade to move earth and rocks.

11 This machine or ship is used for removing sand and mud from the bottom of a river or a harbour.

12 This machine is used for rolling tarmac or asphalt flat on a road surface.

3 A civil engineer is showing an international visitor around. Complete the text with words from *Roads* from the opposite page.

Here we are on one of our town streets. As you can see the road is not flat, it has a (a) _____. This is to allow rain water to run off the surface and into the drains at the side. The highest part of the road is the (b) _____ in the centre. A (c) _____ carrying waste water runs below the surface of the road. At certain points along the road you'll find large (d) _____ which allow engineers to go down and inspect electricity and telephone cables which also run below the road. On either side of the road there is a raised (e) _____ for pedestrians which is edged with (f) _____ stones. The black surface we use nowadays is a variety of (g) _____. It was invented by a man of that name whose company was later called Tarmac. As you can see this road needs to be resurfaced. There are a number of (h) _____ following the heavy rain we had last month.

Now, here we are on a (i) _____ road out of town. There are no pavements here. Grass is allowed to grow along the edges and provides a (j) _____ _____. Over there you can see a (k) _____ carrying a small stream under the road.

21 Civil engineering 2

A The functions of civil engineers fall into three categories:

1. before construction (**feasibility studies**, **site investigations**, and **design**),
2. during construction (dealing with clients, consulting engineers, and contractors),
3. after construction (**maintenance**).

Any major civil engineering project starts with a **feasibility study** to assess both financial and engineering aspects. During the feasibility study a preliminary **site investigation** is carried out. Once a scheme has been approved, a more extensive investigation is usually necessary to evaluate the **load-bearing** qualities and **stability** of the ground. This field is called **soil mechanics**. The design of engineering works may require the application of principles of **hydraulics**, **thermodynamics** and **nuclear physics**. During the construction phase, a consulting engineer is often employed to be responsible for **design** of the works, supplying **specifications**, **drawings**, and legal documents to get competitive **tender** prices. In a **turnkey** or package contract the **building contractor** undertakes to finance, design, specify, construct, and **commission** the whole project. **Maintenance** is normally carried out by the contractor as part of the agreement; if there are maintenance problems, it is the responsibility of the contractor to pay for any necessary work.

B Now look at the following statements about the pre-construction phase.

Preliminary feasibility study:
A series of **steps** by which all the **attributes** of each **proposal** are marked, resulting in two or three being selected.

Secondary feasibility study:
A **process** to determine the best of the two or three remaining **schemes**. Rough **dimensions** are put onto the structure at this stage, in order that a more accurate **costing system** can be implemented.

Feasibility study factors:
cost • aesthetic appeal • maintenance • ecology • disruption

Preliminary design:
Dimensions and quantities of materials are roughly **analysed** and calculations are performed to **estimate** prices and construction needs.

Detailed design:
At this stage of the design other factors are considered, such as the exact **geology** of the area. To determine this, **boreholes** and **trial pits** are sunk.

After all calculations have been worked out exactly and checked, detailed **technical drawings** are done. The result of these calculations is a **finished design** which can be built from the drawings produced. Once the detailed design is complete, construction can begin.

C Read the list of the *essential duties and responsibilities* of a civil engineer below:

- to provide detailed fact finding, research and analysis
- to provide support for less experienced staff
- to develop computer models, including detailed and potentially complex spreadsheet analyses
- to assist with engagement planning activities including the development of **draft work plans** and budgets
- to prepare client communications for senior level review

1   Match the following words and phrases with their definitions.

feasibility study	building or installation which is built, supplied, or installed complete and ready to operate
site investigation	activities carried out after the project to ensure problems are solved
maintenance	detailed plan of proposed structures
soil mechanics	dimensions and measurements
specifications	extensive investigation to evaluate the load-bearing qualities and stability of the ground
technical drawings	investigation to assess both financial and engineering aspects of a project
commission a project	offer of a bid for an engineering contract
costing system	procedure to monitor the costs of a project so that management can get information on development
tender	study of the proposed location to assess geology of the area
turnkey project	to order a plan to be carried out

2   Put the following tasks into the appropriate phase of construction.

consulting engineer communications with client • extensive site investigation
consulting engineer contact with contractors • feasibility study • detailed design
maintenance • employment of consulting engineer • preliminary site investigation

Phase	Tasks
Before construction	
During construction	
After construction	

3   The following extract is from a letter written by a qualified civil engineer in response to a job advertisement. Complete the extract by unscrambling the letters in brackets.

I am writing in connection with the job advertisement for a civil (a) _____ (renigeen), which appeared in today's *Civil Engineering*.

I have a degree in (b) _____ (rnlutiasid) engineering. After graduation, I worked for four years at Locke Engineers in the field of (c) _____ (onscorutitcn) consulting. During my time there, I specialized in (d) _____ (ilamsc) preparation and construction (e) _____ (ehdnsgulic). I am particularly interested in the opportunities to further develop my skills, especially in the following areas:

- development of (f) _____ (tdfar) work plans
- (g) _____ (etis) investigations
- preparation of (h) _____ (nictel) communications

22 Mining

A Mining is the process of **extracting** useful **minerals** from the **earth's crust** – the land and the seas. The process involves the physical **removal** of **rock** and **earth**. Excavations take place in different types of mines. **Underground** mines are constructed when any **ore** lies deep below the surface. There are several types of **surface** mining, but the three most common are **open-pit** mining, **strip mining**, and **quarrying**. These differ from one another in:

- their structure
- the mining techniques employed
- the minerals produced.

There are typically four stages to mining:

- **prospecting** – looking for mineral **deposits**
- **exploring** – assessing the size, shape, location, and economic value of the deposit
- **developing** – preparing **access** to the deposit so that the minerals can be **mined**
- **exploiting** – extracting the minerals

Mining is an extremely dangerous activity. The health and safety of mine workers and the protection of the public are achieved by regular mine safety **audits** and mine site **inspections**.

B Various *professionals* are employed in mining to extract minerals. The output from mines can be divided into *metalliferous*, *nonmetalliferous* and *building and ornamental stones*.

Professionals in mining

drill supervisor • environmental engineer • geochemist • geologist • geophysicist
hydrogeologist • miner • mining engineer • prospector • safety engineer

Minerals: metalliferous ores

copper • gold • iron • lead • manganese • tin • zinc

Minerals: nonmetalliferous ores

asbestos • bauxite • borax • coal • feldspar
phosphate rock • quartz • talctrona

Building and ornamental stones

granite • limestone • marble • slate • traprock • travertine

What's in a mine?

cage • chute • conveyor • dragline • drift • drill • dump truck
explosive • headframe • mechanical loader • mine car • pump • raise
shovel • skip • stope • stripping machine • sump • ventilation shaft

C Here is a comparison of the properties of different grades of coal:

Peat is the lowest grade of coal. It is composed of 90% water, 5% carbon, and 5% volatile materials. Because of its high water content, it is not commonly used for fuel. The second lowest grade of coal is **lignite.** It is formed in **swamps** and then covered by large amounts of water, usually an ocean or sea. The second highest grade of coal is called **bituminous** or "soft coal". It is formed when the weight of overlying **sediment**, the depth of **burial**, and the length of time are slightly increased. The highest and most desirable grade of coal, called **anthracite**, is formed when previously formed coal deposits are subjected to substantially increased heat and pressure.

1 Match the following words and phrases with their definitions.

deposit	a natural occurrence of a useful mineral in sufficient quantities for exploitation
excavate	a natural resource extracted from the earth for human use, e.g., ores, salts, coal, or petroleum
explore	an open or surface mineral working, usually for the extraction of building stone, such as slate and limestone
extract	examine a territory for its mineral wealth
mineral	remove coal or ore from a mine
mining	remove soil and/or rock materials from one location and transport them to another
ore	search for coal, minerals, or ore
prospect	the naturally occurring material from which a mineral or minerals of economic value can be extracted
quarry	the science, technique, and business of mineral discovery and exploitation

2 Label the following items of mining equipment with words from the box.

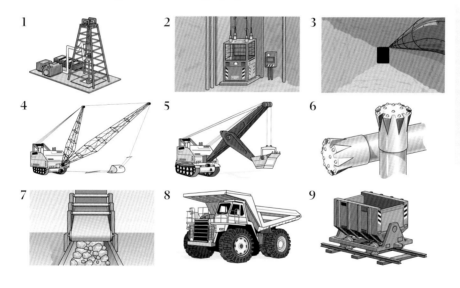

1   2   3

4   5   6

7   8   9

shovel
conveyor
drift
headframe
mining skip
dragline
drill
cage
dump truck

3 Rearrange the letters to complete the short descriptions of the activities of different mining professionals.

There are two main activities in my job. Firstly to make holes in rock so that samples of the rock can be taken and to insert (a) _____ (leoivsxspe) for blasting.

I make evaluations of conditions at a (b) _____ (ienm) and check air pollution, waste disposal, and previously mined areas.

My job is to study the chemistry of (c) _____ (htare) materials. I specialize in the study of the planet and the materials of which it is made. This information helps us to discover (d) _____ (nlriames) and fuels.

I study and investigate phenomena which cause movement of the earth's surface. Through my studies I help others to locate petroleum and mineral (e) _____ (tseopids).

I specialize in various branches of work, including (f) _____ (goespnrctip), surveying, and technical underground management.

My job is to inspect all possible danger spots in the mine, prepare (g) _____ (sutdai) and cooperate with committees to prevent unnecessary dangers.

23 Petroleum 1

A Petroleum is an **oily**, thick, **flammable**, usually dark-coloured liquid that is a form of **bitumen** or a mixture of various **hydrocarbons**. It occurs naturally in various parts of the world and is usually obtained by **drilling**. **Offshore** drilling for oil takes places in oceans, seas or large lakes from **platforms** standing on the bed; **onshore** drilling takes place on land. Because petroleum is found underground, it must be **extracted** by means of **wells**. To check whether there is any oil at a site, an **exploratory** well, or **wildcat**, is **dug**. Scientific methods and technical equipment, such as gravimeters, magnetometers, and seismographs are used to find **subsurface rock formations** that might hold **crude oil**. The petroleum from a new well will usually come to the surface under its own **pressure**. Later the crude oil must be **pumped** out or forced to the surface by **injecting** water, gas, or air into the **deposits**. The oil and gas industry distinguishes between:

upstream – oil and natural gas exploration and production activities; plus gas gathering, processing and marketing operations
downstream – all activities from the processing of **refined crude oil** into petroleum products to the distribution, marketing, and shipping of the products. (➥ 24)

B Accurate *forecasting and measuring* always precedes *drilling and pumping*.

Forecasting and measuring

> downhole • flow rate • layer • pressure • reserves
> reservoir • rock mapping • wellbore • wildcat well

Drilling and pumping

> blowout • casing • (drill) collar • cuttings • derrick • drill bit • drill pipe
> drill string • drilling mud • inject • kelly • licence • oil field/gas field • permit
> platform • pump • recover • rig • trap • turntable/rotary table • well

C Below are some excerpts from professional journals about exploration and drilling.

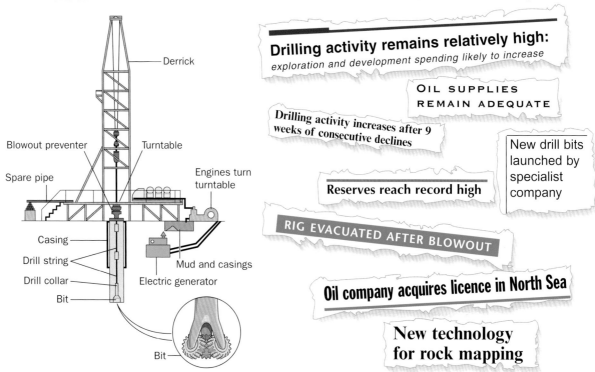

Derrick

Blowout preventer — Turntable

Spare pipe

Engines turn turntable

Casing

Drill string

Drill collar

Mud and casings

Electric generator

Bit

Bit

Drilling activity remains relatively high:
exploration and development spending likely to increase

OIL SUPPLIES REMAIN ADEQUATE

Drilling activity increases after 9 weeks of consecutive declines

New drill bits launched by specialist company

Reserves reach record high

RIG EVACUATED AFTER BLOWOUT

Oil company acquires licence in North Sea

New technology for rock mapping

TASKS

1   Match the following words and phrases with their definitions.

derrick	a hole drilled into the earth to recover oil or gas
drill	a pyramid of steel erected over a bore hole to drill for oil
extract	a structure that contains all the necessary equipment for drilling
flammable	an offshore structure from which wells are drilled
offshore	burns easily
platform	exploration and production activities for oil and natural gas
reservoir	places in oceans, seas or large lakes
rig	rock formation containing oil and/or natural gas
upstream	to cut through rock
well	to take out a solid or liquid

2   The following diagram shows the main parts of an oil rig. Label the parts.

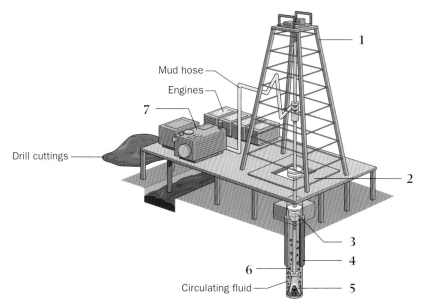

Mud hose

Engines

7

Drill cuttings

1

2

3

4

5

6

Circulating fluid

3   The following text describes the eight basic steps to drill a surface hole – a hole above where the exploration company thinks oil is located. The steps are mixed up and some of the letters of the missing words are also mixed up. Number the steps in the correct order and then rearrange the jumbled words.

___ Add new sections (joints) of drill (a) _____ (ispep) as the hole gets deeper.

___ Allow the (b) _____ (tenecm) to harden.

___ As drilling progresses, circulate drilling (c) _____ (umd) through the pipe and out of the (d) _____ (ibt) to float the rock (e) _____ (gutntsci) out of the hole.

___ Attach the (f) _____ (ylelk) and (g) _____ (lunbretat) and begin drilling.

___ Place (h) _____ (nagsic) pipe sections into the hole to prevent it from collapsing in on itself.

___ Place the drill bit, (i) _____ (rclaol) and drill pipe in the hole.

___ (j) _____ (ppmu) cement down the casing (k) _____ (iepp).

___ (l) _____ (emevor) the drill pipe, collar and bit when the pre-set depth is reached.

24 Petroleum 2

A Petroleum is used in a natural or **refined** state as **fuel**, or **separated** by **distillation** into **petrochemicals** such as **petrol (gasoline)**, **benzene**, **kerosene** and **paraffin**. From the well, the crude is usually **transported** to a **refinery** in **pipelines** or **tanker ships**. There the hydrocarbons are **separated** from each other by various refining processes. In a process called **fractional distillation**, petroleum is **heated** and sent into a **tower**. The **vapours** of the different components **condense** on **collectors** at different heights in the tower. The separated **fractions** are then **drawn** from the collectors and further **processed** into various petroleum products, for example gasoline or **asphalt**.

Cracking processes use heat, pressure, and certain **catalysts** to break up the large molecules of heavy hydrocarbons into small molecules of light hydrocarbons. Some of the heavier fractions find eventual use as **lubricating oils** and paraffins.

Today the world is heavily dependent on petroleum for **power**, **lubrication**, **fuel**, **dyes**, **drugs**, and many **synthetics**. The widespread use of petroleum has created serious environmental problems; air pollution from burnt fuels contaminates the atmosphere and oil **spillages** from tankers and offshore wells pollute oceans and **coastlines**.

B After *refining*, the petroleum is *transported* to the refinery. Depending on the end *use*, the petroleum may be converted into petrochemicals.

Refining

> catalytic cracking • distillation • impurity • refinery
> separation • steam cracking • thermal cracking

Transporting

> barrel • pipeline • spill • store • tanker • terminal • transport

Uses of petroleum fuel

> aeroplanes • automobiles • electrical power supply
> rockets • ships • tractors • trucks

Petrochemicals from petroleum (➔ 12)

> cleansing agents • explosives • fertilizers • jellies • paints
> plastics (➔ 25) • soaps • solvents • synthetic rubber and fibres • waxes

C One way of increasing your vocabulary is to learn the associated words from a key word. Look at the word table below, which shows words related to the key words presented above.

Noun	Verb	Adjective
refinery	refine	refining/refined
separation	separate	separate
distillation	distil	distilling/distilled
heat	heat	hot
vapour	vaporize	vaporous
lubrication/lubricant	lubricate	lubricating/lubricated
synthetics	synthesize	synthetic
pollution/pollutant	pollute	polluting/polluted
spillage	spill	spilt
explosive	explode	explosive

TASKS

1 Find 15 petroleum-related products in the word square below.

P	W	D	T	K	Y	P	E	O	S	I	N	C	B	U
L	U	B	R	I	C	A	T	I	O	N	M	O	J	Q
A	V	I	O	O	S	R	U	K	L	W	F	U	E	L
S	O	A	P	L	W	A	X	G	V	P	Q	L	L	S
T	A	R	G	N	N	F	T	P	E	T	R	O	L	Y
I	Q	U	Z	W	C	F	X	K	N	H	T	M	Y	L
C	B	U	P	W	Z	I	T	B	T	F	K	A	C	V
T	T	E	P	A	I	N	T	A	C	P	L	P	P	X
A	S	D	W	X	T	E	X	P	L	O	S	I	V	E
B	R	E	E	F	G	I	O	U	W	W	S	T	J	P
A	T	D	R	U	G	F	P	Z	D	E	J	B	P	O
O	O	Y	F	H	U	P	A	R	A	R	R	T	H	J
F	F	E	R	T	I	L	I	Z	E	R	U	N	B	V
W	G	H	P	B	O	A	K	T	U	K	L	P	T	Y

2 Complete the following sentences by adding a word derived from the word given.

1 At the first stage in the refining process, crude oil is heated and petroleum products are initially _____.
separation

2 _____ are devices used to remove solids from the gas.
collect

3 _____ converts crude oil into petroleum products by separating the crude oil into its constituent components through evaporation and condensation.
distil

4 In the stack, crude oil is pumped into a boiler and _____.
hot

5 Refining crude involves removing the _____, most of which become valuable products.
pure

6 Synthetic motor oils provide extremely fast _____ of all moving parts compared to conventional mineral oils.
lubricate

7 Fuels generate most of the air _____ in industrialized countries.
pollute

8 In a _____ the various components present in crude oil are separated and converted into usable products.
refine

3 Petronoco refines and transports oil. In the following extract from the chairman's end-of-year presentation, some words are missing. Complete the extract using appropriate words from the box below. You should use each word once.

refineries • distillation • impurities • pipeline • barrel • processed
refining • separate • spillage • tankers • terminal • transporting

I am pleased to report that the supply of crude from our wells is expected to flow for some decades. Further good news is that over the last twelve months we have seen a significant rise in the price per (a) _____. Therefore we will continue to be active in our two core areas: (b) _____ and (c) _____ oil. For the first area, we plan to invest in technology for new (d) _____. In particular, we need to improve the (e) _____ process in order to (f) _____ the hydrocarbons more efficiently. In addition, we need to research new technologies to remove the (g) _____ so that they can be (h) _____ and converted into marketable products. On to transportation. We will continue to lease the (i) _____ from SeaBed Enterprises, since this is the most economical way to transport oil from the fields to the (j) _____. After the major (k) _____ last year, we sold all our (l) _____. This is no longer part of our core business.

25 Plastics

A Plastic is a common name for **polymers**: materials made of long **strings** of carbon and other elements. Each unit in a string is called a **monomer**, and is a chemical derived from oil, coal or natural gas. (➤ 24). Monomers are made into polymers by **joining** the carbon atoms together.

There are many different types of plastic, depending on:

- the starting monomer selected
- the length of the polymer **chains**
- the type of **modifying compounds** added

There are two main groups of plastics: **thermoplastics soften** with **heat** and **harden** with **cooling**, while **thermosets** are **cured** or hardened by heat.

The disposal of plastics causes major environmental problems. Efforts to reduce the environmental impact of waste plastics are:

- source reduction – using less material to manufacture a product
- **biodegradable** plastics – developing plastics that will **disintegrate**
- **incineration** – some plastics can be burned though this is strictly regulated because of **hazardous** air **emissions** and other pollutants
- **recycling** plastics – making the plastics into new products
- collecting and **sorting** used plastics

B Life would be different without *plastics*, as their *features* make them indispensable.

A selection of plastic products

audio cassette • ballpoint pen • bucket • electric cables • milk bottle
plastic bag • refrigerator liner • ruler • shoe soles • water pipes

Features of plastics

attractive • cheap • easy to shape and colour • flexible
good insulators of heat or electricity • hard and slippery • hygienic
lightweight • non-rusting • soft and rubbery • tough and slippery

C Plastics are made into shapes in many ways. Here are some of the processes used.

Extrusion – hot molten plastic is squeezed through a nozzle to make long lengths of special shapes like pipes

Blow extrusion – used for making plastic films and bags

Injection moulding – lots of everyday articles like washers or bowls are made this way

Blow moulding – many bottles and toys are made this way.

Reaction injection moulding – used to make car bumpers and the meat trays in supermarkets

Fabrication – used to make acrylic signs and displays, and industrial tanks and equipment.

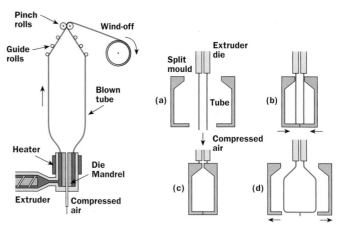

Film blowing   Bottle blowing

1 Are the following statements about plastics true or false? If false, correct the information.

  1 Polymers are made of long strings of carbon and other elements. (   )

  2 Monomers are made into polymers by separating the carbon atoms. (   )

  3 Thermoplastics harden with heat and soften with cooling. (   )

  4 All plastics can be recycled and made into new products. (   )

  5 Incineration is the safest way to dispose of plastics. (   )

  6 Biodegradable plastics will disintegrate. (   )

2 Below is a table showing a list of plastic articles and the types of plastic used. The middle column shows how the plastics are made. Choose the correct method from the list in the box.

> blow extrusion • blow moulding • extrusion (× 2)
> injection moulding (× 4) • reaction injection moulding

Article	How made	Plastic
bucket	a	polyethylene
shoe sole	b	polyurethane
ballpoint pen	c	styrene
electric cable	d	PVC
ruler	e	styrene
plastic bag	f	polyethylene
water pipe	g	PVC
milk bottle	h	polyethylene
audio cassette	i	styrene

3 Below is the contents page from a leading book on plastics. On the left is the title of each chapter; on the right, a short description of the contents of each chapter. Link the chapter title to the correct contents.

1 Environmental aspects of plastics _____

2 Physical properties _____

3 Thermoplastics _____

4 Thermosets _____

5 Features of plastics _____

6 Plastic products _____

7 Extrusion process _____

8 Injection moulding process _____

9 Blow moulding _____

10 Environmental aspects of plastics _____

a pushing heated plastic through a nozzle

b using compressed air to blow bubbles inside the plastic

c combining carbon atoms

d heat-hardening processes

e safe disposal of plastics

f from audio cassettes (A) to zips (Z)

g monomers and polymers

h heat-softening and cool-hardening processes

i squeezing heated plastic into a mould

j attractive, flexible, lightweight .... the ideal material

26 Agroindustry

A **Agroindustry** includes a number of industries connected to the growing, **processing** and transporting of food and food-related products. In its widest sense, it covers the outputs and inputs of **agriculture** and the food industry, including:

- food production and supply
- **dairy farming** and produce
- animal **feed**
- food and drink for consumption

Agroprocessing can be divided into:

- upstream industries which are engaged in the initial processing of agricultural commodities such as **rice milling** and **flour milling**, leather **tanning**, oil **pressing**, and fish **canning**
- downstream industries which carry out further manufacturing operations on intermediate products made from agricultural materials. Examples are bread and biscuit **baking**, textile **spinning** and **weaving**, paper production, and clothing and **footwear** manufacturing

Agribusiness covers businesses that:

- supply farm inputs, such as **fertilizers**, **pesticides** or equipment
- are involved in the marketing of farm products, such as warehouses, processors, wholesalers, transporters, and retailers

Finally, **agriculture** is the art, science, and industry of managing the **growth** of plants and animals for human use. In a broad sense agriculture includes **cultivation** of the **soil**, growing and harvesting **crops**, **breeding** and **raising livestock**, dairy farming, and forestry.

B *Agricultural engineering* is the application of engineering principles to agricultural production systems, processing systems, and conservation of land and water resources. It covers:

> conservation • drainage • food engineering • post-harvest handling
> power and machinery development • processing of commodities
> resource management and utilization • sanitary engineering
> soil and water management

Agricultural chemistry deals with the chemical compositions and changes involved in the production, protection, and use of crops and livestock.

> additive • animal feed supplement • fertilizer • fungicide
> herbicide • insecticide • plant growth regulator • soil makeup

Food packing and processing covers the activities needed to distribute the food and prevent it from spoiling

> canning • dehydration • drying • fermentation • food preservation
> freezing • irradiation • pasteurization • quick-freezing • refrigeration
> reverse osmosis • spoilage • spray drying • thermal processing

C Below are the course contents of a food hygiene programme – essential training for all food handlers in the catering, food retailing or food processing environments.

- Introduction to food hygiene
- Personal hygiene
- Food poisoning
- Premises, equipment and pest control
- Bacteriology
- Cleaning and disinfection
- Prevention of contamination and food poisoning
- Legislation

1 Find 10 agroindustrial terms in the word square opposite.

L	U	C	R	G	R	O	W	T	H
I	S	U	J	A	B	H	D	H	Y
V	R	B	R	E	E	D	I	N	G
E	W	T	I	F	E	Z	D	B	I
S	F	I	C	I	B	A	B	F	E
T	O	F	E	E	D	T	A	E	N
O	X	L	Z	H	T	H	K	R	E
C	R	O	P	S	P	R	I	T	I
K	B	U	Q	U	I	R	N	I	V
O	D	R	A	I	N	A	G	E	R

2 Combine a word in A with a word in B to form ten agroprocessing and food processing terms. Finally, choose the best definition for the term in C.

A	B	C
bread	weaving	to convert animal skin into a material that can be worn
fish	baking	to make paper
flour	drying	to extract liquid by squeezing
footwear	freezing	to cook by dry heat especially in an oven
leather	grinding	to make chilled with cold
oil	manufacturing	to make cloth
pulp	pressing	to make from raw materials by machinery
quick	producing	to make grains into very small particles for human food or animal feed
spray	tanning	to preserve by sealing in airtight containers
textile	canning	to remove liquid

3 Below are the details of a course in food hygiene. Link the correct description on the right to the course component on the left.

FOOD HYGIENE COURSE DETAILS

Introduction to food hygiene	Cross-contamination can easily occur when one food touches (or drips onto) another, or indirectly, for example from hands, equipment, work surfaces, or knives and other utensils.
Food handling	Floors, walls, ceilings and surfaces (which come into contact with food) must be adequately maintained, easy to clean and, where necessary, disinfected.
Bacteriology	Food handlers must protect food and ingredients against risks which may make them unfit for human consumption or a health hazard.
Prevention of contamination	Hygiene is important for anyone working in a food business. Good hygiene prevents food poisoning and protects your reputation with customers.
Premises	Owners and managers of food businesses must ensure that their businesses comply with the law.
Cleaning and disinfection	People who work in food areas can spread food poisoning germs very easily.
Staff	The place where you work has to be kept clean, maintained in good repair and be designed and constructed to permit good hygiene practices.
Legislation	While you are working, clean up any spills immediately and clean work surfaces, equipment and floors frequently.

27 Pulp and paper

A Paper is used for a wide range of writing, printing, **wrapping** and **packaging** products. There are two main raw materials: primary **wood pulp** from **felled** trees and recycled **waste**. For the cheapest **grades** of paper, such as **newsprint**, only pulp is used; for better grades, chemical wood, pulp from which undesirable materials have been chemically removed, or a mixture of pulp and **rags** (from **cotton** or **linen**) is used; and for the finest papers, such as the highest grades of writing papers, only rag **fibre** is used.

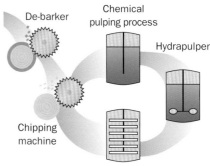

De-barker Chemical pulping process Hydrapulper Chipping machine Mechanical pulping process

Wood pulp is prepared by removing the **bark** (the outer layer of a **log**). Then the logs are **chopped** into **chips** (very small pieces). There are two types of **pulping**: chemical and mechanical. In the chemical process, the **woodchips** are cooked with chemicals in a **digester**. In the mechanical process, the woodchips are **ground** mechanically in a **refiner** to separate the fibres.
At this stage, different pulps in the form of **slurry** from the chemical, mechanical and waste pulp processes can be combined in a **blend chest**. Also at this stage, **additives** such as **dyes** and **bleach** may be added. The mixture, the **papermaking stock**, is treated to separate the fibres. This is known as the **refining** stage.

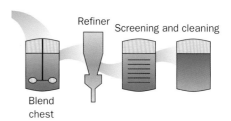

Refiner Screening and cleaning Blend chest

Finally this pulp is **pressed** and **dried** in a **mill**. The finished paper is **wound** onto large **rolls**. It is converted into smaller rolls or sheets for ease of transport and use.

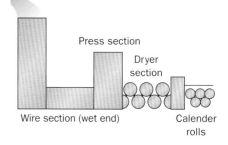

Press section Dryer section Wire section (wet end) Calender rolls

B Different *grades of paper* have different *properties*; and paper also comes in different *sizes and quantities*.

Paper grades

Bible • bond • book • bristol • groundwood
kraft • newsprint • paperboard • sanitary

Paper properties

absorbance • brightness • colour • durability • gloss
opacity • porosity • stiffness • strength • water resistance

Paper sizes and quantities

octavo • quire • ream • sheet

C Paper has many uses. Here are some of them:

brochures • cartons • catalogues • envelopes • games
magazines • maps • matchboxes • money • newspapers
packaging • paper bags • posters • serviettes • stamps
tickets • tissues • wallpaper • wrappers • wrapping paper

1 Match the following words with their definitions.

fell	chemical to whiten paper
bark	to convert wood into a fibrous material by a mechanical or chemical process
chop	to crush into particles
pulp	to cut down a tree
grind	to cut into small pieces
slurry	liquid mixture consisting of fibres in water used in papermaking process
bleach	outer layer of a log
press	quantity of paper formed into a large cylinder or ball
wind	to squeeze out water between rollers
roll	to turn around so as to form a roll

2 Organize the following stages in the papermaking process into the correct order in the flowchart.

blending the pulp   cooking woodchips with chemicals   felling trees
grinding woodchips   pressing and drying   removing the bark
winding onto rolls

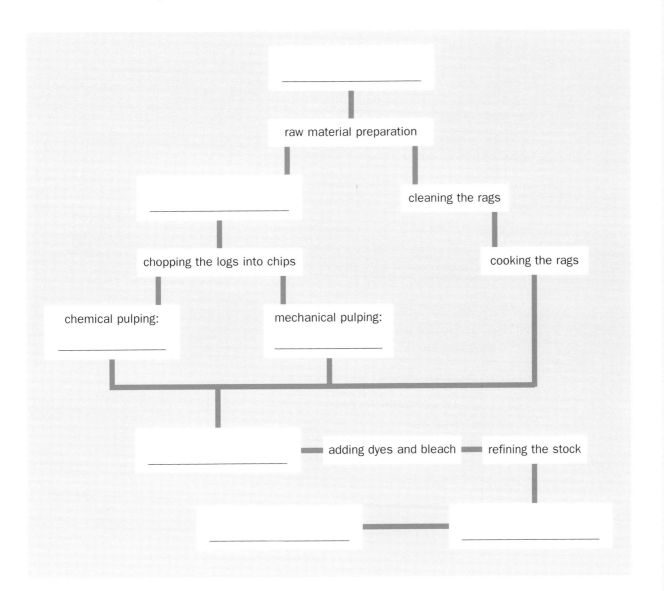

28 Telecoms 1

A Telecommunications technology **transmits** information by **electromagnetic** means over media such as telephone **wires** or radio **waves**. The information may be voice, facsimile, data, radio, or television signals. The electronic **signals** that are transmitted can be either **analogue** or **digital**. The advantages of digital transmission are high reliability and low cost. Digital **switching systems** are much cheaper than analogue systems.

In analogue **modulation**, the signals are transmitted directly (without **converting** them to digital form) by **amplitude modulation** or **frequency modulation**. For digital transmission the analogue signals must be converted to a digital form. Then the digitized signal is passed through a **source encoder**, which reduces redundant **binary** information. After source encoding, the digitized signal is processed in a **channel encoder**, which introduces **redundant** information that allows errors (**degradation** by **noise** or **distortion**) to be detected and corrected. The encoded signal is made suitable for transmission by modulation onto a **carrier wave**. When a signal reaches its destination, the device on the receiving end converts the **electronic** signal back into an understandable message – sound on a telephone, images on a television, or words and pictures on a computer.

B There are three main methods of electromagnetic signal transmission: *wire*, *radio* and *optical*.

wire transmission

amplify • attenuation • coaxial cable • copper wire • metallic-pair circuit
multipair cable • open-wire pair • repeater • restore • retransmit • single-wire line

radio transmission

antenna • dish • electromagnetic wave • microwave • radio wave • receiver
reflected propagation • satellite • surface propagation • transmitter • transponder

optical transmission

fibre optic cable • high bandwidth • interference immunity • laser • lightweight
light-emitting diode (LED) • low attenuation • low cost • wavelength

C Telecommunications is the fastest growing segment of technology today. Telecommunications technologists are needed to plan, install and maintain state-of-the-art telephone systems, cable TV and computer networks. Although technologists have knowledge of theoretical topics, they tend to focus on solving practical design and application problems. Training covers a wide range of telecoms-related topics. Here is the content from one such course:

COURSE CONTENT

Part 1: Operating Systems

Part 2: Analogue Communications

Part 3: Telecommunications Fundamentals

Part 4: Telecommunications Fundamentals Lab

Part 5: Digital Electronics

Part 6: Telecommunications Networking

Part 7: Fundamentals of Optical Communications

Part 8: Data Communications Networking

1 Match each of the following words with its definition.

wire	a device which maps the binary strings into coded bits or waveforms for transmission
wave	a device which maps the source into a set of binary strings
analogue	a system in which data is represented as 0 or 1
digital	a system in which data is represented as a continuously varying voltage
amplitude modulation	a thin piece of metal for conducting electrical current
frequency modulation	a wave suitable for modulation by an information-bearing signal
source encoder	an electric, electromagnetic, acoustic, mechanical or other form whose physical activity rises and falls as it travels through a medium
channel encoder	the deterioration in quality, level, or standard of performance
degradation	to fail to reproduce accurately the characteristics of the input
distort	where audio signals increase and decrease the amplitude of the carrier wave
carrier wave	where voltage levels change the frequency of a carrier wave

2 The following words are taken from three modes of transmission: wire, radio and optical. Link each term with the most appropriate mode of transmission.

antenna • coaxial cable • copper wire • fibre optic cable
laser • light-emitting diode • microwave • repeater • satellite
single-wire line • transmitter • wavelength

wire _____

radio _____

optical _____

3 The following extract is taken from a description for a telecommunications technology course. Complete the text by choosing a suitable word or phrase from the box.

sharing • laser • information • electromagnetic transmission
direct • converting analogue • transmit signals

TELECOMMUNICATIONS TECHNOLOGY CERTIFICATE COURSE

COURSE NAME	COURSE DETAILS
Telecommunications Fundamentals	Introduction to the _____ _____ of information
Telecommunications Fundamentals Lab	Hands-on practical experiments to _____ _____
Analogue Communications	_____ transmission of signals
Digital Electronics	_____ _____ signals
Fundamentals of Optical Communications	The advantages of _____ technologies
Fundamentals of Telecommunications Networking	Introduction to _____ information
Data Communications Networking	Sharing _____ between networks

29 Telecoms 2

A A wide variety of information can be **transferred** through a telecommunications system, including **voice** and **music**, **still-frame** and **full-motion** pictures, computer **files** and **applications**, and telegraphic **data**.

The telephone is an **instrument** used for **sending** and **receiving** voice **messages** and data. Most phone **calls** involve two people, but the phone **network** can also be used to pay bills and **retrieve** messages from **answering machines**. Private individuals will usually have their own **phone line**; a large business will usually have its own **switching machine**, called a **Private Branch Exchange (PBX)**, with many lines, all of which can be reached by **dialling** one number.

Radio **transmission broadcasts signals** that are intended for general public **reception**. With an **omnidirectional antenna**, radio signals are **transmitted** over a wide area. In a point-to-point radio **channel**, a **directional** transmitting antenna focuses the wave into a narrow **beam**, which is directed toward a single receiver. Broadcasts may be **audible** only, as in radio, or **visual** or a combination of both, as in television.

B Two applications of telecoms are *telephony* and *television*.

Telephony
A **videophone** is a personal **video camera** and **display**, a **microphone** and **speaker**, and a **data-conversion device**.
A **cordless** telephone is a **device** which plugs directly into an existing telephone **jack**, allowing limited **mobility** within the home, garden or office.
Telephony has been revolutionized by **cellular** (**cell** or **mobile**) telephones, which are personal **portable** devices.
Facsimile, or **fax**, refers to the **transmission** of print: text, fixed **images** or **drawings** by wire or radio channels or undersea **cable**.

Television

aerial •	antenna •	broadcast •	cable television •	dish
relay station •	television set •	television station •	visible	

C Mobile telephony is revolutionizing how we use the phone. Look at the range of features offered by the MobiPhone.

THE MOBIPHONE WORLD

THE MOBIPHONE WORLD is the latest in a line of WAP "smartphones" combining the best of both worlds – mobile phones and handy PDAs. All phones offer the full complement of features,

- 14.4 kbps data and fax transmission
- a vibrating alert
- a clock and alarm
- a currency converter
- a built-in personal organizer that holds up to 1,000 short memos.

THE TOP-OF-THE-RANGE World 1000 is GPRS enabled (General Packet Radio Service) offering:
- 'always-on'
- higher capacity
- Internet-based content
- packet-based data services.

This enables services such as colour internet browsing, email on the move, powerful visual communications, multimedia messages and location-based services. With an LCD screen displaying up to ten times the amount of text you'd get on a traditional cell phone, the MobiPhone is tomorrow's mobile phone today.

Also available: an infra-red computer connection.
Dimensions: 103mm × 51mm × 16mm (including battery). Weight: 69g (including battery).

1 Circle *all* the correct answers that apply.

1 A telecommunications system can transfer
     a voice   **b** pictures   **c** computer files   **d** energy

2 The telephone is an instrument used for
     a sending messages   **b** switching messages   **c** receiving messages
     d retrieving messages

3 Broadcast signals can be
     a tactile   **b** audible   **c** visual   **d** a combination of all three

4 A videophone combines
     a a video camera   **b** a display   **c** a microphone   **d** a speaker

5 Fax can be used to transmit
     a sounds   **b** moving pictures   **c** drawings   **d** images

6 A cordless phone
     a plugs into a jack   **b** allows unlimited mobility   **c** can be used within the home
     d is portable

2 Match a word in the left-hand column with a word on the right to form ten phrases from the field of telecommunications.

answering	antenna
radio	camera
video	jack
relay	machine
cable	messages
television	phone
retrieve	set
transmitting	signal
cordless	station
telephone	television

Now complete the following sentences using phrases from the table opposite.

1 The telephone can be used to pay bills
   and _____ from _____.

2 With an omnidirectional antenna,
   _____ can be transmitted
   over a wide area.

3 A videophone incorporates a _____
   and display, a microphone and speaker.

4 A _____ allows limited mobility in and around the home.

5 _____ allows access to many television stations.

3 Below is an extract from the review of the newly released MobiPhone World. Complete the text using the words/phrases in the box below.

alert • browsing • cell phone • clock and alarm • currency converter
email • organizer • PDA • screen • weight

MobiPhone World 1000 is the latest product from MobiCom. It is a fully-featured, future-proof mobile, packed with exciting applications. Not only a mobile phone, it doubles as a handy (a) _____. As it is GPRS enabled, you can collect your (b) _____ while you are on the move. In addition, the colour internet (c) _____ makes word wide web searching a new experience. This is enhanced by the new LCD (d) _____ which displays up to ten times the amount of text you'd get on a traditional (e) _____. When you go abroad, you don't need to worry about missing that important meeting as the World 1000 comes with a (f) _____. You can also be one step ahead of the bank by checking how much you'll get for your money with the (g) _____. And when you get to the business meeting, you won't disturb your neighbours, as the vibrating (h) _____ lets you know about incoming calls. You can even write short notes of the meeting on the built-in personal (i) _____.

With a (j) _____ of just 69 grams, the MobiPhone World 1000 is a must have.

30 Textiles

A Textiles refers to:

- **fibres** that can be **spun** into **yarn** or made into **fabric** by operations such as **weaving**, **knitting**, **braiding**, and **felting**
- all fabrics (both natural and **synthetic**) produced by mechanically or chemically bonding fibres

Fibres, the basic raw materials, may be:

- obtained from natural sources, such as **wool** from sheep
- produced from various substances by chemical processes

After cleaning and **blending**, the fibres are spun into yarn. This is then processed into fabric in a **weaving mill or knitting mill**. The next stage, called finishing, includes various mechanical and chemical processes for:

- removal of **defects** or **foreign matter**
- removal of moisture
- **bleaching**
- **dyeing**
- printing

The appearance of the fabric may also be improved by **napping**, **shearing**, **pressing**, **brushing**, and **polishing**.

After finishing, the woven material is ready for delivery to:

- a manufacturer of textile products such as **clothing**, household linens and **bedding**, **upholstery**, **rugs** and **carpets**
- a retailer, who sells it to individuals to make **clothes** or household articles such as **curtains**

B Various *techniques and processes* are used to produce *fibres* of different *qualities*.

Fibres

> acetate • cotton • linen • nylon • polyester • rayon • silk • wool

Techniques and processes

> blending • braiding • carding • embroidering • fibre processing
> knitting • lace-making • net-making • spinning • weaving

Qualities of fibres

> ability to withstand laundering or dry-cleaning • absorption • crease control
> elasticity • fineness • flexibility • length • reaction to heat and light
> shrinkage control • strength • wash and wear

C Looking after your fabrics is important if you want to make them last. Care labels tell you about:

washing		indicates that normal (maximum) washing conditions may be used at the appropriate temperature; the number indicates the maximum temperature
bleaching		means that chlorine bleach may be used
ironing		means that a hot iron may be used
dry-cleaning		indicates that the garment must be professionally cleaned
tumble drying		means that the garment may be tumble dried

1 Find eighteen textile-related products in the word square opposite.

S	I	L	K	Q	U	P	F	F	I	O	G	R	A	F
P	S	E	N	Y	L	O	N	B	X	D	R	P	G	B
I	V	C	I	A	Z	L	U	K	A	Y	S	Q	O	P
N	Z	S	T	E	S	Y	N	T	H	E	T	I	C	T
Y	S	G	H	B	L	E	L	W	T	Y	P	Z	T	W
D	L	M	J	L	K	S	H	R	I	N	K	A	G	E
F	I	B	R	E	W	T	H	A	V	I	U	P	W	A
P	N	J	L	A	L	E	R	C	X	Q	C	M	Y	V
S	E	R	T	C	U	R	T	A	I	N	L	T	T	E
G	N	B	F	H	X	H	O	R	A	J	W	U	P	A
P	P	A	X	A	W	Y	K	P	R	E	S	S	I	M
N	F	F	C	R	E	A	S	E	B	W	H	Q	U	W
N	D	I	Q	U	T	R	A	T	P	P	Q	C	C	V
Z	A	F	T	G	T	N	C	E	H	U	K	E	P	C

2 Classify the following fabrics into their fibre type – natural (N) or synthetic (S). Then choose from the box opposite which characteristics best describe each fabric.

Fabric	Fibre type	Characteristics
cotton		a
linen		b
nylon		c
polyester		d
silk		e
wool		f

- Good insulator; luxurious, soft to the touch
- Good strength, twice as strong as cotton; crisp to the touch
- Lightweight; easy to wash: resists shrinkage and wrinkling
- Luxurious; thinnest of all natural fibres
- Soft to the touch; absorbent
- Strong; resistant to most chemicals

3 Below are the instructions for how to look after your fabrics. Complete the texts using the words below.

dry-cleanable • drying • hand-washable • machine-washable
shrinkage • stain • stretching • sunlight

When caring for your fabrics, remember that:

COTTON
is easy to care for. It is (a) _____ and dry-cleanable and has good colour retention.

LINEN
is twice as strong as cotton and is hand-washable or (b) _____.

SILK
is (c) _____ or dry-cleanable, but has poor resistance to prolonged exposure to (d) _____.

NYLON
is easy to wash, resists (e) _____ and wrinkling, is fast (f) _____, but has poor resistance to continuous sunlight.

POLYESTER
is resistant to (g) _____; can be washed or dry-cleaned; is quick drying and wrinkle resistant; because of its low absorbency, (h) _____ removal can be a problem.

31 Present tenses

A Sample sentences

The logistics department dispatches finished goods to our customers and receives raw materials from our suppliers. Delivery documentation is enclosed with the consignment, but the shipping papers aren't prepared in this department. In this area here the goods are loaded onto trucks; and over there incoming goods which have just arrived are unloaded. A consignment is just being delivered over there. We have been using plastic packaging for many years; however, next year we are moving to more environmentally-friendly materials.

B Form

Present simple and *Present continuous*

	Positive	Negative	Question
Present simple active	We *receive* raw materials from our suppliers.	The supervisor *doesn't prepare* the papers.	Where *do* you *store* finished goods?
Present simple passive	All goods *are received* at this depot.	The bill of lading *isn't dispatched.*	Where *are* the goods *stored*?
Present continuous active	The supervisor *is checking* the delivery.	I *am not sending* out a bill of lading with this shipment.	When *are* we *moving* to the new depot?
Present continuous passive	Goods *are being unloaded* over there.	At present the pallets *are not being reused.*	Why *are* those crates *being moved*?

Present perfect

	Positive	Negative	Question
Present perfect simple active	Our contractor *has built* a supporting wall.	They *have not drained* the water yet.	How many tunnels *have* they *dug*?
Present perfect simple passive	The walls *have been built.*	The water *has not been drained.*	*Has* the cable *been laid*?
Present perfect continuous active	The supervisor *has been checking* the walls today.	I *have not been working* on that site since last year.	How long *have* they *been excavating* at the site?

Note: the *present perfect continuous passive* is very rare

C Uses

The *present tenses* are used to express a range of meanings.

The *present continuous* describes:

1 an activity at or around the time of speaking
   At present we are using plastic packaging.
2 a fixed future plan
   Next year we are building a new depot.

The *present simple* describes:

a regular or characteristic happening
How often do you receive shipments?

The *present perfect* describes:

1 an activity at a non-specific time in the past
   Our contractor has built a new supporting wall.
2 an activity which started in the past and continues to the present
   We have been working on this project since last year.

TASKS

1 Choose the correct verb form in each of the following.

1 In this process, the mixture **is heated/is heating** to 120°C.

2 Once the salts **are dissolving/have dissolved**, the heat is reduced.

3 Several people **have survived/are surviving** the earthquake and **are treating/are being treated** in hospital at the moment.

4 For security purposes the employees **change/are changing** their passwords regularly.

5 Up until now people in this area **have taken/take** waste plastic to recycling centres, but at present we **have tried/are trying** a curbside collection system.

2 A journalist is asking some questions. Complete the answers by putting the verb in brackets into the appropriate present tense in the active or passive.

1 A: Do you normally hold these products in stock?
   B: No. They _____*are*_____ normally _____*made*_____ to order. (make)

2 A: Is the chief engineer here at the moment?
   B: I'm afraid not. He _____ currently _____ the plant in the north of Scotland. (inspect)

3 A: Can I see the new design?
   B: Yes, of course. It _____ just _____ off the production line. (come)

4 A: How many units do you produce a month?
   B: We _____ 5,000 units a month and only a very small number _____ . (produce) (reject)

5 A: How long have you been using imported raw materials?
   B: We _____ (import) rayon for many years but we _____ only just _____ (begin) using imported polyester.

6 A: Is this the natural colour of the fabric?
   B: No, this fabric _____ (dye).

7 A: And how long will it be kept in store?
   B: Not long at all. We _____ (dispatch) this load tomorrow afternoon.

3 Complete the following text with the correct form of the verbs in brackets.

Over the past ten years, this area (a) _____ (experience) severe flooding. Houses (b) _____ (damage) and roads (c) _____ (destroy). The local authority (d) _____ (decide) to introduce a flood control system. At present our workforce (e) _____ (build) a dam on the west side of the town and dikes along the river bank (f) _____ (heighten). We must complete the work within two months, so at present we (g) _____ (work) 24 hours a day. We (h) _____ (believe) that these measures will solve the problem in the short term but on 1st May we (i) _____ (start) work on a new watercourse. The plans (j) _____ already _____ (draw up) and we (k) _____ (be) ready to start next week.

32 Past tenses

A Last year we began a study of airbags on our four wheel drive vehicles. First we analysed the results of the tests that we had carried out. After the results had been compiled, we used modelling software to evaluate the performance of the airbags. This showed how well they had performed under different conditions. While we were evaluating the physical performance, another study was assessing the materials that we were using. All the results were then recorded into a database.

B **Form**

Past simple and *Past continuous*

	Positive	Negative	Question
Past simple active	Last year we *began* a new study.	We *didn't develop* the software ourselves.	Where *did* you *record* the results?
Past simple passive	The performance of the air bags *was assessed*.	The results *weren't recorded*.	Where *were* the findings *published*?
Past continuous active	While the analyst *was carrying* out the test …	… the other technicians *were not recording* the results.	What *were* you *doing* during the test phase?
Past continuous passive	While the test *was being* carried out …	… the results *were not being* recorded.	Why *were* the findings *being written* down?

Past perfect

	Positive	Negative	Question
Past perfect simple active	After we *had compiled* the results …	Because they *had not* recorded the data …	*Had* they *carried* out all the tests?
Past perfect simple passive	… after the results *had been compiled*.	… because the data *had not been recorded*.	*Had* all the tests *been carried* out?
Past perfect continuous active	The analyst *had been checking* the walls yesterday …	We *had not been evaluating* the physical characteristics …	How long *had* you *been working* on the project?

Note: the *past perfect continuous active* is quite unusual and the *past perfect continuous passive* is very rare

C **Uses**

All the *past tenses* are used to express activities at a definite time in the past.

The *past simple* describes:
an activity at a definite time in the past
The study of airbags was started last year.

The *past continuous* describes:
an activity which is a time frame for another activity
While we were studying the airbags, we made a significant discovery.
While our team was studying performance, another team was looking at the characteristics.

The *past perfect* describes:
an activity that happened earlier than another activity in the past
Our studies showed how well the equipment had performed.

Notes:
We use the *past tenses* with these expressions:

yesterday	**yesterday** *morning/afternoon,/evening*
last	**last** *night/week/month/year*
ago	*one hour/two weeks/three months/four years* **ago**
in	*in 2005/the 1990's/the 19th century*

TASKS

1   Six of the following sentences contain mistakes. Find the mistakes and correct them.

1   Sydney Harbour Bridge was building in 1932.

2   While they were carrying out tests in the laboratories, researchers were analysing past results.

3   The first real road builders in Britain was the Romans.

4   The Romans built roads of layers of broken stones of various sizes and were covering them with flat stones.

5   The system didn't working because the loudspeaker had been wrongly connected.

6   Before factories were told to stop polluting the environment, waste was being dumped in rivers and in the sea.

7   Louis Pasteur was discovering the action of germs while he was studying fermentation in wines.

8   The production process had already been shut down when the leak in the fuel tank was found.

9   Nuclear energy began to be used from the mid-1950s.

10   In the second half of the 20th century, the electronics industry transforming the way we work in factories.

2   Make past tense questions and answers using the words given.

1: When were fibre optics first developed?

1   When / be / fibre optics / first / develop?

2   The boxes / break / because they / make / of low quality materials.

3   The power supply / cut off / because / cables / come down / during the storm.

4   They / not complete / the foundations / by the time the building materials / arrive.

5   When / they / install / the solar panels?

6   be / this / the first hydroelectric scheme/ in Scotland?

7   They / not use / wood chip / for heating / when the engineer / visit / the factory.

8   How / they / produce / gas / before they / discover / North Sea gas?

9   be / the oil pollution along the coastline / cause / by an oil tanker spillage?

10   How / they prepare access to this mine?

3   Complete the following report of an accident which happened in a factory with the correct form of the verbs in brackets.

On Friday morning at 9.25 a worker in the chemical plant (a) _____
(find) by a female colleague. He (b) _____ (lie) on the floor. His colleague
(c) _____ (check) that he (d) _____ still _____
(breathe) and then (e) _____ (call) the emergency services. The injured man
(f) _____ (take) to hospital where he later (g) _____ (recover).
An investigation at the factory (h) _____ (find) that a bottle containing a
dangerous chemical liquid (i) _____ (leave) open. Vapour from the liquid
(j) _____ (escape) into the air. While he had been working in the room he
(k) _____ (become) unwell. He (l) _____ (become) drowsy and
then (m) _____ (fall) unconscious. Investigating officers are interviewing
everyone who (n) _____ (work) in the factory that morning.

33 Future forms

A Sample sentences

A: When are we going to treat the first patients with the new drug?
B: The results from the tests won't be available before next year.
A: When is PharEurop going to register the drug?
B: They are preparing the preliminary forms next month. So they'll be ready before the summer.
A: And when are you going to publish that paper on the results?
B: I am submitting it to the medical journal after the summer.

B Form

1 There is no *to* after *will* or *shall*:
 The results of the tests will be ready after the summer.
2 You need the verb *to be* with the *present continuous* and the *going to* forms:
 I am submitting it to the medical journal after the summer.
 When is PharEurop going to register the drug?

C Uses

Look at the differences in meanings between the following pairs of sentences:
I am going to upload the new web page next week. (I intend to do it: future with *going to*)
I am uploading the new web page next week. (It is my fixed plan to do it: future with *present continuous*)

We are going to digitize the pictures so that we can upload them to our website. (We intend to digitize them: future with *going to*)
The digital pictures will be uploaded to our website on 1st June. (The upload date is a fact: future with *will*)

Now look at this mini-dialogue. Notice the different shades of meaning between the three future forms:

A: When will the hardware be installed?
B: We are going to lay the network cables next Tuesday.
A: I'm seeing the electrical contractor tomorrow. We're going to review the site plan.
B: Good. So when do you think the system will go live.
A: The file server will be delivered on Friday.
B: And the work stations?
A: They're coming at the beginning of the following week.

Notes:
1 The *present continuous* needs an expression of future time to give it a future meaning.
 The work stations are coming. (now)
 The work stations are coming at the beginning of next week. (in the future)
2 Typical expressions of future time are:
 tomorrow morning/afternoon/evening but *tonight*
 next week/month/year
 in two weeks/months/years
 in the short/medium/long term
3 The negative of *will* is *won't*:
 The results won't be ready this week.

1   Match these present tense situations with the future intention.

1   The building materials are being delivered.
2   There is a backlog of orders.
3   We're shutting down production.
4   The workers need different interesting jobs to do.
5   This is a very slow manual process.
6   There have been too many faulty goods recently.

a   We're going to replace the faulty machine.
b   We're going to build a new warehouse.
c   The assembly line is going to be inspected.
d   We're going to automate it in the near future.
e   The workers are going to work overtime.
f   We're going to introduce job rotation.

2   In the following situations choose the correct sentence, a) or b).

1   You are reminding a colleague about the programme for tomorrow.
  a   Remember that you'll meet the supplier at 12 o'clock.
  b   Remember that you're meeting the supplier at 12 o'clock.

2   Two colleagues are discussing the future visit by inspectors.
  a   The inspectors won't allow us to store chemicals in this cupboard.
  b   The inspectors are not allowing us to store chemicals in this cupboard.

3   Designers are discussing the car models with airbags.
  a   The use of airbags is going to save more lives in the future.
  b   The use of airbags is saving more lives in the future.

4   Two managers need the results from some research before November.
  a   They won't be able to complete the research before November.
  b   They aren't completing the research before November.

5   A senior manager isn't looking forward to next week because he's worried about the tests.
  a   Tests will be carried out next week.
  b   Tests are being carried out next week.

3   A salesman is describing a new product to a customer. Complete what they say with *will* or *won't* and a verb from the box.

give • operate • deal • take • be • contact
install • provide • need • revolutionize • warm • see

S: This is an excellent new material which (a) _____ the use of solar panels.

C: I see, and how many hours of sunshine (b) _____ we _____ to produce energy?

S: It (c) _____ necessary to have sunshine. It (d) _____ in daylight only.

C: (e) _____ it _____ enough energy to warm the building in winter?

S: It (f) _____ the building but you may need additional heating when it is very cold.

C: What about installation?

S: We (g) _____ it for you. It (h) _____ long and you (i) _____ soon _____ how effective it is. We (j) _____ you a three year guarantee and if there are any problems we (k) _____ with them immediately.

C: When will you be able to install it?

S: As soon as we receive your order we (l) _____ you to discuss a suitable date.

34 Conditionals

A Sample sentences

If you follow these measures, the risk of burns will be substantially reduced.

If you combined these two substances together there would be a serious risk of explosion.

If you hadn't sealed the container, the vapour would have contaminated the environment.

If you feel unwell, seek medical advice immediately.

In case of contact with eyes, rinse immediately with plenty of water.

B Form

A conditional sentence has two clauses: the *if* clause and the main clause.

There are four principal types of conditional sentences: conditional I, conditional II, conditional III and universal conditions.

Conditional	*if* clause	main clause
I	*present simple*	*future* with *will*
II	*past simple*	*conditional* with *would*
III	*past perfect*	*past conditional* with *would have*
Universal	*present simple*	*present simple*

Note that the following contractions are common in speech:

will – *'ll*, e.g. *I'll*   *would have* – *would've*, e.g. *we would* **'ve**   *would/had* – *'d*, e.g. *they***'d**

C Uses

We use conditional sentences to talk about the relationship between events and their consequences:

If our survey indicates the possibility of oil (event), *then we will do some drilling* (consequence).

Conditional I

Here the speaker sees the event as a real possibility:

If the oil field is productive, we will recover our exploration costs in a short time.

Conditional II

Here the speaker sees the event as a remote possibility:

If there was a blowout, we would evacuate the rig immediately.

Conditional III

Here the speaker recognizes that the event is an impossibility, i.e. cannot be fulfilled:

If we hadn't made this find, we would have leased out our tankers.

Universal Conditions

Here the speaker indicates that the consequence always follows the event:

If a rock is permeable, it allows water or other fluids, such as oil, to pass through it.

Notes:

1   These expressions mean '*if*' and '*only if*':
    provided/providing (that)   on condition that   so long as
    Provided that the results of our surveys are positive, we will continue to drill here.
2   These expressions indicate that a future event may or may not happen.
    in case   in the case of   in the event that   in the event of
    In case of corrosion, stop all activity.
3   *unless* means '*if .... not*'
    Do not return to the rig unless the supervisor gives instructions to do so.

TASKS

1   Match two parts to form conditional sentences.

1 If these tests produce positive results,	**a** the accident would never have happened.
2 If rubber is cooled to –200° C,	**b** download them onto your computer.
3 If safety measures had been followed,	**c** we'd be able to do all the technical specifications in half the time.
4 If you want to study the files from the internet,	**d** we could estimate the experimental error.
5 If we bought a new software package,	**e** they would have taken nearly two months.
6 If you want to use this software package on more than one system,	**f** it becomes brittle and will break.
7 If the goods had been sent by sea,	**g** we'll continue with clinical trials.
8 If we ran an additional test,	**h** you'll have to get a site licence.

2   Complete these sentences using the words in brackets.

1   The tests won't be continued unless _____ (there/be/better safety measures).

2   He wouldn't have been injured if _____ (he/follow/the correct procedures).

3   In the event of a collision, _____ (the airbag/inflate).

4   If all vehicles were fitted with a catalytic converter, _____ (there/be/less/pollution).

5   The reaction would be speeded up if _____ (we/introduce/a catalyst).

6   If heat is applied, _____ (the substance/decompose).

7   As long as disinfectant is used, _____ (infections/not be/ pass on).

8   If iron is left in contact with air and water, _____ (it/rust).

3   Two site workers are discussing the weather. Complete the conversation with the correct form of the verbs in brackets.

A: We'll carry on with the work when the conditions (a) _____ (improve).

B: If we'd known the weather was going to be this bad, we (b) _____ (delay) the start of the project.

A: Well, if the rain (c) _____ (stop) soon, we'll get the foundations laid by evening.

B: It could have been worse. Do you remember building that bridge last year? If we (d) _____ (not build) the dike of sandbags, the river would have flooded the town.

A: And if we hadn't brought in that earthmover, we (e) _____ (not make) it in time.

B: If we get any more rain here, we (f) _____ (have to) repair the potholes in the road before we can use it.

A: Provided it (g) _____ (stop) soon, we'll be able to start preparing the timber. If they'd chosen another time of year, we (h) _____ (not have) these problems. It would be much nicer if we (i) _____ (have) indoor jobs at this time of year!

35 Verb phrases

A Sample sentences

Next month the production department will start to control stock levels every week.
Next month the production department will start controlling stock levels every week.
Do you like working on the assembly line?
Do you like to work on the assembly line?

B Form

After some verbs we can use:
Verb ...*ing* or infinitive + *to*, e.g.
We will continue to automate the process.
We will continue automating the process.
You should never try to operate this machinery unless you are wearing protective clothing.
You should never try operating this machinery unless you are wearing protective clothing.

C Uses

Sometimes the meaning is the same; sometimes it is different.

1 The same meaning:
   We can use both forms after these verbs:

   begin • continue • intend • prefer • start

   We prefer to inspect stock levels on a monthly basis.
   We prefer inspecting them twice a month.

2 A different meaning:
   We can use both forms after these verbs, but with a different meaning:

   forget • remember • try

   Please remember to check the bill of materials. (Don't forget)
   I remember checking the bill of materials. (I checked it and I remember it)
   We tried to mix the two chemicals that you delivered (we attempted to do it)
   We tried mixing the two chemicals that you delivered. (we experimented with it)

3 A slight difference of meaning:

   The employees like rotating jobs, as it increases their motivation. (They enjoy it)
   We like to use a subcontractor to maintain this equipment. (It is a good thing to do)

   Notes:

   1 *We would like _____ (as is)*

   2 *We prefer to use organic products rather than chemical ones.*
      We prefer organic products rather than chemical ones.
      We prefer carrying out thorough lab tests to field trials.
      We prefer carrying out thorough lab tests to trialling the products in the field.

   We would like to introduce quality circles next year. (not *we would like introducing*)

TASKS

1   Choose the correct sentence in each of the following.

1   This new telephone system has been such a success.
  a   I really regret not making a change a long time ago.
  b   I really regret to not make a change a long time ago.

2   This unit is extremely heavy.
  a   Could you try moving it, please?
  b   Could you try to move it, please?

3   Security is very important.
  a   Don't forget changing your password regularly.
  b   Don't forget to change your password regularly.

4   This sounds as though it could work!
  a   Would you like setting up trials?
  b   Would you like to set up trials?

5   It was several years ago but
  a   I remember discussing the advantages of videoconferencing.
  b   I remember to discuss the advantages of videoconferencing.

2   Complete the following sentences with either *to* + infinitive or verb + *...ing*. Choose from the verbs in the box.

produce • scratch • visit • overload • deliver • increase • reduce • switch

1   Installing another machine could risk _____ the electricity supply.

2   Tell him _____ off the power supply.

3   We expect _____ production by 15%.

4   We'll finish _____ that model in November.

5   The suppliers have agreed _____ the amount of packaging.

6   Please avoid _____ the disc.

7   The firm refuse _____ without payment in advance.

8   We want our customers _____ our website for further information.

3   This is part of a memo sent from a computer consultant to a manufacturing company. Complete the memo using the words in brackets.

To:	Helmut Pohl	**MEMO**
From:	Steve Banks	
Re:	computer software	

I have begun work on the software for order processing. I had planned (a) _____ (come) and see you but I've decided (b) _____ (begin) _____ (work) on what I've got here. I am trying (c) _____ (develop) your existing software so that your office staff can keep (d) _____ (use) the existing routine. If we do that we can avoid (e) _____ (create) further training costs. The idea will involve (f) _____ (link) all the modules from quotations, order processing, bill of materials to invoicing. When we link them in this way we will hopefully prevent mistakes (g) _____ (happen). I'd like to invite an associate (h) _____ (join) us on this project and if he agrees (i) _____ (do) this, we can hope (j) _____ (complete) the outline of the programme by July. I don't want (k) _____ (delay) _____ (run) the demonstration and will try (l) _____ (arrange) a suitable time to discuss this further.

36 Active vs passive

A Sample sentences

For our research studies we normally produce a preliminary analysis. We then publish the findings and circulate them to various experts. This is exactly what we did when we applied for the current patent. We are therefore very surprised that you have contacted us in this matter. We can assure you that we completed all the relevant documentation. In the meantime we will investigate your claims further.

For our research studies a preliminary analysis is normally produced. The findings are then published and circulated to various experts. This is exactly what was done when the current patent was applied for. We are therefore very surprised that we have been contacted in this matter. We can assure you that all the relevant documentation was completed. In the meantime your claims will be investigated further.

B Form

Every active sentence has at least two parts:
a subject [1] + an active verb form [2]
We normally produce a preliminary analysis.
[1]   [2]
Every passive sentence has at least two parts:
a subject [1] + a passive verb form [2]
A preliminary analysis   is normally produced.
[1   ] [2   ]

C Uses

We use the *active* verb form in speech and writing to describe actions and events. For example: Paper still plays a vital role in our lives – newspapers tell us the events of the day, and books entertain and educate us. Paper has been with us since 105 A.D. The Chinese first used it to make records; later it spread to all parts of the world.

We can use the *passive* in the following situations:

1 We are not interested in the doer.
   Ancient paper was made entirely of rags; modern paper is made from wood pulp - a faster and cheaper alternative.

2 In process descriptions.
   First the logs are stripped of bark, cut into smaller sections, and made into chips. The chips are put into a large tank called a digester and allowed to stew in a chemical mix under pressure. The wood pulp that is created by this process is then washed to remove any chemicals and pressed through screens to remove chunks and foreign objects. The pulp is then drained of water to form a mass that is then bleached and washed again.

   The first two corresponding *active* sentences would be:
   First we strip the logs of bark, then we cut them into smaller sections, and make them into chips. We then put the chips into a large tank called a digester and allow them to stew in a chemical mix under pressure.

3 In impersonal language.
   The chemicals in this process are toxic: safety clothing must be worn.
   This is the typical style of a written order or instruction. The corresponding *active* sentence would be:
   The chemicals are toxic: wear safety clothing.

TASKS

1 In the following sentences underline the verbs and decide if they are *active* or *passive*.

1 A repeater boosts the electrical signal so that longer cables can be used.
2 Men's ties are usually made of silk or polyester.
3 Nearly all paper can be recycled if it is sorted and contaminants are removed.
4 Geothermal energy is produced below the earth's surface.
5 The main sources of greenhouse gas emissions include fossil fuel generating plants and transportation vehicles.
6 Manufacturers choose plastic containers for many different reasons.
7 Oil was formed in underground rocks millions of years ago.

2 Here is a list of changes which have taken place in a town between 1960 and today. Use these notes and the verbs given to write sentences to describe these changes.

Example: *Four hotels have been built.*

1960	today	verb
no hotels	four hotels	build
wet land	no wet land	drain
small library	new library extension	open
three factories	no factories	close
river polluted	river clean	clean
few offices	new office block	build
no parks	two parks	establish
no airport	plans for airport	plan

3 In the following description of how plastics are shaped, put the verb in brackets in the correct form.

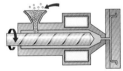 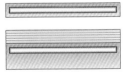 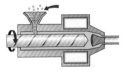

Injection moulding   Laminating   Blow moulding   Tube making – extrusion

There are many ways of shaping plastics. The most common way is by moulding. Blow-moulding (a) _____ (use) to make bottles. In this process, air (b) _____ (blow) into a blob of molten plastic inside a hollow mould and the plastic (c) _____ (force) against the sides of the mould.

Toys and bowls (d) _____ (make) by injection moulding. Thermoplastic chips (e) _____ first _____ (heat) until they melt and then forced into a water-cooled mould under pressure. This method (f) _____ (suit) to mass production.

Laminating (g) _____ (produce) the heat-proof laminate which (h) _____ (use), for example, for work surfaces in kitchens. In this process, a kind of sandwich (i) _____ (make) of layers of paper or cloth which (j) _____ (soak) in resin solution. They (k) _____ then _____ (squeeze) together in a heated press.

Thermoplastics can (l) _____ (shape) by extrusion. Molten plastic (m) _____ (force) through a shaped hole or die. Fibres for textiles and sheet plastic may (n) _____ (make) by extrusion.

37 Causation

A Sample sentences

The application of civil engineering techniques has led to more secure structures.
Tighter environmental controls have made many companies use cleaner sources of energy.
These stains result from the extensive use of dyes.
We have moved over to water turbines because they offer significant cost savings.
Many accidents in mining happen due to poor security procedures.

B Form

We can express the relationship between a cause and an effect in a number of ways.

1 *Verbs* and *verb phrases*

Modern civil engineering techniques **have led to** *the use of better construction methods.*

|_____A_____||__B__||_____C_____|

Here   A = the cause; B = the verb linking the cause to the effect; C = the effect.

Here are other *verbs* and *verb phrases* with a similar meaning.

   account for cause • result in bring about give rise to be responsible for

Alternatively we can reverse the elements in the sentence:

The use of better construction methods **results from** *modern civil engineering techniques.*

|_____C_____||__B__||_____A_____|

Here   A = the effect;   B = the verb linking the effect to the cause;   C = the cause.

Here are other *verbs* and *verb phrases* with a similar meaning.

   arise from • be attributable to • stem from

2 *Clauses of cause*

We have moved over to water turbines **because** *they offer significant cost savings.*
Here a subordinating conjunction links the effect and the cause.
Here are the other main *subordinating conjunctions*:

   as • since

3 *Phrases of cause*

Many accidents in mining happen **due to** *poor security procedures.*
Here an *adverb phrase* introduces the cause.
Other expressions with a similar meaning are:

   as a consequence of • because of • on account of • owing to

C Uses

Look at the following text which shows the above language in use.

Combustion is a reaction in which the oxidization of an element or compound **leads to** the release of energy. If the combustion **results in** a flame, it is called burning. **Since** combustion can be dangerous, it is important to take precautions against injury. However, not all combustions **result in** flames. For example, the combustion of carbon in oxygen **causes** an intense red-white light but no flame. Petroleum, on the other hand, requires special handling **on account of** its volatility.

TASKS

1   Choose the correct phrase in each of the following.

    1   Just-in-time manufacturing methods **result from/result in** a saving on storage costs.

    2   The reject rate has fallen **as a result of/giving rise to** quality control.

    3   Poor quality materials **were responsible for/stem from** product defects.

    4   The machine broke down **and resulted in/because of** poor maintenance.

    5   Steel was used in the construction **caused by/on account of** its strength.

    6   Data was damaged **as a result of/giving rise** to a virus in the system.

    7   Transport costs have increased **accounting for/due** to a rise in oil prices.

    8   Stopping the use of certain chemicals in the process **has brought about/arises from** a reduction in the number of cases of allergic skin reactions.

    9   Most British coal mines have been closed **because/on account of** they have become uneconomic.

   10   The regeneration of plants and wildlife in rivers and waterways **accounts for/is attributable to** new legislation to stop pollution by industry.

   11   There has been a large increase in the number of people who want to buy organic food products **since/as a consequence of** fears about chemicals in food.

   12   Environmental problems resulting from the disposal of plastics **led to/due to** the development of biodegradable plastics.

2   Rewrite the following sentences using the verb or phrase in brackets.

    1: Modern communication systems here resulted in more and more people working from home.

    1   More and more people working from home is a consequence of modern telecommunications systems. (have resulted in)

    2   Cold weather leads to a rise in the volume of electricity required by consumers. (is caused by)

    3   Reduced transportation costs stem from the use of more lightweight parts. (brings about)

    4   Increased energy efficiency accounts for an annual saving of electricity. (is attributable to)

    5   Friction during drilling causes the production of heat. (results from)

    6   A reduction in the amount of waste being discharged into rivers has resulted in rivers beginning to support fish again. (is attributable to)

    7   Cars and aeroplanes are partly responsible for air pollution. (partly stems from)

    8   Water flowing through the turbines causes them to spin. (due to)

3   Place the preposition *of, for, from, about, on, in, to* or <u>no preposition</u> in each space below to complete the following description of global warming.

The earth is kept warm (a) _____ account (b) _____ a layer of gases which surrounds it. However, human activity has brought (c) _____ an increase in greenhouse gases which trap more heat and cause a rise in temperature. Scientists believe that CO_2 accounts (d) _____ nearly half of global warming. CO_2 results (e) _____ the burning of fossil fuels and forests. No one knows exactly what changes will take place because (f) _____ this warming. In addition to CO_2, CFCs may be responsible (g) _____ about 25% of global warming in the future. Most scientists believe that more extremes in the weather will also be attributable (h) _____ global warming. They also expect higher temperatures to result (i) _____ more evaporation from the seas and an increase in rainfall. As a consequence (j) _____ heating, water expands and this will give rise (k) _____ a rise in ocean levels.

38 Obligation and requirements

A Sample sentences

Our quality policy is to develop, produce, and deliver on time. In order to do this, we have implemented quality systems and processes that demand continuous improvement. To achieve this we need to constantly strive to upgrade our performance and inspire others by example. The competitive marketplace in which we operate requires us to be responsive to customer needs. On the other hand, peer needs must not be ignored. Staff have to be trained to enable them to carry out their tasks. Everyone will be encouraged to take on responsibility. However, no-one will be forced.

B Form

We can view the notion of obligation under the following headings:

- obligation to do something
- obligation not to do something, i.e. prohibition
- no obligation

We can also view the notion from the point of view of the person/situation causing the obligation (the obliger), and the person receiving the obligation (the obliged).

For the use of the verbs below see C 1–6.
Here is the range of verbs for the obliger:

1 Oblige someone to do something

> compel • demand • force • make
> oblige • require

2 Oblige someone not to do something

> ban • forbid • prohibit

3 Not oblige someone to do something

> not compel • not force • not make
> not require

Here is the range of verbs for the obliged:

4 Obliged to do something

> be forced to • be required to • be supposed to
> have to • must • need to

5 Obliged not to do something

> be prohibited from • cannot • may not
> must not • not be allowed to • not be permitted to

6 Not oblige someone to do something

> do not need to • need not • not have to

C Uses

1 To oblige someone to do something:
We require the general contractor to supervise and co-ordinate the project.
The general contractor made the sub-contractor sign a compensation clause for delays. (not: made the sub-contractor ~~to~~ sign)

2 To oblige someone not to do something:
The use of asbestos is banned.
Fire regulations prohibit builders from using flammable materials.

3 Not to oblige someone to do something:
The construction engineers don't normally force painters, plasterers and plumbers to use specific products.

4 To be obliged to do something:
The contractor must apply flame-retardant chemicals to slow down the spread of fire.

5 To be obliged not to do something:
A nonload-bearing wall must not support any other load except its own weight.

6 Not obliged:
In this type of soil we needn't dig the foundations deeper than 10 metres.
Architects don't have to/need to have the same qualifications as quantity surveyors.

TASKS

1

Choose one correct sentence for each picture. There are more sentences than you need.

a You must go to this point if there is a fire.

b You are required to wear a hard hat in this area.

c Authorized personnel are obliged to enter.

d You mustn't consume these.

e A fire extinguisher needs to be placed here.

f People without authorization are prohibited from entering.

g You can get fire fighting equipment here.

h Smoking is not allowed after this point.

2 **Each of the following sentences contains a mistake. Find the mistakes and correct them.**

1 You needn't to enclose the invoice. It will be sent separately.

2 The customer will be needed to pay import duty before he can get the goods.

3 When bacteria were found in the food plant, the government made the company to shut down production.

4 They don't required to wear safety clothes in this area.

5 Without just-in-time manufacturing, we would be permitted to hold large stocks of components.

6 Children are not allowed entering this area.

3 **Below is an extract from a letter from an insurance agent to a manufacturing company about regulations. Complete the extract by choosing the correct word from the box.**

needn't • permit • permitted • forcing • have • supposed
prohibited • require • must (2) • banned

Following my visit to your factory last week, I am writing to confirm what we discussed. It is important that these points are followed; otherwise the insurance cover will not be valid.

▪ All empty crates (a) _____ not be stacked in the production area. They are a health and safety problem and we will not (b) _____ you to leave them there.

▪ The government has (c) _____ the dumping of waste chemicals in waste sites and are (d) _____ companies to apply for a licence for waste disposal. However, prior to disposal, these chemicals (e) _____ to be stored in sealed containers in a designated area away from the main plant.

▪ Containers that contain flammable materials (f) _____ be at least 100 metres from the building.

▪ Present air conditioning systems are adequate, so you (g) _____ make any changes there.

▪ Walls are (h) _____ to be kept clear of dust, so we (i) _____ you to arrange to have the walls dusted and cleaned.

▪ The use of water fire extinguishers is still (j) _____ , but they are (k) _____ from use near or on electrical equipment.

39 Cause and effect

A Sample sentences

We are going to convert the assembly line because we believe it will improve overall effectiveness.

Due to the frequent faults in finished products, we are going to install new machinery.

As a result of the high cost of local raw materials, we are going to start importing from China.

Plastics are a versatile family of materials; therefore they are suitable for a wide range of packaging applications.

Since PET (polyethylene terephthalate) is a clear, tough polymer, it is ideal for use in soft drink bottles.

B Form

1 *Clauses of cause:*

Here a *subordinating conjunction* links the effect and the cause:

*The automotive industry uses plastics **because** they are durable, resistant to corrosion and lightweight.*

Here are the other main subordinating conjunctions:

> as • since

2 *Phrases of cause:*

Here an *adverb phrase* introduces the cause:

*Polystyrene manufacturers phased out the use of chlorofluorocarbons (CFCs) in the late 1980s **because of** concerns about the ozone layer.*

Other expressions with a similar meaning are:

> as a consequence of • due to • on account of • owing to

We always put a noun phrase after these expressions:

***Because of** the large number of back orders, we have put extra workers on the night shift. (not: because of the number of back orders is large)*

3 *Sentence connectors of cause:*

Here a cause in one sentence is linked to an effect in the following sentence by a *connector*.

The maintenance team are here; therefore we'll need to shut down the machinery after this shift.

The *connector* 'therefore' points backwards to the cause and forwards to the effect. Other connecting words and expressions are:

> accordingly • as a consequence/result • because of this • consequently
> hence (formal) • so • that's why (informal) • that's (the reason) • therefore
> thus (formal)

C Uses

Look at the following dialogue which demonstrates the use of expressions of cause and effect:

> A: Why are we reviewing our quality control practices?
>
> B: Because management is thinking of introducing a zero defect production initiative.
> So we are starting a project group to look at current practices in production.
>
> A: So, that's why everyone has been called to the meeting.
>
> B: Exactly. We've scheduled a preliminary meeting on account of this new initiative.
>
> B: But I thought productivity levels had increased.
>
> A: Yes, but because of this it seems that the reject rate has risen, too.

1 Match one part of a sentence from A and one from B to form sentences of cause and effect.

A	B
The reject rate has fallen	owing to extensive research and development.
There is now a backlog of orders	due to more effective quality control.
They want to understand why customers buy a product.	Consequently, users can share files and resources.
We have developed an improved product	therefore, all workers should wear masks.
Computer software has been made easier to use	That's why they're studying customer attitudes.
They have set up a computer network.	That's the reason he had an accident.
We are having to increase our prices	as a result of machinery breakdowns.
This is a very dusty environment,	so more people use computers daily.
He was not following safety regulations.	as a consequence of increased carriage charges.

2 The following sentences contain a mistake. Find the mistake and correct it.

1 Owing a danger of falling objects, workers must wear a hard hat.

2 The driver wasn't badly injured in the accident on account from the airbag.

3 The car is cheap but reliable and that's the result for its popularity.

4 The manufacture of paper uses bleach and other chemicals. Consequently of this, the waste must be treated before it can be disposed of.

5 Due to oil is used in the manufacture of so many useful substances, it is a valuable raw material.

6 Optical fibres carry more information more quickly than copper wires, since copper wires are being replaced by optical fibres.

3 Here is part of a dialogue between an architect and someone who is interested in a local housing development. Fill in the blanks with words from the box.

result • because (2) • why
consequence • due • account
consequently • reason • so

A: So, these are the finished plans for the housing development. The site was previously used by heavy industry and (a) _____ of this we will have to remove a thick layer of soil. As a (b) _____ of this, costs will be higher than expected. As far as building design is concerned, the houses will all have a regular shape as you can see here on the plan on (c) _____ of cost considerations.

B: Why does that affect cost?

A: If you measure the surface area of the walls, you'll see that buildings with an irregular shape have a greater surface area. As a (d) _____ , more materials will be required and, (e) _____ , it will cost more.

B: I see. Now what about the foundations?

A: Well, the soil is very stable, (f) _____ shallow concrete foundations will be sufficient. The walls will be wooden frame walls. That's the (g) _____ the houses can be erected very quickly. The external wall cladding will also be made of wood.

B: But won't the wind and rain damage the wood?

A: That's (h) _____ we will use pre-treated wood. As for the roofs – well, (i) _____ to local planning regulations, the roofs will have to be made of blue slate. It's the traditional stone from this area and (j) _____ of this we have to use it.

40 Ability and inability

A Sample sentences

With the new version of Web Discoverer you can specify better search criteria.

Applications are computer programs and systems which enable people to interface with the computer.

Anti-virus software is designed to prevent programs from damaging your data or halting operations on your system.

You can't make this type of jacket out of wool. It'll crease too easily.

This cloth is capable of being dyed; but this one doesn't dye well.

B Form

We can view the concepts of ability and inability in terms of:

1 making someone able or something possible

*The database **allows** you to search for client names and addresses.*

2 being able

*This new monitor **can** display more than two million colours.*

3 making someone unable or something impossible

*The climate **stops** people from wearing this type of heavy jacket – it's just too hot.*

4 being unable

*You **can't** press this material with a hot iron as it is too sensitive.*

Let's look at the use of language for the concepts 1–4 above:

1	2	3	4
make able	be able	make unable	be unable
enable	can	prohibit	cannot
allow	able to	prevent	not able/unable to
permit	capable of	stop	incapable of

C Uses

Now look at the following short text which demonstrates the use of these verbs.

Now you *can* create your own website. So simple, anyone is *capable of* producing a quality site in minutes. You'll be *able to* add graphics and photos. This new software *allows* you to work with all types of graphic files. The text editing function *enables* you to work directly from your word processor. Remember: only one registered user *is permitted* to use this software.

Note:

1 We use the infinitive with *to* after *able/unable*, e.g.

*You'll be **able to** add graphics and photos.*

*Synthetic fibre is **unable to** replace natural fibre.*

2 After *capable/incapable* we use *of* + verb ....*ing*, e.g.

*Anyone is **capable of** producing a quality site in minutes.*

*They are **incapable of** producing these shirts in a wider range of colours.*

3 After *prohibit*, *prevent* and *stop*, we use the following constructions:

*Local regulations **prevent/stop** us from importing tee shirts from certain countries.* (from + verb...ing)

*Local regulations **prevent/prohibit** the importation of tee shirts from certain countries.* (noun)

TASKS

1 Match one part of a sentence from A and one from B to form sentences of ability and inability.

A	B
Improving quality control will enable us	the storage of chemicals in plastic containers.
Shortage of space prevents us from	carrying the volume of data required today.
Regulations prohibit	see the person you are talking to.
A machine breakdown means that we can't	producing more product lines.
Old copper cables are incapable of	now be used to send emails.
Using a videophone allows you to	to become more profitable.
Mobile phones can	unauthorized users accessing a network.
A firewall is used to stop	finish the order this week.

2 There is a mistake in each of the following sentences. Underline the mistake and correct it.

1 All unauthorized personnel are prohibited to entering this area.

2 Building regulations do not allow of the use of asbestos in public buildings.

3 Only fully qualified electricians should be permitted repairing these appliances.

4 Deep pile foundations are capable to support a high building.

5 Water is unable to passing through the vapour barrier.

6 Designers can to design complex structures using computer-aided design tools.

7 Scientists are not yet able of curing cancer.

8 Aspirin is known to prevent people of having a heart attack.

3 Read the following extract from a brochure advertising car features. Look at the prompts in bold and change them for a verb or verb phrase from the opposite page, changing the grammar to fit the sentence.

One feature common to all our models is the airbag. If the driver is involved in a crash, the airbag inflates and ~~make unable~~ **stops/prevents** the driver or the passenger hitting the steering wheel or front panel. It (a) **make unable** serious injury.

The anti-lock brake system equips the vehicle with speed sensors. If a driver brakes hard, this system (b) **make unable** wheel lockup. Valves control the brake pressure and (c) **make able** the driver to steer the car safely. All our models are fitted with disc brakes, which means the car (d) **be able** operate more efficiently in wet weather. Disc brakes also (e) **make able** better performance at high temperatures.

The catalytic converter is part of the car's exhaust system and (f) **make able** the exhaust gases to be converted into less harmful products. With a catalyst the car (g) **be able** of meeting new international pollution levels.

A very popular feature is four-wheel drive. In this range of vehicles the driver (h) **be able** select two or four wheel drive. Together with these off-road tyres, the vehicle (i) **be able** perform well on rough ground.

But if you are more concerned about economical driving, you may be interested in the overdrive facility. Here the highest gear ratio is less than a one-to-one ratio. This (j) **make able** you to save fuel and as a result also (k) **make unable** the engine wearing out so quickly.

The turbocharger forces more air into the cylinder than it can normally draw and (l) **make able** the engine to burn more fuel. As a result, the car is capable of greater speed and faster acceleration.

41 Scale of likelihood

A Sample sentences

The term engineering can have different meanings.
A scientist is unlikely to be able to solve engineering problems.
We are likely to see significant advances in robotics in the coming years.
The generators and turbines are bound to use a lot of electrical power.
These rainproof seals can't possibly let water into the switchboard.

B Form and uses

If we consider that the scale of likelihood goes from 100% certainty to 0% certainty, we can identify the following segments. (The numbers below are only a general indication, not exact values.)

certainty (100%)
probability (75%)
possibility (50%)
improbability (25%)
impossibility (0%)

Now let's look at the language for each of these categories.

certainty	I am (absolutely) *sure/certain/positive* that power requirements will increase. Power requirements will *definitely/certainly* increase. Power requirements are *certain/sure/bound* to increase.
probability	It is *(very) likely/probable* that the pumps will use more electricity. The pumps are *(quite) likely* to use more electricity. They *could* use more electricity.
possibility	We *may/might* need more pumps on site.
improbability	It is *(very/highly) unlikely/improbable* that the pumps will use more electricity. The pumps *probably* won't use more electricity. The pumps are *(quite) unlikely* to use more electricity. The pumps *shouldn't* use more electricity.
impossibility	I am *sure/certain/positive* that power requirements won't increase. Power requirements *definitely/certainly* won't increase. Power requirements *can't (possibly)* increase.

C Uses

1 *Definitely* and *certainly*
Notice the position of the adverbs in certainty and impossibility:
*We will **definitely/certainly** replace the fuses.* (after *will*)
*The fuses **definitely/certainly** won't fail.* (before *won't*)

2 *Likely* and *unlikely*
These adjectives can take two constructions:
*It is **likely/unlikely** that the pumps will use more electricity.* (adjective + *that* + clause)
*The pumps are **likely/unlikely** to use more electricity.* (adjective + *to* + infinitive)

3 *May* and *might*
Some speakers feel there is a slight difference in the strength of these two words:
*We **may** need more pumps on site.* (50% likelihood)
*We **might** need more pumps on site.* (45% likelihood)

TASKS

1   Put the following words in the correct order to form sentences.

1   The goods/ until next week/ won't /be delivered/ probably.

2   I'm/ these crates/ sure/ are strong enough/ absolutely/ that.

3   The goods/ to remain in the warehouse/ unlikely/ for long/ are.

4   It/ take long/ to load the ship/ shouldn't.

5   They/ be sent by air freight/ won't/ definitely.

6   The goods/ in transit/ be/ for four days/ may.

7   They're/ the volume of imports/ quite/ to increase/ likely.

2   Rewrite the following sentences so that the meaning does not change. For example:

The local authorities probably won't accept the plans for a concrete arch bridge.
The local authorities are unlikely to accept the plans for a concrete arch bridge.

1   I'm absolutely sure that there will be advances in heat-exchange technology.

2   It's unlikely that we will see more robots being used in the home in the next ten years.

3   Glass fibre optics will very probably be replaced by plastic in the near future.

4   Washing machines and dishwashers are certain to become more energy-efficient.

5   A mat foundation can't possibly support a high building.

6   We may need extra sound-deadening material in these walls.

7   They definitely won't want to use wood for the ceiling.

8   It is very probable that she's suffering from an allergy.

9   Research being carried out at the moment may help find a cure for cancer.

3   Complete the following text about future sources of energy by choosing a suitable verb or phrase from the table in B on the opposite page. The figure in brackets indicates the likelihood.

At present most of the energy we use comes from oil and gas, and scientists are becoming increasingly concerned about our future energy needs. Many scientists believe that fossil fuels are (a) _certain bound_ (100%) to run out by the middle of this century, while others think that they are (b) _____ (75%) to run out before then. Whatever the time scale, fossil fuels (c) _____ (100%) run out sooner or later, and we must consider alternative sources of energy. In the short term, it (d) _____ (25%) that alternative energy will be able to supply the world's needs, however, in the long term, our energy needs (e) _____ (0%) be met by fossil fuels. The future of nuclear power is also uncertain. It (f) _____ (50%) provide enough power, but public opinion is (g) _____ (75%) to prevent any expansion. Some countries have promised to stop nuclear power production but it seems increasingly (h) _____ (25%) that they will be able to do so. Atomic power is considered much safer and we (i) _____ (50%) see an expansion of this in the future. Alternative sources of energy are (j) _____ (100%) increase but they (k) _____ (25%) won't provide 100% of our needs within the next 50 years. Solar thermal power will (l) _____ (100%) be one of our future sources, but no one is sure what percentage it will provide. The US Department of Energy thinks that solar power plants are (m) _____ (75%) be able to produce electricity almost as cheaply as fossil fuel plants within the next 50 years. However, due to global warming there (n) _____ (50%) be changes in the pattern of sunshine as changes in climate are (o) _____ (75%). There (p) _____ (50%) be more cloud in the future which is (q) _____ (100%) to have a serious effect on solar concentrators.

87

42 Relative clauses

A Sample sentences

Logistics is the business function which controls the movement of physical materials in a factory.
Our logistics department, which controls the movement of physical materials in the factory, is headed by Barry Perks.
A mine is a place where ores, coal, and precious stones may be obtained.
A miner is a person who works in a mine.
You need to speak to John Martin, who is in charge of the coal mine.

B Form

A *relative clause* is a type of *subordinate clause*.
Relative clauses begin with a relative pronoun.
Who and *which* are typical relative pronouns.
Blowholes are air or gas vents   which   *carry off fumes from tunnels or underground passages.*
[main clause   ] [relative pronoun] [subordinate clause   ]

There are two types of *relative clauses*:

defining relative clauses and *non-defining relative clauses*
Logistics is the business function which controls the movement of materials. (defining)
Our logistics department, which controls the movement of materials in the factory, is headed by Barry Perks. (non-defining)
A *defining relative clause* is written without commas; a *non-defining relative clause* is written in commas.

The table shows the range of relative pronouns

person	who, whom, whose	time	when
things	which, that	place	where

C Uses

1 *Defining relative clauses* give information which is essential to understand the sentence.
   The packing list is a document which describes the contents of each package.
   The clause *which describes the contents of each package* identifies the document; without this information, the sentence has a different meaning.
   A haulier is a company or person who specializes in transporting goods by truck.
   The clause *who specializes in transporting goods by truck* identifies the company or person.

2 *Non-defining relative clauses* give additional, non-essential information.
   The packing list, which describes the contents of each package, is sent with the goods.
   The clause *which describes the contents of each package* gives additional information; we can still identify the packing list without this information.
   The mine, which has extracted diamonds since the 19th century, will be closed in two years.
   The clause *which has extracted diamonds since the 19th century* gives additional information.

Notes:

1 The relative pronoun after the reason:
   *Thank you for explaining to us the reasons **why/that** the consignment was delayed.*
   (not: ~~the reason because~~)

2 The relative pronoun after *all, each, every* and compounds:
   *All the mining shafts **which/that** lead to the surface are blocked.*

TASKS

1 Choose the appropriate relative pronoun in each of the following sentences.

1 A load-bearing wall is a wall **that/where** supports a vertical load as well as its own weight.

2 An architect is someone **whose/who** draws up plans for buildings and other structures.

3 An unheated building, a cellar or a basement are examples of places **which/where** are often damp.

4 Manufacturing takes place in factories **when/where** finished products are made.

5 Marconi was the scientist **who/whom** first received signals across the Atlantic.

6 You are invited to attend the meeting on Tuesday **which/when** details of the project will be discussed.

7 The company has opened a new workshop **where/which** engineering parts will be produced.

8 The operations manager, wh**om/whose** office is on the first floor, is dealing with the problem.

2 In the following article, underline the relative clauses and write *defining* (D) or *non-defining* (ND) beside each one.

THERE HAS BEEN a lot of controversy surrounding the Three Gorges Dam, which is being built in China. The dam, which will be 181 metres high, is expected to produce 18.2 million kilowatts of power. However, this is the reason why many people are unhappy. 15 million people, who used to live in the valley, have had to move. These people, whose homes have been covered in water, complain that they have been given land where very little grows. They also say that the living conditions, which they have to live in now, are unsatisfactory. But those who are in favour of the project say that the dam will provide extra electricity, which will stimulate the economy in eastern and central China, where development has been held back. However, critics say there will be an oversupply of power, which they will not be able to sell. There are people who are deeply worried about the effects of the dam on the environment. They say there is a danger to animals and fish which live in the area. But there are other people who claim that hydroelectric power is much cleaner than burning coal. There will be fewer emissions which contribute to the greenhouse effect. New ship locks, which are expected to increase shipping and reduce transportation costs, will be built. Navigation on the river, which is currently dangerous, will become much safer. But critics say there will be sedimentation which could increase flood levels.

3 Use the information in brackets to complete the following sentences.

For example: (The manufacturers provided some information.) We have used the information that ...
We have used the information that the manufacturers provided.

1 (The assembly line produces car parts.) They have automated the assembly line that _____ .

2 (Water is stored in a tank.) The water tank where _____ is underground.

3 (Circuits can store large amounts of information.) Computers contain many circuits which _____ .

4 (W.C. Röntgen discovered X-rays by accident.) X-rays have been used since 1895 when _____ .

5 (Faraday was born in the south of England.) Faraday, who _____ , developed the process of electromagnetic induction.

6 (The manager's signature appears on the document.) The manager whose _____ . is responsible for purchasing.

7 (Several people work in this area.) Everyone who _____ is responsible for regular maintenance of the machinery.

43 Subordinate clauses of result and purpose

A Sample sentences

Benton have defined quality standards (in order) to meet minimum product specifications.
Last year Markham introduced new quality standards so (that) they detected defective products before completion.
Mansell have initiated a quality review programme so as to meet customer expectations.
We sample and monitor all processes so that customers' needs are exceeded.
For zero defects to be achieved, we will have to introduce tighter prevention controls.

B Form

Clauses of result and *purpose* are subordinate clauses. There are three possible constructions:

1 (*in order/so as*) *to* + infinitive
   *Benton have defined quality control standards **(in order) to meet** minimum product specifications.*
2 a *subordinating conjunction* followed by a verb
   *We sample and monitor all processes **so that** customer needs **are exceeded**.* (purpose)
   *Last year Markham introduced new quality standards **so (that)** they **detected** defective products before completion.* (result)
3 *for* + noun followed by an infinitive + *to*
   ***For** zero defects **to be achieved**, we will have to introduce tighter prevention controls.*
   (= ***so that** zero defects **can be achieved**, we ...*)

The main *subordinating conjunctions* are: in order that • so that

Before the infinitive + *to* you can put: for • in order (to) • so as (to)

Note the negative forms:
***So as not to** pay for unnecessary reworking, we sample all raw materials.*
***In order not to** lose customers, we have a policy of continuous process improvement.*

C Uses

Clauses of purpose answer the question *why* or *what ... for*. They present the purpose of the information in the main clause.
Clauses of result also answer the question *why* or *what ... for*. In contrast to *clauses of purpose*, they typically look to the past to see what result an action achieved.
Electricity is usually transmitted at the highest voltages possible to minimize energy losses. (purpose)
We tied together the electric utilities into large systems so that power was exchanged. (result)

Now look at the differences between the constructions in *clauses of purpose* and *result*.

1 We use *to, in order to* and *so as to* + infinitive when the subject of both clauses is the same.
   *Energy is generated from different fuels in order **to** avoid reliance on one source.*
2 We use *so that* or *in order that* where the subject of the clauses is different.
   Electricity producers are able to exchange power so that one utility can assist another
3 We use *so that* + clause for *clauses of result*.
   These electric utilities were then combined into larger systems so that power was exchanged.

Notes:
The following sentences are wrong:
We use coal ~~for make~~ energy. (to make)
We changed to gas ~~for to make~~ energy. (in order to make)
We started producing hydroelectric power ~~for making~~ cleaner energy. (to make)

TASKS

1 Rewrite the following sentences using the words in brackets.

1 They introduced computer-guided robots because they wanted to increase efficiency. (in order to).

2 Close the valve. That way the system won't overheat. (so that)

3 Scientists are carrying out research. They want to find a cure for AIDS. (so as to)

4 Circuit breakers have been installed because they don't want the system to overload. (so that ... not)

5 The system is sealed. They want to stop water and dust getting in. (in order to)

6 He is taking anti-malarial drugs. He doesn't want to get malaria. (so that)

2 An architect is explaining the features of an ecological house to some interested builders. Complete the following description choosing phrases from the box.

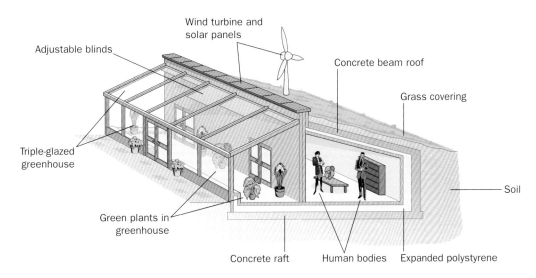

heat doesn't escape • use too much power within the house
the temperature can be controlled • produce power for the house
provide insulation • receive the maximum amount of sun
save energy • purify the air • prevent the loss of heat • be kept dry

As you can see, there are several features in this house that have been designed to (a) _____ but still provide a comfortable living area. On one side you can see a large glazed greenhouse that faces south so as to (b) _____ . It is in fact triple glazed in order to (c) _____ . Inside this greenhouse, we would recommend plenty of green plants to (d) _____ . Of course it can get quite hot on summer days so adjustable blinds are fitted on all the glass windows so that (e) _____ . Wind turbines and solar panels are fitted to the roof in order to (f) _____ . For the house to (g) _____ , the foundations consist of a concrete raft. The inner layer is made of expanded polystyrene which is used to (h) _____ . The roof comprises concrete beams with a thick soil covering and grass so that (i) _____ . Of course, there are also people in the house to generate a certain amount of heat too. In addition, so as not to (j) _____ , low energy equipment and lighting are used.

44 Countable and uncountable nouns

A Sample sentences

The engineers in the production department regularly assess the accuracy of the finished goods. We are concerned about the level of pollution; so the test equipment is checked each day for reliability.

Tools must be stored in a safe place after use.

B Form

We can identify two classes of nouns:

countable   *uncountable*

A *countable noun* typically has both a singular and plural form. Look at the following (production) words:

component/components • cycle/cycles • defect/defects
factory/factories • line/lines • machine/machines

An *uncountable noun* typically has only one form, which normally takes a singular verb. Look at the following (health and safety) words:

dust • environment • friction • harm • inhalation • waste

Notes:

1 A small number of *countable nouns* only have a plural form:
The report identified six major **findings***.*

2 A small number of *uncountable nouns* take a plural verb:

briefs (textiles) • *clothes* (textiles) • *eaves* (construction)
goods (production) • *jeans* (textiles)

Also: *gasworks* (energy), *waterworks* (energy) and other compound words with *works*.

3 A small number of *uncountable nouns* look plural, but take a singular verb:
electronics (electronics)   *hydraulics* (energy)
Hydraulics is a branch of science that deals with practical applications (like the transmission of energy or the effects of flow) of liquid (like water) in motion.

C Uses

Look at the following sentences from the field of textiles which contrast *countable* and *uncountable nouns.*

We produce our *cloth* by knitting natural fibres. This *cloth* is then used in the manufacture of a range of *clothes*, mainly menswear. Our products include *jackets* and *trousers*. This *jacket* has been produced using our latest *equipment* which streamlines the sewing and final pressing of the garment.

TASKS

1 Decide if the following nouns are *countable* or *uncountable* and write them in the appropriate column below.

drill • dye • electronic mail • equipment • factory • fault • information • laboratory machine • machinery • packaging • pollution • reliability • silk • tunnel

Countable	Uncountable

2 Complete the sentences with a suitable noun from the box. Make it *plural* or add *a/an* if necessary.

study • paint • pavement • storage • prevention • disposal • reservoir • inspection

1 The European Community has prepared guidelines on waste _____ .

2 Companies usually want to deliver goods as soon as they have been completed because _____ takes up a lot of room and is very expensive.

3 Government officials have carried out _____ of the factory.

4 The main aim of the training is accident _____ .

5 Painters often use hot air guns to burn off old _____ .

6 During icy weather, the _____ at the side of the road may become slippery.

7 Drinking water for the local population comes from _____ in the mountains.

8 Scientists are carrying out _____ of children's eating habits.

3 In each of the **numbered lines** below there is a mistake. Underline the mistake and write in the correction.

1 The weather affects the <u>cloths</u> (*clothes*) that people choose to wear. In a warm

2 dry climate, a man may choose a pair of short and a short-sleeved shirt

3 made of cottons while a woman may prefer a thin dress. In colder climates

4 a thick jumper and a warm trousers would be more suitable and out of doors, a

5 coat, scarf and glove are necessary.

6 Different natural fibres was used by ancient cultures to produce textiles.

7 Linen were made in Egypt as long ago as 5000 BC, and cotton in India in

8 3000BC. Today, there are many different type of fibres available.

9 Synthetic fibres, often mixed with natural fibres, are used widely and provide a wide choice for the fashion industry.

45 Comparison of adjectives

A Sample sentences

Working in a factory is more dangerous than working in a chemical laboratory.
There is a higher risk of accidents in a factory than in a chemical laboratory.
Flammable materials have a lower flash point and are combustible; therefore we need to handle them with more care.
A bipolar transistor is the most common form of transistor.
A bit is the smallest unit of binary data.

B Form

Many *adjectives* have three forms: positive, comparative and superlative.
*Manson's factory is **noisy**. (positive adjective)*
*Burton's factory **is noisier than** Manson's. (comparative adjective)*
*Denham's factory is **the noisiest**. (superlative adjective)*

1   If the positive adjective has one syllable, we form the comparative by adding - *er* and the superlative by adding -*est*:

positive	comparative	superlative
safe	safer	safest
clean	cleaner	cleanest

If we compare two objects, we use *than* in the comparison:
*Burton's factory is noisier **than** Manson's.*
If we compare more than two objects, we use *the* in the superlative.
*Denham's factory is **the** noisiest.*

2   If the positive adjective has two syllables and ends in -*y*, -*ow* or -*le*, we form the comparative by adding -*er* and the superlative by adding -*est*:

positive	comparative	superlative
healthy	healthier	healthiest
narrow	narrower	narrowest
simple	simpler	simplest

3   For other adjectives with two syllables or more, we form the comparative with *more* and the superlative with *most*:

positive	comparative	superlative
dangerous	more dangerous	most dangerous
flammable	more flammable	most flammable

4   There is a small group of adjectives with irregular comparative and superlative forms:

positive	good	bad	little	much	far
comparative	better	worse	less	more	farther/furthest
superlative	best	worst	least	most	farthest/furthest

C Uses

1   If we compare two objects, we use *than* in the comparison:
TV's today are smaller than ever before.
2   If we compare more than two objects, we use *the* in the superlative:
Today we have the cheapest and the most reliable electronic appliances.

TASKS

1 Complete the table.

adjective	comparative	superlative
accurate	more accurate	the most accurate
pure		
stable		
hard		
heavy		
thin		
far		
impractical		
bad		

2 Five of the sentences below contain a mistake. Find the mistake and correct it.

1 This silk fabric is the best quality we produce.

2 Following the fire, many more people have been affected by smoke as we had originally thought.

3 Pollution of the ground is most serious in area A than in area B.

4 Please wear ear protection because it's noisier here than in the other areas.

5 The locked cabinet contains some of most poisonous chemicals there are.

6 That was the loudest explosion I've ever heard.

7 These chemicals should be kept in good containers than these.

8 Sending the goods by air is certainly the most quick but it's also the most expensive.

3 Use the information from the table to complete the sentences below.

Bridge	Type of bridge	Length of span in metres	Built
Humber Bridge, England	suspension	1410	1981
Golden Gate Bridge, USA	suspension	1280	1937
Verrazano Narrows, USA	suspension	1298	1964
Quebec Bridge, Canada	cantilever	549	1917
Firth of Forth Railway Bridge, Scotland	cantilever	521	1890
Commodore John Barry, USA	cantilever	501	1974
New River Gorge, USA	steel arch	518	1981
Sydney Harbour Bridge, Australia	steel arch	509	1932

The Humber Bridge is the (a) _____ (long) bridge listed in the table above.

It is (b) _____ (long) than the Golden Gate Bridge in the USA but it isn't as (c) _____ (old). The Verrazano Narrows Bridge in the USA is (d) _____ (new) than the Golden Gate Bridge but (e) _____ (old) than the Humber Bridge. The (f) _____ (long) cantilever bridge is the Quebec Bridge in Canada. It is 28 metres (g) _____ (long) than the Firth of Forth Railway Bridge in Scotland which is over 110 years (h) _____ (old). The (i) _____ (new) cantilever bridge is the Commodore John Barry which is also the (j) _____ (short). The Sydney Harbour Bridge is (k) _____ (short) and (l) _____ (old) than the New River Gorge.

46 Adjectives and adverbs

A Sample sentences

R and D aims to develop new products and the means to produce them cheaply.

Qualitative research investigates current product positioning; and why customers currently use a particular product.

A coal field is an area containing significant coal deposits; the deposits in this coal field have been significantly reduced in recent years.

B Form

Adjectives and *adverbs* are grammatical units.

1 Here are some typical *adjective* endings and *adjective* forms:

-ate/-ite	accurate	-ic	scientific
-ful	harmful	-ous	dangerous
-al/-ial	artificial	-ing	mining
-ive	active	-ed	finished
-able/-ible	renewable	-ant/-ent	transparent

2 Other *adjectives*, particularly short ones, do not have special endings

bad • big • good • old • small • young

3 Most *adverbs* are formed by adding -ly to the *adjective*

adjective	harmful	active	scientific	dangerous	transparent	artificial
adverb	harmfully	actively	scientifically	dangerously	transparently	artificially

4 Some *adjectives* have the same form as adverbs

early • fast • hard • late • straight

A cage provides fast access to the mine. (adjective)
The cage raises and lowers miners fast. (adverb)

C Uses

We use an *adjective*:

1 to give more information about a *noun*
  We carry out   pure   research.
        [adjective] [noun]
  What type of research? **Pure** *research*

2 after the verb *be*
  All research is scientific.

We use an *adverb*:

1 to give more information about a *verb*
  The miners reached the surface safely.
        [verb]   [adverb]
  How did they reach the surface? **Safely**

2 to give more information about an *adjective*
  The mine is extremely dangerous.
        [adverb] [adjective]
  How dangerous is the mine? **Extremely**

3 to give more information about an *adverb*
  Miners work   very   hard.
        [adverb] [adverb]

4 to give more information about a *sentence*
  Firstly, *I'll present the coal cutting equipment.*

TASKS

1 Form an adjective from the following words by adding the correct suffix: -ful, -ic, -ous, -y, -ant, -al, -able, -ent, -ed, -ial, -ive, -ible.

danger	rely	experiment
dirt	origin	wash
magnet	expense	flex
use	excel	resist
industry		

2 Complete the following sentences with the adjective and adverb in brackets. Use each word once only.

1 The system will shut down _____ . There is an _____ temperature control. (automatic/automatically)

2 New testing methods have made the process much more _____ . Quality control now runs more _____ . (efficient/efficiently)

3 Our aim is to ensure the _____ operation at the plant. The manufacturing process should run _____ . (smooth/smoothly)

4 Demand for electricity is _____ lower in the evening. Statistics show that there is a _____ fall in demand after 10 p.m. (general/generally)

5 People are becoming more interested in _____ friendly products. There is a growing interest in _____ issues. (environmental/environmentally)

6 Safety procedures must be _____ observed to avoid accidents. The manager in a coal mine must be _____ about activities underground. (strict/strictly)

3 Here is part of a presentation about the textile industry in the UK. Choose the correct word in bold.

The number of people who work in the textile (a) **manufactured/manufacturing** industry in the UK has fallen (b) **considerable/considerably** over the last 50 years. Today, it employs (c) **approximately/approximate** 130,000 people. Textiles for clothing and carpets have always been (d) **important/importantly** but today there is (e) **increasing/increasingly** trade in fabrics for (f) **industrial/industrially** applications. Fabrics are used (g) **increasing/increasingly** in the healthcare and automotive industries. The export of wool and (h) **woollen/wool** products has remained fairly (i) **constantly/constant** over the last 15 years. The UK also has a (j) **significant/significantly** silk industry, which produces over £170 million worth of goods (k) **annual/annually**. The UK linen trade has an (l) **excellent/excellently** reputation for quality and service and British exports remain very (m) **healthy/healthily**. The UK's expertise in chemistry is (n) **extensive/extensively** and this is (o) **important/importantly** to the (p) **dying/dyed** industry.

The manufacturing of dyestuffs is (q) **relative/relatively** strong. The sale of carpets contributes to the sale of textiles (r) **significant/significantly**. The carpet industry has (s) **particular/particularly** strengths in the (t) **high/highly** quality end of the market.

47 Prepositions of time

A Sample sentences

The timetable looks like this. We will install the software on Monday afternoon. That means your system will be out of action from 2 o'clock till about 5 o'clock. We also need to download some programs before starting the system again. Then we'll start testing. That'll take until Wednesday. After that, we need to configure all the modules. We hope to finish that by Wednesday evening. That means that you'll be up and running with a brand new system on Thursday morning. So, please inform everyone that we will need to shut down the system next Monday.

B Form

A *preposition* comes before a *noun*, e.g.　　on　　Monday afternoon
　　　　　　　　　　　　　　　　　　　　[preposition] [noun]
Where the *preposition* is followed by a *verb*, we use the *-ing* form of the verb, e.g.
We also need to download　　**before**　　**starting**　　*the system again.*
　　　　　　　　　　[preposition]　[verb ... ing]
Note: *We also need to download before the system again.*

The most important *prepositions of time* are:

> after • at • before • between • by • during • for
> from ....in • on • since • to .... • until/till • up to

*The drug testing programme will start **on** 1ˢᵗ July.*
*We hope to get approval for sale of the drug **by** 2005.*

C Uses

1　*At, in, on,* and *by*
　At + clock time: *at 8 o'clock*
　On + days of the week: *on Tuesday*
　In + parts of the day: *in the morning*
　but: *at night*

　On + dates: *on 1st July*
　In + months and years: *in August*
　By + a deadline:
　*We hope to get approval **by** 2005.*

2　*By* and *until/till*

　We use *by* for an action which happens at or before a deadline:
　*We hope to finish configuring the system **by** Wednesday evening.*

　We use *until/till* for an action which continues up to a deadline:
　*We will work on configuring the system **until/till** Wednesday evening.*

3　No preposition
　In some time phrases, we do not use a *preposition of time.*
　a. before *this, last* and *next*
　We will need to shut down the system next Monday. (not: ~~on next Monday~~)
　b. with speed and frequency expressions
　Megahertz is a unit of measurement equal to one million electrical vibrations or cycles a second. (not: ~~in a second~~).
　This laser printer prints twenty pages of text a minute. (not: ~~in a minute~~)
　You can also say *per* second, *per* minute, etc.

TASKS

1 Five of the following sentences contain mistakes. Find the mistakes and correct them.

1 The interim report was completed to the end of last month.

2 These products have been on the market since nearly ten years.

3 The meeting has been arranged for 16th April at 10 a.m.

4 The results will be evaluated after the tests have been completed.

5 We intend to continue production during the new machinery is installed.

6 The road will be closed from 7 p.m to 7 a.m.

7 The jacquard loom for weaving cloth was created at 1801.

8 During the 19th and 20th centuries, great advances were made in treating illnesses.

2 Complete the following telephone conversation by adding the correct prepositions of time. If no preposition is required, leave the space blank.

ERIK: I was wondering if we could arrange a meeting (a) _____ next week?

MIRJAM: Yes, of course! I'm going to Washington (b) _____ Friday evening so can we arrange something (c) _____ that?

ERIK: Eh, Yes. I'm pretty busy (d) _____ the beginning (e) _____ the week but perhaps we could meet some time (f) _____ Wednesday?

MIRJAM: Could we meet (g) _____ the morning (h) _____ 9.30?

ERIK: That's fine. I should have received the test results we've been waiting for (i) _____ then.

MIRJAM: I'm looking forward to seeing the latest results. I haven't heard anything (j) _____ we spoke (k) _____ last month.

3 Look at the Gantt chart and complete the memo. If no preposition is required, leave the space blank.

The project is running according to plan so far. (a) _____ October, negotiations for the site were carried out and a contract signed. (b) _____ the beginning (c) _____ November we had meetings with the architects. Plans were submitted to the local planning authority (d) _____ 12 December. Services to the site were laid (e) _____ November and completed (f) _____ December. Planning permission was received (g) _____ last week and we intend to start construction of the building early (h) _____ next month. We expect construction to take about three months. (i) _____ the middle (j) _____ April, work will begin on fixtures and fittings and plant and machinery is due for delivery (k) _____ 4 May. Commissioning of the machines will last (l) _____ about two weeks (m) _____ June. (n) _____ the same time, training courses will begin for operators and maintenance staff. These will continue (o) _____ mid-July. All going well, start up will be (p) _____ 8 months' time (q) _____ 6 August and if all goes smoothly we hope to be working at full capacity (r) _____ the middle (s) _____ September.

	Oct	Nov	Dec	Jan	Feb	Mar	Apr	May	Jun	Jul	Aug	Sep
negotiations												
architect												
✳ plans submitted												
services to site												
✳ planning permission received												
building construction												
fixtures and fittings												
plant and machinery												
commissioning												
training												
✳ start up												
full capacity												

48 Prepositions of place

A Sample sentences

Let me give you a brief update about developments in the production area. On Monday, components will be moved from the old storage area to the new one. This means that fork lift trucks will need to move components out of warehouse 1 and into warehouse 2. You will find more details in the email I sent last week. There are two stages to the movement of old parts. In the new storage area, the parts will be stored on pallets on the top two shelves. From there they will be moved to their final destination according to the plan in the email attachment.

B Form

A preposition comes before a noun, e.g.   *in*   the production area

                                         [preposition]   [noun]

The most important *prepositions of place* are:

| at • from • in • into • on • out of • to |

*Oil is transported **from** the oil field **to** the terminal by pipeline.*
*Corrosion **in** the pipes is extremely dangerous.*

C Uses

1 *at*

We use *at* to describe a place in general rather than specific terms:
*In the event of a blowout **at** the terminal we evacuate everyone immediately.*
*We employ some 30 people **at** the pumping station.* cf *Twenty men sleep **in** the terminal,* i.e. inside

2 *to*

We use *to* to describe movement to a place:
*Then the oil is transported **to** the terminal.*
*The roughnecks fly out **to** the oil rig on a Sunday evening.*

3 *from*

We use *from* to describe movement from a place:
*After the blowout we managed to pull everyone **from** the water.*
*The safety officer has just arrived **from** headquarters.*

4 *in* and *into*

We use *in* to describe a place:
*Corrosion **in** the pipes is extremely dangerous.*
We use *into* to describe movement into a place:
*The drill bit is fitted **into** the drill.*

5 *into **and** out of*

Into and *out of* describe movement; they describe opposite movements:
*Drilling mud is pumped **into** and **out of** the well during drilling.*

6 *on **and** onto*

We use *on* with objects which have a surface:
*We've found some new deposits **on** the Continental Shelf.*
We use *onto* to describe movement onto a place which has a surface:
*The oil is then loaded **onto** tankers.* (Here the tanker is seen as a two-dimensional floating object.) cf. *The oil is then loaded **into** tankers.* (Here the tanker is seen as a three-dimensional object.)

TASKS

1 Complete the following texts using the correct preposition.
You may have to use some prepositions more than once.

between • from • on • along
above • through • to

Signals pass (a) _____ a telephone (b) _____ the local exchange

(c) _____ copper cables. Most exchanges are linked by optical fibre cables

(d) _____ which the signals travel as pulses of laser light. Microwave beams sent

(e) _____ dishes (f) _____ tall towers, link some signals. International calls go

(g) _____ undersea optical fibre cables or via satellites high (h) _____ the Earth.

around • at • of • from • to

Refrigerators keep food (a) _____ a temperature (b) _____ about 5°C. They

work by evaporation. When a liquid changes (c) _____ a vapour, it takes heat

(d) _____ its surroundings. In a fridge, the cooling process is done by a refrigerant

which circulates (e) _____ a system (f) _____ sealed pipes.

2 Complete the following description of an oil rig with the correct prepositions. Choose from those in the box. You will need to use some more than once.

above • on • in • from • to • in between
around • close to • of • beside • at • along • below

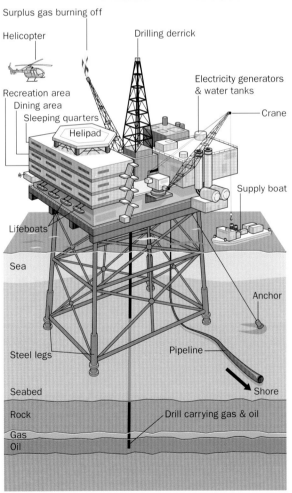

Surplus gas burning off

Helicopter

Drilling derrick

Electricity generators & water tanks

Recreation area
Dining area
Sleeping quarters
Helipad

Crane

Supply boat

Lifeboats

Sea

Anchor

Steel legs
Pipeline

Seabed
Shore

Rock
Drill carrying gas & oil

Gas
Oil

The Magnus oil rig stands (a) _____ huge steel legs resting (b) _____ the seabed. To prevent movement, a large anchor is firmly embedded (c) _____ the seabed. A production platform is built (d) _____ sea level. (e) _____ the centre (f) _____ the platform, (g) _____ the well, is the drilling derrick. Oil and gas are separated (h) _____ the bottom (i) _____ the derrick and a pipeline takes oil (j) _____ the platform (k) _____ shore. Helicopters carrying operators land (l) _____ the helipad located on one side of the platform. (m) _____ this pad there is an accommodation block. The recreation area is found (n) _____ the first level and (o) _____ the top floor the workers sleeping quarters are to be found. The dining area is on the floor (p) _____. Walkways run (q) _____ one side of the accommodation block and (r) _____ the outside of the platform. Lifeboats can be found (s) _____ the accommodation block. Supply boats, carrying supplies for the rig, can tie up (t) _____ one side (u) _____ the rig and goods are lifted (v) _____ the boats using a crane. Drinking water is stored (w) _____ large tanks located (x) _____ the electricity generators.

49 Quantifiers

A Sample sentences

If you have no customer feedback, it is very difficult to understand their needs. That's where qualitative research comes in. It has many common uses. It can help you to understand why some customers buy and use a product. It can also investigate a lot of alternative communication messages. Most of our clients use our services to understand their customers better. And all of them use this information in the development of new products.

B Form

Countable	all	most	many	a lot of	some	a few	few	no
Uncountable	all	most	much	a lot of	some	a little	little	no

We use *countable quantifiers* with *plural countable nouns*; we use *uncountable quantifiers* with *uncountable nouns.* ➤ 44

Qualitative market research has **many** common uses.
       [quantifier]   [countable noun]

If you have **no** customer feedback, it is difficult to understand their needs.
  [quantifier] [uncountable noun]

C Uses

Below are some examples of *quantifiers* in use, first in a short dialogue and then in an extract from a presentation.

A: Is there much demand for civil engineers these days?

B: You wouldn't believe it, but most of the vacancies are for civil engineers.

A: Really? With what type of qualifications?

B: All our vacancies require people with a thorough knowledge of surveying.

A: Don't most civil engineers need to know about surveying?

B: Yes, but there are some jobs in areas not directly linked to construction.

A: Such as?

B: We have a few vacancies for engineers to work in the aircraft industry.

A: Anything in nuclear power?

B: No vacancies in that area at the moment, I'm afraid.

A: Well, please let me know if anything turns up.

> In *all* turnkey contracts we undertake to finance, design, specify, construct, and commission the whole project. As *many of* our clients ask for a follow-up maintenance agreement, *most* maintenance will be included in the project price . However, there are *some* repairs which will not be covered. But, I wish to assure you that in other contracts there have been very *few* of these.

TASKS

1 Put the following in order from the most to the least.

1 Some of our clothing is made of silk.

2 None of our clothing is made of silk.

3 Most of our clothing is made of silk.

4 Little of our clothing is made of silk.

5 Much of our clothing is made of silk.

6 A lot of our clothing is made of silk.

7 A little of our clothing is made of silk.

8 All of our clothing is made of silk.

2 Complete the sentences with the words given in brackets.

1 There aren't _____ people working at night. _____ of the staff work during the day. (most, many)

2 _____ of the timber which was delivered last week was of very poor quality. We had to return _____ of the boards. (a few, some)

3 We don't manufacture _____ jackets of pure wool. There isn't _____ demand for them. (many, much)

4 Fibre optic cabling will be used in the future for _____ land-based communications. But, today, only _____ of these communications use fibre optics. (all, some)

5 At present, only a _____ paper is recycled in the UK. In the future, a _____ more paper will have to be collected and recycled. (little, lot)

6 In the UK, _____ electricity is generated from nuclear energy or fossil fuels and very _____ renewable energy sources have so far been developed. (few, most)

3 The table below shows how the methods of transportation used by a company have changed over a period of 30 years. Complete the text below with words from the table in B on the opposite page.

Year	1970	1980	1990	2000	2010
rail	100%	85%	60%	40%	0%
road	0%	12%	35%	40%	70%
air	0%	3%	5%	20%	30%

In 1970 (a) _____*all*_____ transportation was carried out by rail. (b) _____ goods were carried by road or by air. Ten years later, (c) _____ goods were transported by rail and a (d) _____ were taken by road. For the first time goods were being transported by air but there weren't (e) _____ goods being transported in this way. In 1990 the picture had changed. A (f) _____ _____ goods were still being transported by rail. However, (g) _____ more transportation was by road and a (h) _____ transportation was being done by air. By the year 2000, (i) _____ transportation was by rail, (j) _____ by road and a (k) _____ was by air. By the year 2010, it is expected that (l) _____ goods will be transported by rail. (m) _____ goods will be transported by road and (n) _____ will be taken by air.

50 Contrasting ideas

A Sample sentences

Although email is a very convenient form of personal communication, most people have never sent one. But the number of users is increasing very quickly. Despite improvements in telecoms networks, connection speeds are often very slow; however ADSL promises faster connections.

B Form

We can use the following language techniques to contrast ideas:

1 *Clauses of contrast*
   These consist of two clauses: the *main clause* and the *contrast clause*.
   Even though the number of mobile phones users has increased,   call charges remain high.
   [contrast clause   ]   [main clause   ]

   The main *conjunctions of contrast* are:

   | although • but • even though • though • whereas • while |

   Notice the difference in use between *but* and the others:
   *Videoconferencing is very convenient, **but** (it) is not as personal as face-to-face contact.*
   [main clause   ]   [main clause   ]
   ***Although** videoconferencing is very convenient, it is not as personal as face-to-face contact.*
   [contrast clause   ] [main clause   ]

2 *Phrases of contrast*
   The *phrase of contrast* consists of a *preposition* (or prepositional phrase) + a noun.
   ***Despite** improved security, hackers can still access many networks.*
   [phrase of contrast   ]
   The phrase of contrast can also come at the end of the sentence.
   *Hackers can still access many networks **despite** improved security.*
   The main words to introduce a phrase of contrast are:

   | despite • in spite of |

3 *Sentence connectors of contrast*
   These words or expressions link two sentences together which are in contrast to each other.
   *You can download Google from many sites worldwide. **However**, some are faster than others.*
   The main sentence connectors are:

   | all the same (informal) • but • even so • however • nevertheless • still • yet |

C Uses

Study the mini dialogue below.

A: *Although* we can share many resources, some are not shared. *Even so*, we should see this as a vast improvement.

B: I don't understand why all the printers aren't available to all.

A: In fact, everyone can use all the printers; *however*, one has been designated as default for each work group.

A: I'd prefer to use the colour laser printer.

B: I know you would, *but* it's very expensive to print each page in colour. And in most cases, colour isn't necessary.

1 Complete the following sentences by choosing a suitable ending from the box.

- accidents sometimes occur.
- those are a mixture of polyester and wool.
- people in developing countries often have to drink polluted water.
- there are places in the country where it doesn't work.
- careful packing.
- he washed it.

1 The contents of the crate were broken despite ...

2 Although the care label said the coat should be dry-cleaned, ...

3 These carpets are 100% wool whereas ...

4 Mobile phone coverage is fairly extensive; however, ...

5 In spite of strict safety regulations, ...

6 While we enjoy clean piped drinking water, ...

2 Complete the following text by using one of the words in the box.

whereas • however • but • despite • while

The first cantilever bridges were built in China and Tibet (a) _____ they were made of timber and could not carry heavy loads. (b) _____, once cheap, reliable steel became available in the 1870s, it was possible to build long spans capable of carrying rail traffic. (c) _____ the first modern cantilever bridge was built in Germany, the Forth Railway Bridge in Scotland held the record for the longest for over 30 years. The Forth Railway Bridge is made of huge steel tubes, (d) _____ the Oosterschelde Bridge in Holland is made of pre-stressed concrete. Some bridges look a little confusing in design. (e) _____ having cable stays, Lake Maracaibo Bridge in Venezuela is a cantilever type bridge.

3 A small company is looking for a new site to build a new factory. The Director is discussing three possible sites. Join the sentences in A and B using the connector in C to form part of her speech.

Example *Site 1 provides a suitable amount of space but it's the most expensive.*

A	B	C
Site 1 provides a suitable amount of space.	It's the most expensive.	but
It could be difficult.	It's worth considering.	although, still
Road and rail connections are not far away.	It will be necessary to build a bridge across the river.	although
It's surrounded by trees and close to the mountains.	It's only four kilometres from the nearest town.	however
There is a large labour market.	Workers in this area are unskilled.	even though
Site 1 is close to road and rail connections.	Site 2 is close to the airport.	while
Government finance is available for companies moving into the area.		nevertheless
Site 2 is fairly small.	Site 3 is almost too big.	whereas
Site 3 is not expensive.	It's in the centre of town.	despite
It may be difficult to get planning permission for new industrial buildings.		even so

Glossary of grammatical terms

The following list will help you understand the terms used in this book.

Active A verb or verb phrase which is not in the passive voice, e.g. *We normally produce a preliminary analysis.* See also **Passive** and **Voice**.

Auxiliary verb The verbs *be*, *have* and *do* when used in the following constructions:
continuous verbs (*be*), e.g. *the supervisor is/was checking the delivery.*
passive verbs (*be*), e.g. *all goods are/were received at this depot.*
the perfect (*have* and *had*), e.g. *our contractor has/had built a supporting wall.*
interrogative and negative verbs in the present and past simple tenses (*do*), e.g. *where does the company store finshed goods? We don't store them in the depot.*

Clause A group of words with a subject and verb and acting as a full sentence or part of a sentence. The verb may be:
a finite verb, e.g. *We began a study last year* (finite clause)
a non-finite verb, e.g. *Having begun the study, ...* (non-finite clause)

Conjunction A word which links words, phrases or clauses, e.g. *and, but, or, because,* etc.

Connector A word which links clauses which are separated by a full stop or a semi-colon, e.g. *however, therefore, similarly.*

Continuous (aspect) A verb construction comprising *be* + present participle. See also **Simple**.

Countable A noun which has a singular and plural form, e.g. *component – components.* See also **Uncountable**.

Expression A group of words, e.g. *last week, technical English, in colder climates.*

Infinitive without *to* The base form of a verb, e.g. *develop, receive, deliver.*

Infinitive + *to* The base form of a verb with the particle *to*, e.g. *to develop, to receive, to deliver.*

Main clause A group of words with a subject and verb, normally between full stops, e.g. *We manufacture packaging.*

Modal verb The following verbs and their negative forms are modals: *can, could, may, might, must, shall, should, will, would.* Modal verbs are followed by an infinitive, e.g. *This new monitor can display more than 2 million colours.*

Participle A non-finite verb form, e.g. *researching* (present participle); *researched* (past participle).

Particle A grammatical word which does not belong to the main classes, e.g. *to* (in the infinitive) or *not*.

Passive A passive construction has a verb or verb phrase with *be* + past participle, where the doer of the action is expressed as the agent rather than the subject, e.g. *We normally produce a preliminary analysis* (active) vs *A preliminary analysis is (normally) produced* (passive). See also **Active** and **Voice**.

Perfect (aspect) A verb construction comprising *has/have* + past participle which places the activity or event in a different time zone from the time of speaking or writing. The present perfect combines the present tense and the perfect aspect. It indicates that the action is seen as completed by reference to now, the time of speaking or writing, e.g. *Our contractor has built a supporting wall.* The past perfect combines the past tense and the perfect aspect. It indicates that the action is seen as completed by reference to an earlier point of time, e.g. *They had already compiled the results.* See also **Continuous** and **Simple**.

Phrase A group of words, but less than a clause, i.e. not containing a subject and verb.

Quantifier Words which describe quantity and amount, e.g. *all, many, some, few* and *no*.

Relative clause A clause beginning with a relative pronoun (*who, whom, whose, which, that* or zero) or a relative adverb (*when, where, why*).

Simple A verb construction in either the present simple or past simple tense. See also **Continuous** and **Perfect**.

Subordinate clause A group of words with a subject and verb which depends on a main clause, e.g. *We sample and monitor all processes so that customers needs are exceeded.* See also **Main Clause**.

Subordinating conjunction A word which introduces a subordinating clause, e.g. *because, as, when.*

Tense The grammatical form of verbs which differentiates the present from the past.

Time line A line which shows the three real-world times of past, present and future, in order to show tenses in terms of their relative position on the line.

past   present   future
|---------------|-----------------|

Time marker A phrase to describe the timing of an event, e.g. *last year, at the moment, next week.*

Uncountable A noun which has only one form, which normally takes a singular verb, e.g. *Dust has a damaging effect on health.* See also **Countable**.

Verb...ing The same as the present participle e.g. *researching.*

Voice The grammatical category of either active or passive verb form. See also **Active** and **Passive**.

Answer key

UNIT 1

Exercise 1

quality control   finished products   industrial process
production manager   large-scale manufacturing
assembly lines   raw material   productivity levels

1 quality control
2 industrial process
3 raw material
4 productivity levels
5 finished products
6 assembly lines
7 large-scale manufacturing
8 production manager

Exercise 2

1 batch
2 assemble
3 outputs
4 purchasing
5 component
6 optimize

Exercise 3

a factory
b site
c layout
d fixtures
e equipment
f machinery
g workshops
h breakdowns
i maintain
j repair
k stock
l faulty

UNIT 2

Exercise 1

1 c   2 a   3 b   4 b   5 a   6 c

Exercise 2

workload	the amount of work that has to be done
workforce	all the people who work in a particular company
back order	an order from an earlier time which hasn't been produced yet
material flow	the movement of materials through a production system
throughput	the volume of goods that can be dealt within a certain period of time
output	the volume of goods which are produced
cycle	the series of activities following one another to produce a product
requirement	something that is needed for a particular process

Exercise 3

a demand
b make-to-stock
c to-order
d uncertainty
e forecast
f lead time
g lead time
h overtime
i backlog
j shift
k bottlenecks
l stock-outs
m slack
n idle

UNIT 3

Exercise 1

applied research	looking at how scientific theory can be used in practice
clinical research	looking at the effects of drugs or treatment on patients
pilot study	small-scale experiment
experimentation	the process of tests and trials to see what happens under different conditions
pure basic research	the study of pure scientific principles
product development	changing and improving a product to achieve the best possible result
innovation	a new technique or idea
analysis	the study of the parts and their relationship to one another

Exercise 2

1 analysis
2 analyst
3 analytical
4 innovative
5 inventor
6 invention
7 developers
8 developmental
9 developments
10 experimental
11 experimenter
12 experimentation

Exercise 3

a design
b innovative
c patent
d prototype
e engineers
f developmental
g experiment
h breakthrough

UNIT 4

Exercise 1

a statistics
b median
c mean
d mode
e distribution
f sampling
g random
h scale
i frequency
j 14.99
k 14.98
l 14.99

Exercise 2

1 compiled
2 recorded
3 investigate
4 improve
5 search
6 find

Exercise 3

h g d e c a b f

UNIT 5

Exercise 1

Printer   Keyboard   Monitor   Screen   Mouse   Scanner   Laptop   Workstation

Exercise 2

create files: to make new programs, utilities or documents
central processing unit: the principal microchip that the computer is built around
software products: these enable a computer to perform word processing, to create databases, and to manipulate numerical data
display information: a monitor will do this on a computer screen
digital data: this describes the format of 0 and 1 in which information is stored
expansion card: you plug this into a slot to add features such as video, sound, modem and networking
integrated circuits: when two or more components are combined and then incorporated into a single package
computer network: a group of electronic machines connected by cables or other means which can exchange information and share equipment (such as printers and disk drives)

Exercise 3

1 display information
2 digital data
3 software products
4 integrated circuits
5 create files
6 computer network
7 central processing unit
8 expansion card

UNIT 6

Exercise 1

1 b 2 a 3 c 4 a 5 c 6 b

Exercise 2

1 downtime
2 interconnected
3 transmitted
4 compatible
5 intranet
6 upload
7 connections
8 combine

Exercise 3

e a j d f b h i c g

UNIT 7

Exercise 1

1 d 2 f 3 g 4 a 5 b 6 i 7 c 8 e 9 h

Exercise 2

1 bill of lading
2 materials management
3 import
4 depot
5 package
6 cargo
7 channel
8 in transit
9 load
10 carriage

Exercise 3

a dispatched
b consignment
c carrier
d crate
e packing list
f delivery note
g shipped
h delivery
i warehouse

UNIT 8

Exercise 1

1 check
2 bar
3 detect
4 prevent
5 inventory
6 repair
7 failures
8 scrap
9 prioritize
10 value

Exercise 2

Let us consider what happened when Japanese cars were first imported into the UK and America.
Local manufacturers thought they were cheap and of low quality. But soon people noticed that they didn't break down as often as British or American cars.
At the same time, Japanese manufacturers started trying to meet customer needs in terms of style and design.
Customers were delighted with the new cars which exceeded their expectations.
The cars did more than simply satisfy customers' requirements, they provided value for money.

Exercise 3

a cause/effect
b improvement
c defective
d Pareto
e sampling
f monitor
g analysis
h prevent
i defects
j continuous
k zero

UNIT 9

Exercise 1

1 well-ventilated
2 wash
3 recycled
4 toxic
5 disposed
6 handling
7 cancer
8 defects
9 impaired
10 drains
11 Avoid
12 fumes

Exercise 2

1 protective
2 contamination
3 explosion
4 harmful
5 precautionary
6 occupational
7 dangerous
8 flammable
9 tightly
10 fumigation

Exercise 3

a risks
b goggles
c protection
d noise
e dust
f accidents
g smoke
h poisonous
i burns
j fumes
k drowsiness

UNIT 10

Exercise 1

anneal	to make materials tough by cooling them slowly, e.g. glass
anodize	to give a metal a protective coat by using it as an anode in electrolysis, e.g. car components
electroplate	to cover with a thin layer of metal using electrolysis, e.g. car components
forge	to shape metals by heating and then hammering, e.g. horse shoes
found	to melt metal and then pour it into a form, e.g. iron components
galvanize	to protect from rusting by coating in zinc, e.g. food cans
grind	to polish or sharpen by rubbing on a rough surface, e.g. stone
roll	to make thin sheets of metal by passing it between large rollers, e.g. steel
plate	to cover one metal with a thin layer of another, e.g. silver plate
soften	to make something softer, e.g. fibres
temper	to heat and then cool metals to obtain the required hardness and elasticity, e.g. steel

Exercise 2

1 chemical, chemists
2 industrial
3 mechanical
4 structural
5 harden
6 mining, miners

Exercise 3

a physics
b chemical
c civil
d highway
e electronic
f electrical
g mechanical
h develop
i production
j machines

UNIT 11

Exercise 1

e c i d h g a f b

Exercise 2

steering wheel	used by the driver to turn the car
exhaust manifold	carries waste gases to the exhaust pipe
radiator	cools water from the engine
fuel tank	holds fuel
brake line	connects the brake cylinder to the brakes
muffler/silencer	reduces the exhaust noise
battery	stores electricity
clutch	disconnects the engine from the gearbox while the gears are changed
differential	ensures that the rear wheels turn at a different speed to each other when a car corners
engine	provides the power
brake cylinder	holds brake fluid
accelerator	makes the car go faster when it is pressed
distributor	sends an electric current to the spark plugs
alternator	produces electricity

Exercise 3

a tests
b desert
c family
d air conditioning
e sunroof
f electric
g central locking
h Power assisted steering
i advanced braking system
j airbags
k alarm
l immobilizer
m mini
n people carrier
o van
p alloy wheels

UNIT 12

Exercise 1

benzene — contains 6 carbon atoms in a ring
aromatics — chemicals that contain the benzene ring
ethylene — the simplest olefin; it is a sweet-smelling gas that is used to make plastics
olefins — a group of compounds made by cracking alkanes and used to make plastics and antifreeze
fluorides — inorganic compounds of fluorine that are added to toothpastes
carbonates — compounds that react with acids to give off carbon dioxide
chlorides — compounds containing chlorine and another element
methanol — an alcohol with the formula CH_3OH
nitrates — contain NO_3- and a metal cation
oxides — compound of oxygen and another element
polypropylene — made from propene and often used for kitchen tools, for example

Exercise 2

1 insecticide
2 synthetic
3 fertilizers
4 fast drying
5 matt
6 cosmetic
7 flavours
8 stiff

Exercise 3

a soaps
b basic
c acids
d alkalis
e fertilizers
f paints
g glass
h oil
i Intermediate
j processes
k dyes
l textile
m explosives
n plastics
o petrochemical
p tough
q transparent
r resistant

UNIT 13

Exercise 1

1 detection
2 hospital, observe
3 seized
4 inspections
5 labelling
6 therapeutic
7 diagnosis
8 licence

Exercise 2

1 viscosity
2 boiling point
3 aerobic
4 distil
5 ferment
6 inorganic
7 odour
8 preservatives
9 extract

Exercise 3

a treatment
b laboratories
c stringent
d healthy
e patients
f suffering
g disease
h regulatory
i approved
j harmful
k safety
l placebo
m evaluate

UNIT 14

Exercise 1

1 an acute – a chronic
2 unlikely – likely
3 infectious – emotional
4 asthma – malaria
5 walking – breathing
6 digestive – nervous
7 salt – sugar
8 physiotherapist – pharmacist

Exercise 2

1 midwife/obstetrician
2 radiologist
3 anaesthetist
4 nutritionist
5 paramedic
6 occupational therapist
7 dentist
8 physiotherapist
9 paediatrician
10 radiographer

Exercise 3

a heart attack
b tablet
c stroke
d side effect
e cancer
f doses
g chronic
h arthritis

UNIT 15

Exercise 1

1 felt
2 partitions
3 vapour
4 structure
5 ventilating
6 –deadening
7 deep
8 Caisson piers

Exercise 2

1 beam
2 column
3 steel girder
4 curtain wall
5 roof truss
6 lattice girder
7 pile foundations

Exercise 3

a load-bearing
b surveyor
c architect
d quantity surveyor
e foundations
f carpenters
g masons
h roofers
i plasterers
j electricians
k plumbers
l painters

UNIT 16

Exercise 1

1 panelboard
2 watertight
3 rainproof
4 switchboard
5 superconductors
6 explosionproof
7 overload
8 dustproof

Exercise 2

1 laser
2 device
3 signal
4 radar
5 fibre optics
6 robotics
7 branch circuit
8 short circuit
9 (circuit) breaker
10 junction (electrical) box

Exercise 3

a turbines
b generators
c transformers
d cables
e power
f transmission lines
g transformers
h cable
i fuse
j circuits
k lighting
l appliances

UNIT 17

Exercise 1

1 Transistors
2 semiconductor
3 electronic
4 receives
5 storage
6 reliability
7 microprocessors
8 communication

Exercise 2

1 amplified, amplifier
2 entertainment
3 generation
4 integrated
5 reliable
6 storage
7 transmission
8 stored
9 Transmission, modulation
10 emitted

Exercise 3

a Transistors
b Resistors
c electrons
d Diodes
e Capacitors
f integrated circuits
g semiconductor
h silicon
i germanium
j devices

UNIT 18

Exercise 1

Devices robot, radio, television, altimeter, computer
Functions develop solutions, transmit data, diagnose problems, evaluate results, provide support
Applications transportation systems, automotive industry, pharmaceutical industry, chemical industry, defence

Exercise 2

1 space technology
2 satellite communications
3 personal computer
4 computer-guided robots
5 navigation aids
6 consumer goods

Exercise 3

a medical
b technicians
c repair
d instrumentation
e examined
f architecture

UNIT 19

Exercise 1

1 sun 2 biofuel 3 wind 4 plutonium 5 wave
6 petroleum

Exercise 2

Across
1 commissioned
3 electrical
7 geothermal
9 gasworks
10 sun
12 uranium
13 solar cell
14 kinetic
15 scheme
16 biofuel

Down
2 open coal fires
4 magnetic
5 greenhouse
6 transport
8 hydraulic
11 petroleum
15 solar

Exercise 3

a fossil fuels
b coal
c power stations
d produce
e gas
f non-renewable
g renewable
h water
i turbines
j generators
k Wave
l tidal
m barrage

UNIT 20

Exercise 1

1 suspension
2 cantilever
3 clapper
4 masonry arch
5 bascule
6 swing

Exercise 2

1 dam
2 dike
3 viaduct
4 aqueduct
5 lock
6 sluice
7 well
8 tunnels
9 desalination
10 bulldozer
11 dredger
12 road roller

Exercise 3

a camber
b crown
c sewer
d manholes
e pavement
f curb
g macadam
h potholes
i main
j soft shoulder
k culvert

UNIT 21

Exercise 1

feasibility study	investigation to assess both financial and engineering aspects of a project
site investigation	study of the proposed location to assess geology of the area
maintenance	activities carried out after the project to ensure problems are solved
soil mechanics	extensive investigation to evaluate the load-bearing qualities and stability of the ground
specifications	dimensions and measurements
technical drawings	detailed plan of proposed structures
commission a project	to order a plan to be carried out
costing system	procedure to monitor the costs of a project so that management can get information on development
tender	offer of a bid for an engineering contract
turnkey project	building or installation which is built, supplied, or installed complete and ready to operate

Exercise 2

Phase	Tasks
Before construction	feasibility study preliminary site investigation extensive site investigation detailed design
During construction	employment of consulting engineer consulting engineer contact with contractors consulting engineer communications with client
After construction	maintenance

Exercise 3

a engineer
b industrial
c construction
d claims
e scheduling
f draft
g site
h client

UNIT 22

Exercise 1

deposit	a natural occurrence of a useful mineral in sufficient quantities for exploitation
excavate	remove soil and/or rock materials from one location and transport them to another
explore	search for coal, minerals, or ore
extract	remove coal or ore from a mine
mineral	a natural resource extracted from the earth for human use, e.g. ores, salts, coal, or petroleum
mining	the science, technique, and business of mineral discovery and exploitation
ore	the naturally occurring material from which a mineral or minerals of economic value can be extracted
prospect	examine a territory under for its mineral wealth
quarry	an open or surface mineral working, usually for the extraction of building stone, such as slate and limestone

Exercise 2

1	headframe	6	drill
2	cage	7	conveyor
3	drift	8	dump truck
4	dragline	9	mining skip
5	shovel		

Exercise 3

a	explosives	e	deposits
b	mine	f	prospecting
c	earth	g	audits
d	minerals		

UNIT 23

Exercise 1

derrick	a pyramid of steel erected over a bore hole to drill for oil
drill	to cut through rock
extract	to take out a solid or liquid
flammable	burns easily
offshore	places in oceans, seas or large lakes
platform	an offshore structure from which wells are drilled
reservoir	rock formation containing oil and/or natural gas
rig	a st that contains all the necessary equipment for drilling
upstream	exploration and production activities for oil and natural gas
well	a hole drilled into the earth to recover oil or gas

Exercise 2

1	derrick	5	drill bit
2	rotary table/turntable	6	cuttings
3	blowout preventer	7	mud pump
4	casings		

Exercise 3

1 Place the drill bit, (**a**) *collar* and drill pipe in the hole.
2 Attach the (**f**) *kelly* and (**g**) *turntable* and begin drilling.
3 As drilling progresses, circulate drilling (**c**) *mud* through the pipe and out of the (**d**) *bit* to float the rock (**e**) *cuttings* out of the hole.
4 Add new sections (joints) of drill (**a**) *pipes* as the hole gets deeper.
5 (**l**) *Remove* the drill pipe, collar and bit when the pre-set depth is reached.
6 Place (**h**) *casing* pipe sections into the hole to prevent it from collapsing in on itself.
7 (**j**) *Pump* cement down the casing (**k**) *pipe*.
8 Allow the (**b**) *cement* to harden

UNIT 24

Exercise 1

```
P  W  D  T  K  Y (P  E  O  S) I  N  C  B  U
(L  U  B  R  I  C  A  T  I  O  N) M  O  J  Q
 A  V  I  O  O  S  R  U  K  L  W (F  U  E  L)
(S  O  A  P) L  W  A  X  G  V  P  Q  L  L  S
 T  A  R  G  N  N  F (P  E  T  R  O  L) Y
 I  Q  U  Z  W  C  F  X  K  N  H  T  M  Y  L
(C  B  U  P (W  Z  I  T  B (T) F  K  A  C  V
 T  T  E (P  A  I  N  T) A  C (P  L  P  P  X
 A  S  D  W (X) T (E  X  P  L  O  S  I  V  E)
 B  R  E  E  F  G  I  O  U  W  W  S  T  J  P
 A  T (D  R  U  G) F  P  Z  D (E) J  B  P  O
 O  O  Y  F  H  U  P  A  R  A  R) R  T  H  J
 F (F (E) R  T  I  L  I  Z  E  R) U  N  B  V
 W  G  H  P  B  O  A  K  T  U  K  L  P  T  Y
```

Exercise 2

1	separated	5	impurities
2	Collectors	6	lubrication
3	Distillation	7	pollution
4	heated	8	refinery

Exercise 3

a	barrel	g	impurities
b	refining	h	processed
c	transporting	i	pipeline
d	refineries	j	terminal
e	distillation	k	spillage
f	separate	l	tankers

UNIT 25

Exercise 1

1 T
2 F Monomers are made into polymers by joining the carbon atoms together.
3 F Thermoplastics soften with heat and harden with cooling.
4 T
5 F Incineration is a hazardous way to dispose of plastics because of air emissions and other pollutants.
6 T

Exercise 2

Article	How made	Plastic
bucket	injection moulding	polyethylene
shoe soles	reaction injection moulding	polyurethane
ballpoint pen	injection moulding	styrene
electric cable	extrusion	PVC
ruler	injection moulding	styrene
plastic bag	blow extrusion	polyethylene
water pipes	extrusion	pvc
milk bottle	blow moulding	polyethylene
audio cassette	injection moulding	styrene

Exercise 3

1 g   2 c   3 h   4 d   5 j   6 f   7 a   8 i   9 b   10 e

UNIT 26

Exercise 1

```
L  U  C  R (G  R  O  W  T (H)
I  S  U  J  A  B  H  D  H) Y
V  R (B (R  E  E  D  I  N  G)
E  W  T  I  F  E  Z  D  B) I
S  F  I  C  I  B  A (B) F  E
T  O (F  E  E  D) T  A  E  N
O  X  L  Z  H  T  H  K  R (E)
(C  R  O  P  S) P  R  I  T  I
K) B  U  Q  U  I  R  N  I  V
O (D  R  A  I  N  A (G) E) R
```

Exercise 2

A	B	C
bread	baking	to cook by dry heat especially in an oven
fish	canning	to preserve by sealing in airtight containers
flour	grinding	to make grains into very small particles for human or animal feed
footwear	manufacturing	to make from raw materials by machinery
leather	tanning	to convert animal skin into a material that can be worn
oil	pressing	to extract liquid by squeezing
pulp	producing	to make paper
quick	freezing	to make chilled with cold
spray	drying	to remove liquid
textile	weaving	to make cloth

111

Exercise 3

Introduction to food hygiene	Hygiene is important for anyone working in a food business. Good hygiene prevents food poisoning and protects your reputation with customers.
Food handling	While you are working, clean up any spills immediately and clean work surfaces, equipment and floors frequently.
Bacteriology	Cross-contamination can easily occur when one food touches (or drips onto) another, or indirectly, for example from hands, equipment, work surfaces, or knives and other utensils.
Prevention of contamination	Food handlers must protect food and ingredients against risks which may make them unfit for human consumption or a health hazard.
Premises	The place where you work has to be kept clean, maintained in good repair and be designed and constructed to permit good hygiene practices.
Cleaning and disinfection	Floors, walls, ceilings and surfaces (which come into contact with food) must be adequately maintained, easy to clean and where necessary disinfected.
Staff	People who work in food areas can spread food poisoning germs very easily.
Legislation	Owners and managers of food businesses must ensure that their businesses comply with the law.

UNIT 27

Exercise 1

fell	to cut down a tree
bark	outer layer of a log
chop	to cut into small pieces
pulp	to convert wood into a fibrous material by a mechanical or chemical process
grind	to crush into particles
slurry	liquid mixture consisting of fibres in water used in papermaking process
bleach	chemical to whiten paper
press	to squeeze out water between rollers
wind	to turn around so as to form a roll
roll	quantity of paper formed into a large cylinder or ball

Exercise 2

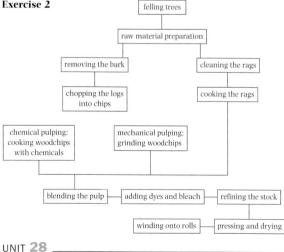

UNIT 28

Exercise 1

wire	a thin piece of metal for conducting electrical current
wave	an electric, electromagnetic, acoustic, mechanical or other form whose physical activity rises and falls as it travels through a medium
analogue	a system in which data is represented as a continuously varying voltage
digital	a system in which data is represented as 0 or 1
amplitude modulation	where audio signals increase and decrease the amplitude of the carrier wave
frequency modulation	where voltage levels change the frequency of a carrier wave
source encoder	a device which maps the source into a set of binary strings
channel encoder	a device which maps the binary strings into coded bits or waveforms for transmission
degradation	the deterioration in quality, level, or standard of performance
distort	to fail to reproduce accurately the characteristics of the input
carrier wave	a wave suitable for modulation by an information-bearing signal

Exercise 2

wire   coaxial cable   copper wire   repeater   single-wire line

radio   antenna   microwave   satellite transmitter

optical   fibre optic cable   laser   light-emitting diode   wavelength

Exercise 3

Telecommunications Fundamentals	Introduction to the *electromagnetic transmission* of information
Telecommunications Fundamentals Lab	Hands-on practical experiments to *transmit signals*
Analogue Communications	*Direct* transmission of signals
Digital Electronics	*Converting analogue* signals
Fundamentals of Optical Communications	The advantages of *laser* technologies
Fundamentals of Telecommunications Networking	Introduction to *sharing* information
Data Communications Networking	Sharing *information* between networks

UNIT 29

Exercise 1

1   a, b, c, d   4   a, b, c, d
2   a, b, c, d   5   a, b, c, d
3   b, c, d   6   a, b, c, d

Exercise 2

answering machine   radio signal   video camera   relay station   cable television   television set   retrieve messages   transmitting antenna   cordless phone   telephone jack

1 The telephone can be used to pay bills and *retrieve messages* from *answering machines*.
2 With an omnidirectional antenna, *radio signals* can be transmitted over a wide area.
3 A videophone incorporates a *video camera* and display, a microphone and speaker.
4 A *cordless phone* allows limited mobility in and around the home.
5 *Cable television* allows access to many television stations.

Exercise 3

a   PDA   f   clock and alarm
b   email   g   currency converter
c   browsing   h   alert
d   screen   i   organizer
e   cell phone   j   weight

UNIT 30

Exercise 1

```
S I L K Q U P F F I O G R A F
P S E N Y L O N B X D R P G B
I V C I A Z L U K A Y S Q O P
N Z S T E S Y N T H E T I C T
Y S G H B L E L W T Y P Z T W
D L M J L K S H R I N K A G E
F I B R E W T H A V I U P W A
P N J L A L E R C X Q C M Y V
S E R T C U R T A I N L T T E
G N B F H X H O R A J W U P A
P P A X A W Y K P R E S S I M
N F F C R E A S E B W H Q U W
N D I Q U T R A T P P Q C C V
Z A F T G T N C E H U K E P C
```

Exercise 2

Fabric	Fibre type	Characteristics
cotton	natural	Soft to the touch; absorbent
linen	natural	Good strength, twice as strong as cotton; crisp to the touch
nylon	synthetic	Lightweight; easy to wash: resists shrinkage and wrinkling
polyester	synthetic	Strong; resistant to most chemicals
silk	natural	Luxurious; thinnest of all natural fibres
wool	natural	Good insulator; luxurious, soft to the touch

Exercise 3

a   machine-washable
b   dry-cleanable.
c   hand-washable
d   sunlight
e   shrinkage
f   drying
g   stretching
h   stain

UNIT 31

Exercise 1

1   is heated
2   have dissolved
3   have survived, are being treated
4   change
5   have taken, are trying

Exercise 2

1   are, made
2   is, inspecting
3   has, come
4   produce, are rejected
5   have been importing, have ... begun
6   has been dyed
7   are dispatching

Exercise 3

a   has experienced
b   have been damaged
c   (have been) destroyed
d   has decided/decided
e   is building
f   are being heightened
g   are working
h   believe
i   are starting
j   have been drawn up
k   are

UNIT 32

Exercise 1

1   was built
2   —
3   were
4   covered
5   work
6   —
7   discovered
8   —
9   —
10 transformed

Exercise 2

1   When were fibre optics first developed?
2   The boxes broke because they were made/had been made of low quality materials.
3   The power supply was cut off because cables came down during the storm.
4   They had not completed the foundations by the time the building materials arrived.
5   When did they install the solar panels?
6   Was this the first hydroelectric scheme in Scotland?
7   They were not using wood chip for heating when the engineer visited the factory.
8   How did they produce gas before they discovered North Sea gas?
9   Was the oil pollution along the coastline caused by an oil tanker spillage?
10 How did they prepare access to this mine?

Exercise 3

a   was found
b   was lying
c   checked
d   was still breathing
e   called
f   was taken
g   recovered
h   found
i   had been left
j   had escaped
k   had become
l   had become
m   (had) fallen
n   was working

UNIT 33

Exercise 1

1 b   2 e   3 c   4 f   5 d   6 a

Exercise 2

1 b   2 a   3 a   4 a   5 b

Exercise 3

a   will revolutionize
b   will we need
c   won't be
d   will operate
e   will it provide
f   will warm
g   will install
h   won't take
i   will soon see
j   will give
k   will deal
l   will contact

UNIT 34

Exercise 1

1 g   2 f   3 a   4 b   5 c   6 h   7 e   8 d

Exercise 2

1   there are greater safety measures
2   he had followed the correct procedures
3   the airbag will inflate
4   there would be less pollution
5   we introduced a catalyst
6   the substance will decompose/decomposes
7   infections won't be passed on
8   it rusts

Exercise 3

a   improve
b   would have delayed
c   stops
d   hadn't built
e   wouldn't have made
f   'll have to
g   stops
h   wouldn't have had
i   had

UNIT 35

Exercise 1

1 a   2 b   3 b   4 b   5 a

Exercise 2

1   overloading
2   to switch
3   to increase
4   producing
5   to reduce
6   scratching
7   to deliver
8   to visit

Exercise 3

a   to come
b   to begin working
c   to develop
d   using
e   creating
f   linking
g   happening
h   to join
i   to do
j   to complete
k   to delay running
l   to arrange

UNIT 36

Exercise 1

1   boosts (active); can be used (passive)
2   are ... made (passive)
3   can be recycled (passive); sorted (passive); are removed (passive)
4   is produced (passive)
5   include (active)
6   choose (active)
7   was formed (passive)

Exercise 2

Four hotels have been built.
The wet land has been drained.
A new library extension has been opened.
The factories have been closed.
The river has been cleaned.
A new office block has been built.
Two parks have been established.
A new airport is/has been planned.

Exercise 3

a   is used
b   is blown
c   is forced
d   are made
e   are first heated
f   is suited
g   produces
h   is used
i   is made
j   are soaked
k   are then squeezed
l   be shaped
m   is forced
n   be made

UNIT 37

Exercise 1

1   result in
2   as a result of
3   were responsible for
4   because of
5   on account of
6   as a result of
7   due to
8   has brought about
9   because
10 is attributable to
11 as a consequence of
12 led to

Exercise 2

1   Modern communications systems have resulted in more and more people working from home.
2   A rise in the volume of electricity required by consumers is caused by cold weather.
3   The use of more lightweight parts brings about reduced transportation costs.
4   An annual saving of electricity is attributable to increased energy efficiency.
5   The production of heat results from friction during drilling.
6   Rivers beginning to support fish again is attributable to a reduction in the amount of waste being discharged into rivers.
7   Air pollution partly stems from cars and aeroplanes.
8   Turbines spin due to water flowing through them.

Exercise 3

a on   b of   c about   d for   e in   f of   g for   h to
i in   j of   k to

UNIT 38

Exercise 1

1 h   2 g   3 e   4 f   5 b   6 d

Exercise 2

1   needn't enclose
2   will need to
3   made the company shut down
4   are not required to
5   required
6   to enter

Exercise 3

a must   b permit   c banned   d forcing   e have
f must   g needn't   h supposed   i require   j permitted
k prohibited,

UNIT 39

Exercise 1

The reject rate has fallen due to more effective quality control.
There is now a backlog of orders as a result of machinery breakdowns.
We have developed an improved product owing to extensive research and development.
They want to understand why customers buy a product. That's why they're studying customer attitudes.
Computer software has been made easier to use so more people use computers daily.
They have set up a computer network. Consequently, users can share files and resources.
We are having to increase our prices as a consequence of increased carriage charges.
This is a very dusty environment, therefore all workers should wear masks.
He was not following safety regulations. That's the reason he had an accident.

Exercise 2

1   Owing– Owing to
2   from – of
3   result – reason
4   Consequently – Because
5   Due to – As
6   since – hence/thus

Exercise 3

a   because
b   consequence
c   account
d   result
e   consequently
f   so
g   reason
h   why
i   due
j   because

UNIT 40

Exercise 1

Improving quality control will enable us to become more profitable.
Shortage of space prevents us from producing more product lines.
Regulations prohibit the storage of chemicals in containers.
A machine breakdown means that we can't finish the order this week.
Old copper cables are incapable of carrying the volume of data required today.
Using a videophone allows you to see the person you are talking to.
Mobile phones can now be used to send emails.
A firewall is used to stop unauthorized users accessing a network.

Exercise 2

1   to – from
2   of
3   repairing – to repair
4   to support – of supporting
5   passing – pass
6   to
7   curing – to cure
8   of – from

Exercise 3

a   make unable prevents
b   make unable prevents
c   make able enable/allow/permit
d   be able is able to operate/ is capable of operating/ can operate
e   make able allow/enable/permit
f   make able allows/enables/permits
g   be able can/ is able to
h   be able can /is able to

i ~~be able~~ can perform /is able to perform/ is capable of performing

j ~~make able~~ allows/enables

k ~~make unable~~ prevents/stops

l ~~make able~~ allows/enables

UNIT 41

Exercise 1

1 The goods probably won't be delivered until next week.
2 I'm absolutely sure that these crates are strong enough.
3 The goods are unlikely to remain in the warehouse for long.
4 It shouldn't take long to load the ship.
5 They definitely won't be sent by air freight.
6 The goods may be in transit for four days.
7 They're quite likely to increase the volume of imports.

Exercise 2

1 I'm absolutely certain that there will be advances in heat-exchange technology.
   There are bound to be advances in heat-exchange technology.
2 It is improbable that we will see more robots being used in the home in the next ten years.
   We probably won't see more robots being used in the home in the next ten years.
3 Glass fibre optics could very probably be replaced by plastic in the near future.
   Glass fibre optics are likely to be replaced by plastic in the near future.
4 Washing machines and dishwashers will definitely become more energy efficient.
   Washing machines and dishwashers are bound to become more energy efficient.
5 A mat foundation definitely won't support a high building.
6 We might need extra sound-deadening material in these walls.
7 I am certain they won't want to use wood for the ceiling.
8 It is very likely that she's suffering from an allergy.
   She is quite likely to be suffering from an allergy.
9 Research being carried out at the moment might help find a cure for cancer.

Exercise 3

Suggested answer. Other forms are possible.

a	certain to	**j**	certain to
b	are likely	**k**	probably won't
c	will definitely	**l**	definitely
d	is unlikely	**m**	likely to
e	definitely won't	**n**	might
f	could	**o**	likely
g	quite likely to	**p**	could
h	unlikely	**q**	bound
i	could		

UNIT 42

Exercise 1

1	that	**5**	who
2	who	**6**	when
3	which	**7**	where
4	where	**8**	whose

Exercise 2

There has been a lot of controversy surrounding the Three Gorges Dam, <u>which is being built in China</u> (ND). The dam, <u>which will be 181 m high</u> (ND), is expected to produce 18.2 million kilowatts of power. However, this is the reason <u>why many people are unhappy</u> (D).
15 million people, <u>who used to live in the valley</u> (ND), have had to move. These people, <u>whose homes have been covered in water</u> (ND), complain that they have been given land <u>where very little grows</u> (D). They also say that the living conditions <u>which they have to live in now</u> (D) are unsatisfactory. But those <u>who are in favour of the project</u> (D) say that the dam will provide extra electricity, <u>which will stimulate the economy in eastern and central China</u> (ND), <u>where development has been held back</u> (ND). However, critics say there will be an oversupply of power, <u>which they will not be able to sell</u> (ND).
There are people <u>who are deeply worried about the effects of the dam on the environment</u> (D). They say there is a danger to animals and fish <u>which live in the area</u> (D). But there are other people <u>who claim that hydroelectric power is much cleaner than burning coal</u> (D). There will be fewer emissions <u>which contribute to the greenhouse effect</u> (D).
New ship locks, <u>which are expected to increase shipping and reduce transportation costs</u> (ND), will be built. Navigation on the river, <u>which is currently dangerous</u> (ND), will become much safer. But critics say there will be sedimentation <u>which could increase flood levels</u> (ND).

Exercise 3

1 produces car parts
2 water is stored
3 can store large amounts of information
4 W.C. Röntgen discovered them by accident
5 was born in the south of England
6 signature appears on the document
7 works in this area

UNIT 43

Exercise 1

1 They introduced computer-guided robots in order to increase efficiency.
2 Close the valve so that the system doesn't overheat.
3 Scientists are carrying out research so as to find a cure for AIDS.
4 Circuit breakers have been installed so that they don't overload the system./ Circuit breakers have been installed so that the system isn't overloaded.
5 The system is sealed in order to stop water and dust getting in.
6 He is taking anti-malarial drugs so that he doesn't get malaria.

Exercise 2

a save energy
b receive the maximum amount of sun
c prevent the loss of heat
d purify the air
e the temperature can be controlled
f produce power for the house
g be kept dry
h provide insulation
i heat doesn't escape
j use too much power within the house

UNIT 44

Exercise 1

Countable: drill   dye   factory   fault   laboratory   machine   tunnel
Uncountable: electronic mail   equipment   information   machinery   packaging   pollution   reliability   silk

Exercise 2

1	disposal	**5**	paint
2	storage	**6**	pavements
3	inspection	**7**	a reservoir
4	prevention	**8**	a study

Exercise 3

1	cloths – *clothes*	**6**	was – were
2	short – shorts	**7**	were – was
3	cottons – cotton	**8**	type of fibres – types of fibre
4	—	**9**	Synthetic – Synthetics
5	glove – gloves		

UNIT 45

Exercice 1

adjective	comparative	superlative
accurate	*more accurate*	*the most accurate*
pure	purer	the purest
stable	more stable	the most stable
hard	harder	the hardest
heavy	heavier	the heaviest
thin	thinner	the thinnest
far	farther/further	the farthest/furthest
impractical	more impractical	the most impractical
bad	worse	the worst

Exercise 2

1 —
2 as – than
3 most – more
4 —
5 some of ... most – some of the most
6 —
7 good – better
8 most quick – quickest

Exercise 3

a longest
b longer
c old as
d newer
e older
f longest
g longer
h old
i newest
j shortest
k shorter
l older

UNIT 46

Exercise 1

dangerous, reliable, experimental, dirty, original, washed, magnetic, expensive, flexible, useful, excellent, resistant, industrial

Exercise 2

1 automatically, automatic
2 efficient, efficiently
3 smooth, smoothly
4 generally, general
5 environmentally, environmental
6 strictly, strict

Exercise 3

a manufacturing
b considerably
c approximately
d important
e increasing
f industrial
g increasingly
h woollen
i constant
j significant
k annually
l excellent
m healthy
n extensive
o important
p dying
q relatively
r significantly
s particular
t high

UNIT 47

Exercise 1

1 to – at
2 since – for
3 —
4 —
5 during – while
6 from – between
7 at – in
8 —

Exercise 2

a for   b on   c before   d at   e of   f on   g in   h at
i by   j since   k in

Exercise 3

a In   b At   c of   d on   e in   f in   g —   h —
i In   j of   k on   l for   m in   n At   o until   p in
q on   r by   s of

UNIT 48

Exercise 1

Text 1

a from   b to   c along   d through   e between   f on
g along   h above

Text 2

a at   b of   c to   d from   e around   f of

Exercise 2

a on   b on   c in   d above   e In   f of   g above   h at
i of   j from   k to   l on   m Below   n on   o on
p in between   q along   r around   s close to   t on   u of
v from   w in   x beside

UNIT 49

Exercise 1

100%   0%
  8   3   5   6   1   7   4   2

Exercise 2

1 many, Most
2 Some, a few
3 many, much
4 all, some
5 little, lot
6 most, few

Exercise 3

a all   b No   c most   d few   e many   f lot of   g much
h little   i some   j some   k little   l no   m Most
n some

UNIT 50

Exercise 1

1 careful packing
2 he washed it
3 those are a mixture of polyester and wool
4 there are places in the country where it doesn't work
5 accidents sometimes occur
6 people in developing countries often have to drink polluted water

Exercise 2

a but   b However   c While   d Whereas   e Despite

Exercise 3

Site 1 provides a suitable amount of space but it's the most expensive.
Although it could be difficult, it's still worth considering.
Although road and rail connections are not far away, it will be necessary to build a bridge across the river.
It's surrounded by trees and close to mountains. However, it's only four kilometres from the nearest town.
Even though there is a large labour market in this area, workers are unskilled.
While site 1 is close to road and rail connections, site 2 is close to the airport.
Nevertheless, government finance is available for companies moving into the area.
Site 2 is fairly small whereas site 3 is almost too big.
Site 3 is not expensive despite being in the centre of town.
Even so, it may be difficult to get planning permission for new industrial buildings.

Checklist

The checklist below contains all the items which appear in the relevant vocabulary unit. For the definitions, refer to the glossary.

PROFESSIONAL ACTIVITIES

1 Production 1
2 Production 2
3 Research & Development 1
4 Research & Development 2
5 Information technology 1
6 Information technology 2
7 Logistics
8 Quality
9 Health and safety

COMPANY PROFILES

10 Engineering
11 Automotive
12 Chemical
13 Pharmaceutical 1
14 Pharmaceutical 2
15 Construction
16 Electrical
17 Electronics 1
18 Electronics 2

19 Energy
20 Civil engineering 1
21 Civil engineering 2
22 Mining
23 Petroleum 1
24 Petroleum 2
25 Plastics
26 Agroindustry
27 Pulp & paper

28 Telecomms 1
29 Telecomms 2
30 Textiles

1 Production 1
analyse
assemble
assembly line
batch
breakdown
component
controlling
convert
distribute
effectiveness
efficiency
equipment
evaluate
factory
failure
fault
finished product
fixtures
flow
input
inventory
layout
line
logistics
lot
machinery
maintain
manufacturing
materials handling
maximize
measure
operations
optimize
planning
plant
process
produce
productivity
quality
raw materials
repair
site
stock
storage
store
unit
workshop

2 Production 2
aggregate
backlog
back order
bottleneck
breakdown
capacity
component
cycle
delivery
demand
downtime
flow
forecast
idle
lead time
lot
machinery
make-to-order
make-to-stock
material
optimization
output
overtime
productivity
prototype
requirement
run
satisfy
schedule
sequence
set up
set-up time
shift
slack
stock
stock-out
throughput
uncertainty
update
workforce
work in progress
workload
workshop

3 Research & Development 1
academic research
analyse
analysis
analyst
analytical
applied research
basic research
breakthrough
carry out
clinical research
develop
developer
development
development and evaluation
    research
developmental
engineer
experiment
experimental
experimental development
experimentation
experimenter
feasibility
feasible
file a patent
findings
improve
innovate
innovation
innovative
innovator
lab technician
laboratory (lab)
me-too product
patent
pilot
pipeline (in the pipeline)
practical application
product development
prototype
pure basic research
pure research
register a patent
research assistant
scientific
scientist
search
strategic basic research
technical know-how (TKH)
technician

4 Research & Development 2
analyse
assess
compile
constant
correlation
determine
develop
deviation
discover
distribution
evaluate
experiment
explore
feedback
frequency
identify
improve
innovate
interview
investigate
mean
measurement scale
median
mode
modify
norm
qualitative research
random
record
reliability
report
research
response
sampling
search
standard
statistics
study
survey
test
trial
validity
variable
variance

5 Information technology 1

analog
analogue
applet
application software
browser
central processing unit (CPU)
collect
computer network
CPU
create
database software
desk top (desktop)
digital
digital communications
display
dot matrix printer
email software
expansion card
file
graphic software
hardware
inkjet printer
integrated circuit
keyboard
lap top (laptop)
laser printer
mainframe
maintain
manipulate
monitor
mouse
note book (notebook)
operating system
organize
process
program
query
RAM (Random Access Memory)
record
retrieve
scanner
screen
search engine
server
software (program)
spreadsheet
storage device
store
terminal
transfer
word processing
work station (workstation)

6 Information technology 2

bandwidth
baud
bits per second (bps)
communicate
compatible
configure
connect
database
downtime
download
electronic message
gateway
hack
hub
install
interactive

interconnect
internet
internet service provider (ISP)
intranet
ISP
LAN (local area network)
link
local area network
network
optical fibre
packet
physical connection
protocol
receive
share files
signal
switch
technique
transfer
transmission speed
transmit
twisted pair
upload
WAN (wide area network)
web page
website
wide area network
World Wide Web

7 Logistics

air freight
bill of lading
cargo
carriage
carrier
carton
channel
consignment
deliver
delivery
delivery note
depot
dispatch
distribution
distribution centre
documentation
envelope
export
factory
flow
forklift truck
forward
freight
haul
import
in transit
lading
load
lorry
material
materials management
movement
pack
packaging
packing list
pallet
picking list
ship
shipment
shipper
storage

tanker
transportation
truck
unload
van
warehouse

8 Quality

accurate
add value
analysis
axis
bar graph
cause/effect analysis
check
commitment
comply with
continuous process
    improvement
control
customer needs
defect prevention
defective
define
delighted
detect
error
exceed
expectation
facilitate
failure
improvement
inspect
inspection
inventory control
meet
monitor
needs (usually plural)
Pareto chart
pie chart
prevent
prevention
prioritize
process
process control
rectify
repair
requirements (usually plural)
rework
sampling
scrap
specification
system failure analysis
variability
variable
zero defects

9 Health and safety

accident
adverse effects
avoid contact with
birth defect
burn
cancer
combustion
contamination
dangerous
dispose of
dizziness
drains
drowsiness

dry
dust
explosion
flammable
friction
fumes
fumigation
gas
genetic damage
goggles
handle
hard hat
harmful
hazard
impair fertility
irreversible effects
keep dry, clean, away from
    children, etc.
machinery
noise
noisy
occupational health
poison
precautionary
protect
protection
protective
radiation
recycle
regulated
rinse
risk
seal
shock
smoking
spraying
substance
tightly
toxic
vapour
vibration
vomiting
wash
well-ventilated

10 Engineering

anneal
anodize
apparatus
boiler
chemical
chemistry
civil
construct
crane
design
develop
electrical
electronic
electroplate
engine
engineer
forge
found
galvanize
gas engine
grind
harden
highway
hydraulic
industrial

machine part
machine tool
manufacturing process
mathematics
mechanical
mechanics
mining
mint
petroleum production
physical
physics
plate
production
pump
rate process
roll
soften
structural
structure
systems analysis
temper
thermodynamics
tinplate
transfer process
turbine

11 Automotive

ABS (= Advanced Braking System)
accelerator
advanced braking system
air conditioning
airbag
alarm
alloy wheel
alternator
Arctic cold
automobile
body panel
brake line
brake pedal
brake system
bus
cast
central locking
climate control
coil spring
component
construct
coolant reservoir
crash
cut
desert heat
design
development
differential
disc brake, disk brake
distributor
drawing board
drum brake
dust tunnel
electric window
electrical system
engine
executive
exhaust manifold
exhaust system
feature
fibreglass
forge
4 × 4

fuel line
fuel system
fuel tank
immobilizer
intake manifold
lorry
luxury
machine operator
master brake cylinder
medium
mini
model
mould (AmE mold)
MPV
muffler (AmE)
multi-purpose vehicle
paint shop
part
PAS
people carrier
pickup
power assisted steering
power train
press shop
prototype
radiator
research
set up
shock absorber
showroom
silencer (AmE muffler)
small family
sports
spray gun
stamp
steel
steering system
steering wheel
sunroof
supermini
support system
tail pipe
test
track
transmission
truck
van
water-proof
wind tunnel

12 Chemical

acid
agricultural chemical
agriculture
aircraft
alcohol
alkali
aromatic
artificial
automobile
bake
basic and intermediate chemicals
beauty aid
benzene
carbonate
chemical
chloride
coal
crack resistant
dye

easy flow
ethylene
explosive
fertilizer
fibre
flame resistant
flame-retardant
flavour
fluoride
fungicide
glossy
hard
heat resistant
herbicide
industrial gas
insecticide
matt
methanol
nitrate
nutrient management
oil
olefin
oxide
paint finish
paints and coatings
pest management
pesticide
petrochemical
pharmaceuticals
plastic
plastics and fibres
polyethylene
polypropylene
process
propylene
reaction
rubber
salt
soap
soil management
specialty chemicals
stiff
sustainable production systems
sweetener
synthetic
synthetic fibre
tough
toxic
transparent

13 Pharmaceutical 1

aerobic
affliction
approve
biological product
boiling point
certificate
chemical purity
chronic depression
clinical
concentrate
crude drug
cultivate
cure
density
detection
diagnosis
disease
distil
double-blind technique
evaluate

exemption
extract
factory inspection
FDA
ferment
Food and Drug Administration
harmful
harvest
healthy
hospital
illness
inorganic elements and compounds
inspect
investigate
laboratory (lab)
licence
MCA
medicinal drug
Medicines Control Authority
melting point
mitigation
observe
odour
organic compound
particle size
patient
placebo
plant
preservative
product labelling
purity standards
regulatory authority
safety risk
safety standard
seize
solubility
stringent conditions
substance
suffer
test
therapeutic practice
treatment
validate
viscosity

14 Pharmaceutical 2

abnormality
acute
ageing
AIDS (= Acquired Immuno-deficiency Syndrome)
allergy
anaesthetist
arthritis
asthma
bronchitis
cancer
carer
chronic
congenital
dentist
diabetes
disorder
dispersion
dosage
drug
epilepsy
haemorrhage
heart attack
hereditary

impairment
infectious
influenza (flu)
malaria
midwife
multiple sclerosis
neurosis
nurse
nutritionist
obstetrician
occupational therapist
orthodontist
orthopaedist
osteopath
paediatrician
paramedic
pharmacist
physiotherapist
pill
pneumonia
poison
psychosis
radiation
radioactive dosage form
radiographer
radiologist
recurrent
severe
solid dosage form
solution
sterile medicament
stroke
surgeon
symptom
tablet
tuberculosis
tumour
ulcer

15 Construction

acoustical
air conditioning
architect
assembly
beam
bracing connection
caisson
carpenter
column
curtain wall
deep
electrician
environmental control
erection
exterior skin
exterior wall
floor
foundation
friction pile
girder
heating
interior partition
lighting
load-bearing wall
mason
mat
nonload-bearing wall
painter
pile
plasterer
plumber

power
quantity surveyor
reinforced-concrete
rigid connection
roof
roofer
roofing felt
shallow
shelter
sound-deadening material
spread footing
stability
structure
support
truss
vapour barrier
ventilating
wall
waste disposal
water supply

16 Electrical

appliance
assembly
branch circuit
cable
circuit
(circuit) breaker
communications
computer
control system
device
dustproof
electronic circuit
explosionproof
feeder
fibre optics
fixture
fuse
generator
ground
ground fault
junction (electrical) box
laser
light
lighting system
machinery
motor
overcurrent
overload
panelboard
power
radar
rainproof
raintight
robotics
service panel
short circuit
signal
solid-state electronics
superconductor
switch
switchboard
system
transformer
transmission line
turbine
watertight
weatherproof

17 Electronics 1

absorb
activate
activation
active
amplification
amplify
audio signal
capacitor
cellular radiotelephone system
computer-aided design
control
demodulation
device size
digitalization
diode
electron
electronic processing
electronic system
emission
emit
energy
entertain
entertainment
extract
extraction
fidelity
generate
generation
generative
generator
germanium
high speed
image
increased reliability
inductor
information extraction
integrate
integrated circuit
integration
integrative
manufacturing cost
modulation
passive
radio wave
receive
reception
receptive
recover
recovery
recovery (of audio signal)
reliability
reliable
rely
resistor
semiconductor
silicon
storage
storage capacity
storage system
store
supercomputer
transducer
transistor
transmission
transmit
transmittable
ultrahigh image definition
vacuum tube (AmE)
valve (BrE)
video signals
weapons system

18 Electronics 2

accurate
aerospace
automotive
chemical
(circuit) board
computer
consumer goods
defence
design
develop
device
diagnose
documentation
electronics lab
energy
environmental
evaluate
firmware
home computer
imaging equipment
industrial automation
manufacture
medical instrumentation
navigation
oil and gas
pharmaceutical
power
product approval
pulp and paper
radar
radio
release
repair
robot
satellite communications
semiconductor
space technology
specification
stereo
technical support
technician
telecommunications
television
test
transmit
transportation
vendor
video game

19 Energy

atomic energy plant
biofuel
coal
commission
distribution network
electrical appliance
electrical energy
fire
fossil fuel
fuel
gas
gas fired central heating
gas power
gas station
gasworks
generating station
generation
generator
geothermal energy
greenhouse effect
heat exchanger

heating
high voltage
hydraulic power
hydroelectric energy
hydroelectric scheme
kinetic energy
magnetic energy
motor
natural gas
nuclear energy
nuclear plant
nuclear power plant
oil
open coal fire
petroleum
plutonium
power plant
power station
powerhouse
solar cell
solar energy
solar panel
steam power
sun
tidal barrage
tidal power
tide mill
town-gas
transmission network
transport fuel
turbine
uranium
water
water power
waterfall
waterworks
wave
wave power
wind
wind farm
wind power
windmill

20 Civil Engineering 1
aircraft,
airport
aqueduct
arch
barrage
bridge
bulldozer
cable
camber
canal
chemical process plant
communal environment
crossover
crown
culvert
curb
dam
dike
docks (also dock)
drainage
dredger
earthmover
energy
excavator
fluid mechanics
flume
footbridge

harbour (AmE harbor)
hydraulics
irrigation
kerb (AmE curb)
lift bridge
lock
macadam
main
manhole
mechanics
metal
nuclear power station
paddle
pavement
pedestrian crossing
pier
plate girder
pothole
pylon
railway line
road
road roller
sewer
shovel
sluice
soft shoulder
soil
span
strand
structural works
structure
survey
suspender
suspension bridge
swing bridge
tarmac
tower
tunnel
underdrain
viaduct
water desalination
water main
watercourse
water-supply system
waterway
weir
well

21 Civil Engineering 2
analyse
attribute
borehole
building contractor
commission
costing system
design
detailed design
dimension
draft
drawings
estimate
feasibility study
finished design
geology
hydraulics
load-bearing
maintenance
nuclear physics
preliminary design
preliminary feasibility study
process

proposal
scheme
secondary feasibility study
site investigation
soil mechanics
specification
stability
step
technical drawings
tender
thermodynamics
trial pit
turnkey
work plan

22 Mining
access
anthracite
asbestos
audit
bauxite
bituminous
borax
burial
cage
chute
coal
conveyor
copper
crust
deposit
dragline
drift
drill
drill supervisor
dump truck
earth
environmental engineer
excavate
exploit
explore
explosive
extract
feldspar
geochemist
geologist
geophysicist
gold
granite
headframe
hydrogeologist
inspection
iron
lead
lignite
limestone
manganese
marble
mechanical loader
metalliferous
mine
mine car
miner
mineral
mining
mining engineer
nonmetalliferous
open-pit
ore
ornamental
peat

phosphate rock
prospect
prospector
pump
quarry
quartz
raise
removal
rock
safety engineer
sediment
shovel
skip
slate
stope
strip mining
stripping machine
sump
surface
swamp
talc
tin
traprock
travertine
trona
underground
ventilation shaft
zinc

23 Petroleum 1
bitumen
blowout
casing
collar
crude oil
cuttings
deposit
derrick
dig
downhole
downstream
drill
drill bit
drill pipe
drill string
drilling mud
evacuate
exploratory
extract
flammable
flow rate
formation
gas field
hydrocarbon
inject
kelly
layer
licence
mapping
offshore
oil field
oily
onshore
permit
platform
pressure
pump
recover
reserves
reservoir
rig

rock formation
rock mapping
rotary table
subsurface
trap
turntable
upstream
well
wellbore (= borehole)
wildcat (wildcat well)
wildcat well

24 Petroleum 2
aeroplane
air pollution
asphalt
automobile
barrel
benzene
catalyst
catalytic cracking
cleansing agent
coastline
collector
condense
crack
distil
distillation
draw
drug
dye
electrical power supply
explode
explosive
fertilizer
fraction
fractional distillation
fuel
gasoline (AmE)
heat
impurity
jelly
kerosene (AmE)
lubricant
lubricate
lubricating oil
lubrication
paint
paraffin (BrE)
petrochemical
petrol (BrE)
pipeline
plastic
pollutant
pollute
pollution
power
process
refine
refinery
rocket
separate
separation
ship
soap
solvent
spill
spillage
steam cracking
store
synthesize

synthetic rubber and fibre
synthetics
tanker
tanker ship
terminal
thermal cracking
tower
tractor
transport
transportation
truck
vaporize
vaporous
vapour
wax

25 Plastics
acrylic sign
biodegradable
blow extrusion
blow moulding
bowl
car bumper
chain
compound
compressed air
cool
cure
disintegrate
display
disposable
electric cable
emission
extrusion
fabrication
flexible
harden
hazardous
heat
hygienic
incineration
injection moulding
insulator
join
lightweight
modifying compound
molten
monomer
mould (AmE mold)
non-rusting
nozzle
polymer
react
reaction injection moulding
recycle
roll
rubbery
shoe sole
sign
slippery
soften
sort
squeeze
string
thermoplastics
thermoset
toy
washer

26 Agroindustry
additive
agribusiness
agricultural chemistry
agricultural engineering
agriculture
agroindustry
agroprocessing
animal feed supplement
bacteriology
baking
breeding
can
catering
commodity
conservation
consumption
contamination
crops (often plural)
cultivation
dairy farming
dehydration
disinfection
drainage
drying
feed
feed supplement
fermentation
fertilizer
flour milling
food hygiene
food packing
food poisoning
food preservation
footwear
freeze
fungicide
grow
growth
  growth regulator
herbicide
hygiene
insecticide
irradiation
livestock
pasteurization
pest
pesticide
pest control
post-harvest handling
press
processing
quick-freezing
raise
refrigeration
regulator
reverse osmosis
rice milling
sanitary engineering
soil
soil makeup
spin
spoilage
spray drying
supplement
tan
thermal processing
weave
pesticide

27 Pulp & paper
absorbance (also absorbency)
additive
bark
bible
bleach
blend chest
bond
book
brightness
bristol
brochure
carton
chip
chop
cotton
digester
dry
durability
dye
fell
gloss
grade
ground
groundwood
kraft
linen
log
matchbox
mill
newsprint
octavo
opacity
packaging
paperboard
papermaking stock
porosity
poster
press
pulp
quire
rag
ream
refine
refiner
roll
sanitary
serviette
sheet
slurry
stiffness
tissue
wallpaper
waste
water resistance
wind (wound - wound)
wood pulp
woodchip
wrap
wrapper
wrapping paper

28 Telecomms 1
amplify
amplitude modulation
analogue
antenna
attenuation
bandwidth
binary
cable TV

carrier wave
channel encoder
coaxial cable
convert
copper wire
degradation
digital
dish
distort
electromagnetic
electromagnetic wave
electronic
fibre optic cable
frequency modulation
high bandwidth
interference
interference immunity
laser
LED (light-emitting diode)
lightweight
light-emitting diode
low attenuation
metallic-pair circuit
microwave
modulation
multipair cable
noise
open-wire pair.
optic cable (also optical cable)
optical communications
optical transmission
radio transmission
radio wave
receiver
redundant
reflected propagation
repeater
restore
retransmit
satellite
signal
single-wire line
source encoder
surface propagation
switching system
transmit
transmitter

transponder
wave
wavelength
wire
wire transmission

29 Telecomms 2

aerial
alert
answering machine
antenna
application
audible
beam
broadcast
cable
cable television (cable TV)
call
cell
cellular
channel
cordless
currency converter
data
data-conversion device
device
dial
directional
dish
display
drawings
facsimile
fax
file
full-motion
General Packet Radio Service
  (GPRS)
image
infra-red computer connection
instrument
jack
LCD screen
location-based service
memo
message
microphone
mobile

mobility
network
omnidirectional antenna
packet-based
PBX
PDA (Personal Digital
  Assistant)
personal organizer
phone line
portable
Private Branch Exchange
  (PBX)
receive
reception
relay station
retrieve
signal
speaker (= loudspeaker)
still-frame
switching machine
telephony
television station
transfer
transmission
video camera
videophone
visible
visual
voice
wallpaper
WAP (Wireless Application
  Protocol)

30 Textiles

absorption
acetate
bedding
bleach
blend
braiding
brocade
brush
card
carpet
chlorine bleach
clothes
clothing

corduroy
cotton
crease control
curtains
defect
dry-cleaning
dye
embroider
fabric
felting
fibre
fibre processing
foreign matter
gauze
knit
knitting mill
lace-making
launder
linen
nap
net-making
nylon
polish
polyester
press
rayon
reversible fabric
rug
satin
shear
shrinkage
silk
spin
synthetic
textile
tumble dry
twill
upholstery
velvet
wash and wear
weave
weaving mill
wool
yarn

Glossary

The number(s) after each entry show the vocabulary unit(s) in which the word/phrase appears.

4 × 4, 11
a drive system where both axles get power from the engine

abnormality 14
something which is not normal or regular; a physical or mental defect or disorder

ABS (= Advanced Braking System) 11
See advanced braking system

absorb 17
to take in

absorbance (also absorbency) 27
the ability of paper to absorb fluids such as water or printing ink

absorption 30
the property of a fibre, yarn or fabric to attract and hold gases or liquids

academic research 3
study that is carried out for theoretical purpose without a practical application

accelerator 11
car pedal which regulates the amount of fuel sent to the engine

access 22
the way to the entrance of a mine

accident 9
something unpleasant that happens unexpectedly and causes loss, damage or injury

accurate 8, 18
correct (according to the specifications)

acetate 30
a man-made fibre (made of cellulose acetate) which is crease and shrink resistant, soft to the touch and luxurious in appearance

acid 12
a water-soluble, sour chemical compound that produces positive ions in solution. An acid is the opposite of an alkali; together, an acid and an alkali neutralize each other and react to form water and a salt. See also alkali.

acoustical 15
describing materials that can absorb sound

acrylic sign 25
a notice made from a plastic synthetic resin

activate 17
to make active

activation 17
the state of being active

active 17
an active device needs energy for its operation. See also passive.

acute 14
severe, serious, very painful

add value 8
to increase the worth (value) of a product or service from the perspective of the customer

additive 26, 27
a substance added to food improve it

advanced braking system 11
an automated way of applying braking. With ABS sensors detect if the wheels are locking; if so, then the system takes over, pumping the brake much faster than is humanly possible (also known as anti-lock brakes).

adverse effects 9
unpleasant results, e.g. loss, damage or injury

aerial 29
a radio or TV antenna, especially one suspended in or extending into the air

aerobic 13
living in air; requiring oxygen

aeroplane 24
a vehicle that carries passengers or goods by air

aerospace 18
describing the air around the earth and the space beyond it

affliction 13
an illness

ageing 14
the process of getting old

aggregate 2
total, e.g. of all planned production

agribusiness, 26
term which includes producers and manufacturers of agricultural goods and services, such as fertilizer and farm equipment makers, food and fibre processors, wholesalers, transporters, and retail food and fibre outlets

agricultural chemical 12
a substance (chemical) that is used in agriculture, e.g. pesticide, insecticide, herbicide

agricultural chemistry 26
the discipline which deals with areas of chemistry, biochemistry and soil science relevant to agricultural (including food) and environmental sciences

agricultural engineering 26
the discipline which applies physical and biological sciences and engineering to the production and processing of food and fibre, and to the preservation of environmental quality

agriculture 26, 12
the science or practice of cultivating the soil, producing crops, and raising livestock and in varying degrees the preparation and marketing of the resulting products

agroindustry 26
term describing the industry of agriculture

agroprocessing 26
term describing all the activities in processing outputs from the industry of agriculture

AIDS (= Acquired Immunodeficiency Syndrome) 14
an epidemic disease caused by an infection by human immunodeficiency virus

air freight 7
goods which are sent by plane

air pollution 24
the effect caused by making the air dirty

airbag 11
a safety device which will cause an air-filled pillow to prevent your head from hitting the dashboard

air-conditioning 11, 15
equipment that can heat, cool, clean, and circulate air in a house, car, etc.

aircraft 20, 12
an aeroplane

airport 20
a place where planes can take off and land

alarm 11
the equipment that gives a warning signal if someone tries to break into the car

alcohol 12
a family of organic compounds, the most common of which is ethyl alcohol or ethanol, CH_3CH_2OH

alkali 12
a group of water soluble mineral compounds. An alkali is the opposite of an acid; together, an acid and an alkali neutralize each other and react to form water and a salt. Also called base. See also acid.

alert 29
a written or acoustic signal that warns or informs the user of a special situation

allergy 14
an extreme reaction or sensitivity to something eaten, breathed in or touched

alloy wheel 11
any non-steel road wheel, usually made of aluminium or magnesium

alternator 11
a device which produces alternating current (AC) by converting the engine's turning (mechanical) energy into alternating electrical current

Relay terminal / F terminal
RAT terminal
GRD terminal

amplification 17
the activity of making a signal stronger

amplify 17, 28
to make a signal, e.g. sound, stronger
amplitude modulation 28
a change in the level of a signal
anaesthetist 14
a doctor who is qualified to give an anaesthetic
analog 5
See analogue
analogue 5, 28
a system in which data is represented as a continuously varying voltage, as opposed to digital which can only be distinct whole numbers. See also digital.
analyse 1, 3, 4, 21
to examine carefully
analysis 3, 8
the study of the parts and their relationship to one another
analyst 3
a person who carries out a detailed examination (analysis)
analytical 3
describing an approach that is based on carrying out a detailed examination
animal feed supplement 26
what is added to food for livestock to make it more effective
anneal 10
to make materials tough by cooling them slowly, e.g. glass
anodize 10
to coat a metallic surface with a protective oxide, e.g. car components
answering machine 29
a tape recorder which serves as a telephone answering device
antenna 28, 29
a device used to transmit and/or receive radio waves
anthracite 22
a hard, black shiny coal containing a high percentage of fixed carbon and a low percentage of volatile matter (also called hard coal)
apparatus 10
equipment
applet 5
a program written in the Java™ programming language that can be included in an HTML page. The applet's code is transferred to your system and executed by the browser's Java Virtual Machine (JVM).
appliance 16
a piece of equipment, e.g. a TV, washing machine
application 29
a computer program
application software 5
this gives a computer instructions which provide the user with tools to perform a task, e.g. word processing
applied research 3
branch of research that looks at how scientific theory can be used in practice
approve 13
to agree to, give permission to

aqueduct 20
a structure which carries water (canal or river) across land, usually over a valley

arch 20
a curved structure, e.g. under a bridge
architect 15
a person who designs and supervises the construction of buildings or other structures
Arctic cold 11
very cold conditions used to test cars
aromatic 12
an organic compound with a benzene-like ring
arthritis 14
a disease which causes pain in the joints
artificial 12
not natural
asbestos 22
a fibrous material made from silica. As it is very heat resistant, it was often used in the past in buildings for insulation. It is now banned because it is a health risk.
asphalt 24
a petroeum-based black sticky material used to cover roads
assemble 1
to put pieces together to make a finished product
assembly 15, 16
1. the process of putting building elements together; 2. a collection of (electrical) parts in an appliance
assembly line 1
the layout of workers and machines where the work passes from one worker to the next, usually along a moving belt, until it is finished
assess 4
to measure and evaluate something
asthma 14
a disease which causes problems of breathing
atomic energy plant 19
a power station which produces nuclear energy. See also nuclear plant.
attenuation 28
the loss in power of a signal between transmission and reception
attribute 21
a special feature or requirement
audible 29
that can be heard
audio signal 17
a signal intended to be heard
audit 22
1. to examine officially; 2. an official examination
automobile 11, 12, 24
a car
automotive 18
relating to cars and other vehicles, e.g. automotove industry

avoid contact with 9
not to touch, usually with a part of the body
axis 8
a line, usually horizontal or vertical, used as a reference on a graph

backlog 2
tasks that have not been done on time
back order 2
an order for goods that has not been processed on time
bacteriology 26
the science that deals with bacteria and their relations to agriculture, medicine, and industry
bake 12
to heat, often at high temperatures to make hard
baking 26
the activity of cooking food, e.g. bread and cake, by dry heat especially in an oven
bandwidth 6, 28
the range of frequencies, expressed in Hertz (Hz), that can pass over a given transmission channel. The bandwidth determines the rate at which information can be transmitted through the circuit: the greater the bandwidth, the more information that can be sent in a given amount of time. Analogue bandwidth is measured in Hertz (Hz) or cycles per second; digital bandwidth is the amount or volume of data that can be sent through a channel, measured in bits per second, without distortion.
bar graph 8
a chart that uses either horizontal or vertical bars to show comparisons among categories
bark 27
the outer layer of a log
barrage 20
a barrier across a stream with a series of gates to control the water-surface level upstream
barrel 24
a unit of measure for petroleum, equal to 42 gallons
basic and intermediate chemicals 12
basic chemicals are made from mined materials like crude oil, natural gas and minerals, or from crops and other natural substances. Chemical companies use basic chemicals to produce intermediate products like polyethylene, polyethylene oxide (PO), ethylene oxide (EO) and ethylene glycol, or final products like phosphate and nitrogen agricultural fertilizers. These basic and intermediate chemicals are called commodity chemicals and are produced mainly by large companies and as byproducts of petroleum refining, using common manufacturing processes.
basic research 3
a systemic, intensive study, which aims to gain a fuller knowledge or understanding of the subject under study rather than a practical application

batch 1
a quantity of items which are made at the same time

baud 6
the speed at which information is transferred, generally referred to as bps (bits per second)

bauxite 22
the mineral from which aluminium is extracted

beam 15, 29
horizontal structural member that sits on posts or walls and supports the structure above it. Sometimes called a "girder".

beauty aid 12
any product that improves the appearance of skin, hair, etc.

bedding 30
sheets and fabrics used on a bed

benzene 12, 24
a colourless, liquid, flammable, aromatic hydrocarbon that boils at 80.1°C and freezes at 5.4–5.5°C; it is used as a solvent and in making other chemicals, e.g. dyes and drugs

Bible 27
a type of thin printing paper, especially for use in high quality productions; e.g. Bibles and dictionaries

bill of lading 7
a transportation document that is the contract of carriage containing the terms and conditions between the shipper and carrier

binary 28
characters and codes specified as a combination of 0 and 1

biodegradable 25
describing the ability of some plastics to breakdown into safe products by the action of living organisms

biofuel 19
fuel made from biological materials including crops (especially trees) and animal waste

biological product 13
a pharmaceutical product that is derived from a biological source (human plasma or cell culture) rather than being synthesized from a chemical source

birth defect 9
something imperfect that you are born with, e.g. a mark

bits per second (bps) 6
the number of bits that are transferred in one second by a computer

bitumen 23
one of various sticky substances, e.g. crude petroleum, ashphalt or tar, that occur naturally

bituminous 22
containing bitumen, a general name for various solid and semisolid hydrocarbons

bleach 27, 30
1. to treat chemically in order to remove impurities and whiten the fabric; 2. the chemical that removes impurities and whitens a fabric

blend 30
1. to mix different fibres together; 2. a mix of different fibres

blend chest 27
a container in which different pulps are combined according to customer specifications

blow extrusion 25
a process where hot molten plastic is blown up like a balloon, with compressed air. This stretches the plastic and makes it thin. The end of the balloon is pinched together by rollers, to hold the air in and make it flat. The flat tube is then wound on to a big roll.

blow moulding 25
a process in which a little bit of hot soft plastic is squeezed into the end of a mould. Compressed air is used to blow a big bubble inside the plastic. The plastic swells out like a balloon until it fills up the whole mould.

blowout 23
an uncontrolled activity in an oil or gas well

body panel 11
a sheet of metal that forms the outside body of a car

boiler 10
equipment to make water hot

boiling point 13
the temperature at which a liquid boils; for water it is normally regarded as 100°C

bond 27
a type of paper made from either cotton, chemical wood pulp, or a combination of the two. This grade of paper is used for stationery and business forms and is made with superior strength for its weight.

book 27
a type of woodfree or mechanical paper used for printing books

borax 22
a mild alkali used in fine grain developing solutions to speed up the action of the solution [$Na_2B_4O_5(OH)_4.8H_2O$]

borehole 21
a hole drilled in the earth to explore what is below the earth

bottleneck 2
a step in production where a number of stages come together and cause a slow down in production

bowl 25
a deep round container, often made of plastic, which can hold liquid

bracing connection 15
1. a diagonal tie that interconnects scaffold members; 2. a temporary support for aligning vertical concrete formwork

braiding 30
a way of making a textile without a loom. Yarns going in the same direction are crossed over and under other yarns in their paths.

brake line 11
the system of hoses and metal tubes through which the brake fluid flows

brake pedal 11
a foot operated device which operates the brakes to stop or slow the wheels

brake system 11
the equipment in a car which makes it slow and then stop

branch circuit 16
a circuit where the current has a choice of paths

break down 1, 2
to stop working, especially for a machine

breakdown 1, 2
a situation where a machine has stopped working

breaker (circuit breaker) 16
a device that can be used to open or close a circuit manually and can also open a circuit automatically when current is too high

"On"
"Tripped"
"Off"

breakthrough 3
a discovery

breeding 26
the business of keeping animals with the purpose of obtaining young ones for sale

bridge 20
a structure, usually built of wood, iron or stone, which carries a road over a valley or river

brightness 27
a measure of the whiteness of pulp and paper

bristol 27
a grade of paper used for folders, index cards, covers and postcards.

broadcast 29
to transmit a radio or TV programme over the airwaves for public reception

brocade 30
a heavy rich-looking fabric with contrasting surfaces or a multicolour design; it is used in upholstery and evening wear

brochure 27
a small book, often with glossy pages, to advertise a company

bronchitis 14
an illness of the bronchial tubes

browser 5
a program that accesses the World Wide Web and allows the user to use the multimedia resources of the World Wide Web internet

brush 30
to use wire brushes or other abrasive materials to raise a nap on surface of the fabric

building contractor 21
a building firm that agrees to perform work

bulldozer 20
a large powerful vehicle which uses a large blade to move earth and rocks

burial 22
describing a level underground

burn 9
a hurt or injury caused by fire

bus 11
large vehicle, either private or public, to carry passengers either within a town/city or between towns/cities

cable 16, 20, 29
a strong wire used in an electrical system

cable television (cable TV) 28, 29
a system of sending and receiving TV signals by wire (cable). Cable systems normally receive signals by satellite at a central location and then send them by cable to homes for a monthly fee.

cage 22
a lift in a mine shaft to carry workers and materials up and down the shaft

caisson 15
the structural support for a foundation wall

call 29
1. to get or try to get in communication with someone by phone; 2. the act of calling someone on the telephone

camber 20
the rise in the centre of a road which helps the water to flow off

can 26
1. to put food into tins; 2. a tin

canal 20
a narrow manmade waterway for boats and ships

cancer 9, 14
a diseased growth in the body

capacitor 17
a device which can store eletrical energy at the required value

capacity 2
the total number of items that a piece of equipment, workshop, factory can produce within a given time

car bumper 25
the plastic bar attached to the front and back of a car to protect it when it is in an accident

carbonate 12
a compound which contains carbon and oxygen, e.g. calcium carbonate (limestone)

card 30
to open up the wool into an even layer by removing as much vegetable matter as possible and drawing the fibres parallel to each other in order to form a single continuous strand of fibres

carer 14
a person who looks after a sick person

cargo 7
goods loaded into a ship for transportation

carpenter 15
a craft worker skilled in woodwork

carpet 30
any fabric used as a floorcovering

carriage 7
transportation; the act of moving goods from one place to another

carrier 7
a firm which transports goods or people

carrier wave 28
a wave that transports the signal wave. The carrier is modulated or altered by the signal wave.

carry out 3
to do, especially an experiment, a study or research

carton 7, 27
a box made from thick, stiff paper, used to protect goods in transit

casing 23
a steel pipe in a well to strengthen it and stop it from caving in

cast 11
to shape hot metal by pouring it into a mould

catalyst 24
a substance which causes a chemical activity without changing itself

catalytic cracking 24
a refining process by which petrol (gasoline) is made from crude petroleum

catering 26
the activity of providing food

cause/effect analysis 8
a diagram which shows the main causes leading to an effect (symptom). The cause and effect diagram is one of the "seven tools of quality".

cell 29
the type of wireless communication in mobile telephony. It is called 'cellular' because the system uses many base stations to divide a service area into multiple 'cells'. Cellular calls are transferred from base station to base station as a user travels from cell to cell.

cellular 29
See cell

cellular radiotelephone system 17
a high-capacity system of one or more multichannel base stations designed to provide radio telecommunications services to users over a wide area

central locking 11
the locking or unlocking of all the doors by locking from one location, either by turning a key in a door lock or using an electronic device.

central processing unit (CPU) 5
either the main microchip that the computer is built around or the box that houses the main components of the computer.

certificate 13
an official document which shows that something can be done

chain 25
a number of atoms that are linked together

channel 7, 29
the way that goods will be transported, e.g. by road, rail, sea, air

channel encoder 28
a device which maps the binary strings into wave for transmission

check 8
1. to test, examine something in order to see if it is correct; 2. a test, examination to see if something is correct

chemical 10, 12, 18
a substance with a definite molecular composition; concerning the science which deals with the elements that make up the earth, the universe and living things. See also chemistry.

chemical process plant 20
a factory in which chemicals are made and used

chemical purity 13
the extent to which a chemical is clean and free from unclean substances

chemistry 10
the science which deals with the elements that make up the earth, the universe and living things

chip 27
a small piece of wood used to produce pulp

chloride 12
a compound containing chlorine and another element

chlorine bleach 30
a chemical used for cleaning, sterilizing and whitening

chop 27
to cut into small pieces

chronic 14
to describe a medical condition that lasts for a long time

chronic depression 13
a state of deep sadness that lasts for a long time and is a sign of a mental health problem

chute 22
a channel or shaft underground

circuit 16
a set of electrical parts in an appliance, e.g. a TV or radio

(circuit) board 18
a panel or assembly along which the electric current can pass

civil 10
for private people, i.e. not for military purposes

cleansing agent 24
an agent used to clean impurities

climate control 11
a lever or button which you can move to change the temperature in the passenger compartment of a vehicle

clinical 13
connected to a hospital

clinical research 3
branch of research that looks at the effects of drugs or treatment on patients

clothes 30
covering for the human body

clothing 30
covering for the human body; clothes

coal 12, 19, 22
a combustible mineral formed from organic matter (mostly plants) that lived about 300 million years ago

coastline 24
the land next to the sea

coaxial cable 28
one of four basic types of wire found in
telecommunications, this is a conducting
wire in a dielectric insulator and an outer
conducting shell; this type of cable is
commonly used because of its
insensitivity to noise interference. The
other types are single-wire line, open-wire
pairs, and multipair cables.

coil spring 11
a section of spring steel used in both front
and rear suspension systems

collar 23
a thick tube of steel through which
drilling fluids are pumped

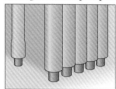

collect 5
to gather together, to bring together

collector 24
equipment which collects different
components as petroleum is broken down

column 15
a supporting pillar consisting of a base, a
cylindrical shaft, and a capital

combustion 9
the act of catching fire and burning

commission 19, 21
1. to place an order for (a power plant);
2. an order (for a power plant)

commitment 8
a promise, an agreement to do something
in a certain way, usually to improve the
way of working

commodity 26
a product of agriculture

communal environment 20
a place where a group or community, e.g.
old people or students, can live comfortably

communicate 6
to send information between two places
or within an area

communications 16
the area that deals with sending
information between 2 places or within
an area

compatible 6
describing the ability of data processing
equipment to accept and process data
prepared by another machine without
conversion or code modification

compile 4
to put together data gathered from several
sources:

comply with 8
to act according to the rules or
regulations

component 1, 2, 11
1. piece of machinery; 2. part that goes
into the final product

compound 25
a substance, e.g. plastic, which is made up
of two or more materials

compressed air 25
air that has been pressed into a volume
smaller than it normally occupies

computer 16, 18
an electronic device that can store and
recall information, and make calculations
very quickly

computer network 5
a group of computers connected
by cables or other means
which exchange
information and share
equipment, such
as printers and
disk drives

computer-aided design 17
the use of computers to assist the design
process

concentrate 13
to remove water

condense 24
to cause a gas to become liquid by making
it cooler

configure 6
1. to arrange in a certain shape; 2. to
prepare all the devices in a computer
system so that they operate

congenital 14
to describe a disease which has existed
since birth

connect 6
1. to join or fasten together; 2. to link
a piece of equipment to an energy
source, e.g. electricity, or to another
piece of equipment; 3. to establish a
communication path for the transfer of
information

conservation 26
protection and management of natural
resources to prevent exploitation,
destruction, or neglect

consignment 7
a collection of goods to be transported
from one place to another

constant 4
something that does not change

construct 10, 11
to build

consumer goods 18
products, e.g. TVs, hi-fis and washing
machines, for personal, domestic or
home use

consumption 26
the act of eating and drinking

contamination 9, 26
the result of mixing something with dirty
or poisonous matter

continuous process improvement 8
the many management practices and
techniques used to find and eliminate
waste and to improve business processes,
quality or costs

control 8, 17
1. to make sure that something is correct;
2. a test that makes sure that something
is correct

control system 16
a system that regulates an operation

controlling 1
stage in a process when you check
what you have done (see also
planning)

convert 1, 28
to change, e.g. from input to output

conveyor 22
a mechanical device like a belt, generally
electrically driven, which transports
material between two points

cool 25
to make cold; cold

coolant reservoir 11
liquid in the cooling system

copper 22
a reddish metallic element that heats
quickly and cools rapidly; its symbol is Cu

copper wire 28
a popular medium, made of copper, for
low-cost networking but limited to a few
hundred metres

cordless 29
without a wire

corduroy 30
a strong, durable, woven fabric with
vertical cut pile stripes or cords with a
velvet-like nap

correlation 4
a measure of the link between two
variables.

costing system 21
a procedure to monitor the costs of a
project so that management can get
information on development

cotton 27, 30
a tall plant with white hair from which
cloth is made

CPU 5
See central processing unit

crack 24
to separate oil into simple compounds

crack resistant 12
describes a finish (paint) that does not
easily split

crane 10
a machine for lifting and moving heavy
objects

crash 11
this happens when one vehicle hits
another vehicle or a stationary object

crease control 30
a fabric finish often used with linen and
cotton to help the fabric resist wrinkles
and creases

create 5
to make something new, e.g. a file

crops (often pl) 26
plants that can be grown and harvested
for profit or subsistence

crossover 20
a place where one road goes over
another

crown 20
the highest point of a road

crude drug 13
any raw or unrefined medicinal
compound in its natural form, especially
one taken from a plant

crude oil 23
untreated oil

crust 22
the outermost layer or shell of the earth

cultivate 13
to cause a plant or other vegetable matter to grow

cultivation 26
the activity of using land to raise crops

culvert 20
a pipe or small bridge for drainage under a road or structure

curb 20
See kerb

cure 13, 25
1. to make a person better; 2. to harden by heat; 3. medicine that makes a person better

currency converter 29
a web service that calculates the value of your money in another currency

curtain wall 15
an exterior wall that provides no structural support

curtains 30, 25
material that hangs in front of a window as a decoration, shade, or screen

customer needs 8
what the customer needs from a product or service

cut 11
to form or shape with a sharp tool

cuttings 23
small pieces of rock that break away due to the action of the bit

cycle 2
the series of activities following one another to produce a product

dairy farming 26
farming that is concerned with the production of milk, butter, and cheese

dam 20
a manmade structure across a river to hold back the water to produce power, improve navigation or control flooding

dangerous 9
likely to cause loss, damage or injury

data 29
information

database 6
a structured set of data

database software 5
a program that allows the user to create a structured set of data (a database) and then to access it and manipulate it

data-conversion device 29
a piece of equipment which translates data from one format to another so that the receiving device can interpret it

deep 15
going far down, usually into the ground

defect 30
something that makes a product imperfect

defect prevention 8
the action to stop a fault from happening, usually before it happens

defective 8
not working (properly)

defence 18
the industry which protects a country against attack

define 8
to state something in detail, e.g. the dimensions of a product

degradation 28
the deterioration in quality, level, or standard of performance

dehydration 26
the removal of all liquid from food

delighted 8
very happy, very satisfied

deliver 7
to carry goods to their destination

delivery 2, 7
a group of goods which are ready to be sent to the customer

delivery note 7
a document which accompanies goods in transit and provides basic information about the goods, the sender and the receiver

demand 2
the number of items that are needed

demodulation 17
the process of extracting the message from a modulated signal for reception by phone, TV or radio

density 13
the amount of darkness or light in an area of a scan

dentist 14
a tooth specialist

deposit 22, 23
a natural occurrence of a useful mineral in sufficient quantities for exploitation

depot 7
the place where goods are (temporarily) stored, either before they are sent out or after they have been received

derrick 23
a pyramid of steel erected over a bore hole to drill for oil

desert heat 11
extremely hot conditions to test a car

design 10, 11, 18, 21
to plan, either in one's mind or with drawings

desktop (desk top) 5
1. the screen background in most graphical user interfaces (GUIs) on which windows, icons, and dialogue boxes appear; 2. a type of computer that sits on a desk and is not easily portable. See also lap top.

detailed design 21
the development stage in which the geology of the area is studied in order to prepare a detailed plan

detect 8
to find out what is causing a particular situation, especially a problem

detection 13
the process of finding out the cause of a problem

determine 4
to find out

develop 3, 4, 10, 18
to change the form of something

developer 3
a person who or organization which produces new ideas or products

development 3, 11
the systematic use of the knowledge or understanding gained from research to produce useful materials, devices, systems, or methods

development and evaluation research 3
the systemic use of scientific knowledge to produce useful materials, devices, systems or methods

developmental 3
describing the systemic use of scientific knowledge to the production of useful materials, devices, systems or methods

deviation 4
the difference between an observed value and the expected value of a variable

device 29, 16, 18
any piece of equipment made for a specific purpose

device size 17
refers to the ability to reduce the size of electronic devices, such as computers, walkmans, etc., mainly as a result of the miniaturization of components

diabetes 14
a disease where there is too much sugar in the blood

diagnose 18
to find the cause of a problem

diagnosis 13
the activity of finding the cause of an illness

dial 29
to make a telephone call or connection

differential 11
a unit that takes the power of the rotating driveshaft and passes it to the axle

dig 23
to make a hole

digester 27
that part of a chemical pulp mill where cooking takes place

digital 5, 28
a system in which data is represented as 0 or 1

digital communications 5
a system of sending information in which data is represented electronically as 0 or 1

digitalization 17
the conversion of analogue data into a digital form (0 or 1)

dike 20
a manmade structure built along the banks of a river or along the coast to hold back water and prevent flooding

dimension 21
a measurement, e.g. length, width, height

diode 17
a component with two terminals (anode and cathode) that passes current primarily in one direction

directional 29
a transmitter with more than one tower to send the station's signal in a particular direction

disc brake, disk brake 11
type of brake that has two basic components: a flat disc that turns with the wheel and a caliper that is stationary

discover 4
to find

disease 13
illness, usually serious

dish 28, 29
a device used for collecting satellite TV signals

disinfection 26
the process of cleaning by destroying harmful organisms

disintegrate 25
to fall apart, especially into small pieces

disorder 14
a disease

dispatch 7
to send out

dispersion 14
the process of spreading a pharmaceutical in a gas, liquid or solid (tablet) form

display 5, 29, 25
1 to show 2 something that is shown, e.g. a graphic 3 a device for showing something i.e. a monitor

disposable 25
describing something that can be thrown away

dispose of 9
to throw away (often because it is dangerous)

distil 13, 24
to make a liquid into gas by heating and then to convert the gas into different liquids again

distillation 24
the process of making a liquid into gas by heating and then converting (separating) the gas into different liquids

distort 28
to fail to reproduce accurately the characteristics of the input

distribute 1
to send goods from the producer to another person or organization

distribution 4, 7
a set of numbers and their frequency of occurrence collected from measurements

distribution centre 7
a large, centralized warehouse that receives finished goods from a factory

distribution network 19
the system of pipes and tubes that carries energy from the production plant to the user

distributor 11
a unit in the ignition system designed to make and break the ignition and to distribute the resultant high voltage to the proper cylinder at the correct time

dizziness 9
unpleasant feeling in one's head that things are going round and round

docks (also dock) 20
a place where ships are loaded and unloaded

documentation 7, 18
all the papers which describe the goods

dosage 14
the amount of a medicine to be taken at one time

dot matrix printer 5
a printer which uses a pattern of dots to form characters or other graphic information.

double-blind technique 13
a type of clinical study in which neither the participants nor the person administering treatment know which treatment any particular subject is receiving. Usually the comparison is between an experimental drug and a placebo or standard comparison treatment. See also placebo.

downhole 23
a well

download 6
to transfer data or code from one computer to another. The distinction between download and upload is not always clear, but download often refers to transfer from a larger server system to a smaller client system.

downstream 23
downstream refers to all activities from the processing of refined crude oil into petroleum products to the distribution, marketing, and shipping of the products. See also upstream.

downtime 2, 6
the time when equipment is not working because of a breakdown or maintenance

draft 21
preliminary

dragline 22
a type of excavating equipment consisting of a bucket on a long rope

drainage 20, 26
the network of pipes through which rainwater runs off

drains 9
the system of pipes and tubes that carry away waste water

draw 24
to take out

drawing board 11
a flat piece of wood on which a piece of paper is put to design a plan

drawings 21, 29
a plan or sketch

dredger 20
a machine or ship used to take away sand and mud from the bottom of a river or a harbour

drift 22
an entry, generally on the slope of a hill, which usually goes in a horizontal direction into a coal seam

drill 22, 23
1. to make a hole through a material with a cutting tool; 2. the cutting tool that makes a hole

drill bit 23
a tool used to crush or cut rock

drill pipe 23
a tube made of steel which connects the rig surface equipment with the bottomhole assembly

drill string 23
the combination of the drill pipe, the bottomhole assembly and any other tools used to make the drill bit turn at the bottom of the wellbore

drill supervisor 22
the person who is in charge of a group of workers who drill (see above)

drilling mud 23
fluids used in drilling

drowsiness 9
a feeling of tiredness

drug 14, 24
a medicine

drum brake 11
a type of brake using a drum-shaped metal cylinder which is attached to the wheel and rotates with it

dry 9, 27
1. to take out the fluid; 2. not wet

dry-cleaning 30
a chemical cleaning process

drying 26
the removal of all liquid

dump truck 22
a vehicle that carries and then dumps rock or ore

durability 27
the ability of a product, e.g. paper, to last a long time

dust 9
a powder made of small particles of waste

dust tunnel 11
a test environment in which a car is exposed to small particles of waste powder

dustproof 16
describing the ability to exclude dust

dye 12, 24, 27, 30
1. to treat chemically in order to change a fabric's colour; 2. a chemical which changes a fabric's colour

earth 22
the soil which must be removed to reach the valuable minerals

earthmover 20
a machine, e.g. a bulldozer to excavate, push or transport large quantities of earth in road building

easy flow 12
describes a liquid that runs easily

effectiveness 1
the ability to do things in the right way

efficiency 1
the ability to do the right things

electric cable 25
the wire used for conducting electricity together with the outer plastic cover

electric window 11
a side window which goes up and down with an electric motor operated by a switch

electrical 10
dealing with electricity

electrical appliance 19
a piece of equipment, e.g. a TV, washing machine, which is powered by electricity

electrical energy 19
electricity

electrical power supply 24
the use of oil to generate electricity which can be used to supply electrical power to users

electrical system 11
the system that generates, stores, and distributes electrical current to the engine to start it and keep it running; the electrical system also gives power to the lights, the heater motor, radio, and other accessories

electrician 15
a craft worker who installs, maintains, and repairs electrical systems in buildings

electromagnetic 28
magnetism developed by a current of electricity

electromagnetic wave 28
a wave generated by an electromagnetic field. Examples includes radio waves, infrared, visible light, ultraviolet, X rays, and gamma rays.

electron 17
one of the elementary particles of an atom

electronic 10, 28
concerning the science (and its application) that deals with the behaviour of electrons in equipment such as TVs and radios

electronic circuit 16
a set of electronic parts in an appliance, e.g. a TV or radio

electronic message 6
a message which is sent and received as data, often through a network

electronic processing 17
the activity of performing calculations with a device, such as a calculator or a computer

electronic system 17
a device which is based on the principles and behaviour of electrons, e.g. a computer

electronics lab 18
the place (laboratory) where a scientist works to examine and test electronic equipment

electroplate 10
to cover with a thin layer of metal using electrolysis, e.g. car components

email software 5
a program that allows you to send and receive electronic messages

embroider 30
to decorate a fabric with needlework stitching, either by hand or machine

emission 17, 25
the production of radiation by a radio transmitting station

emit 17
to send out (electrons)

energy 17, 18, 20
the capacity of a physical system to do work; usable power, such as heat or electricity

engine 11, 10
a device for changing fuel energy to mechanical energy

engineer 3, 10
a person who uses scientific knowledge to solve practical problems.

entertain 17
to amuse, interest or inform, e.g. by means of radio, TV, music, etc.

entertainment 17
programmes on TV, films at the cinema, etc., that give pleasure, amusement or information

envelope 7
a paper covering for a letter

environmental 18
relating to the natural conditions, e.g. air, water and land, in which mankind lives

environmental control 15
a system for remote control of electronic devices. Using it, a person can independently turn lights, radio, and television on and off, answer or make phone calls, and unlock a door.

environmental engineer 22
a techical person who checks that the mining activities do not damage the natural conditions, e.g. air, water and land

epilepsy 14
a diease causing uncontrolled movements

equipment 1
machines used in production

erection 15
a building or structure, or the activity to construct one

error 8
a mistake

estimate 21
1. to make an approximate calculation;
2. an approximate calculation

ethylene 12
the simplest olefin; it is a sweet smelling gas that is used to make plastics

evacuate 23
to take all the people away from a place because of risk to their safety

evaluate 1, 4, 13, 18
to calculate the value of something

excavate 22
to remove soil and/or rock materials from one location and transport them to another

excavator 20
a tool to dig out and take away earth or minerals

exceed 8
to be greater than

executive 11
a range of large, comfortable cars designed for executives

exemption 13
the state of being free from something, often an obligation to pay for something

exhaust manifold 11
the connecting pipes between the exhaust ports and the exhaust pipe

exhaust system 11
the system of pipes and equipment that carry the exhaust gases from the exhaust manifold out into the atmosphere

expansion card 5
you plug this into a slot to add features such as video, sound, modem and networking

expectation 8
how the customer sees an organization's products and services and the extent that these will meet their needs and requirements

experiment 3, 4
a study

experimental 3
describing a situation in which investigators are testing something

experimental development 3
the process of working out something new in a laboratory

experimentation 3
the process of tests and trials to see what happens under different conditions

experimenter 3
a research worker who conducts experiments

explode 24
to undergo a rapid chemical reaction which produces a loud noise

exploit 22
to turn a natural resource into an economic, i.e. saleable, resource. For example, to exploit a mineral deposit

exploratory 23
done to find out if there is oil or gas

explore 4, 22
to investigate, to look for; to search for coal, mineral, or ore

explosion 9
a loud noise made by a bomb or something similar

explosionproof 16
describing the ability to withstand an internal explosion without creating an external explosion or fire

explosive 22, 12, 24
any chemical compound, mixture, or device that is capable of undergoing a rapid chemical reaction, producing an explosion

export 7
a shipment of goods to a foreign country

exterior skin 15
includes all the surfaces of the roof, chimney, exterior walls, woodwork, windows, porches, doors, and the above-ground portion of the foundation

exterior wall 15
an outer wall other than a party wall

extract 13, 17, 22, 23
1. to take out, usually something useful; to remove coal or ore from a mine; 2. the useful thing that is taken out

extraction 17
the processs of taking out information from a signal

extrusion 25
a process in which hot molten plastic is squeezed through a nozzle to make long lengths of special shapes like pipes

fabric 30
a cloth produced especially by knitting or weaving

fabrication 25
a process in which sheets of plastic are cut to shape and then folded by heating a narrow line through the plastic. When it is soft, the sheet will bend along the heated line. Sheets can be joined together by gluing, or by welding. The join is heated with hot air and a thin filler rod is forced into the gap.

facilitate 8
to make easier

facsimile 29
a system of telecommunication for the transmission of fixed images which can be received in a permanent form, usually on paper

factory 1, 7
a place where goods are made

factory inspection 13
a detailed check of a factory, especially to ensure that production meets legal requirements

failure 1, 8
breaking down; stopping working

fast drying 12
describes a finish (paint or other liquid) that dries quickly

fault 1
when a machine does not work properly

fax 29
See facsimile

FDA 13
See Food and Drug Administration

feasibility 3
the possibility that a project or development will completed successfully and within a reasonable time.

feasibility study 21
an investigation to assess both financial and engineering aspects of a project

feasible 3
capable of being done successfully and within a reasonable time

feature 11
an additional characteristic in a car, usually at an extra cost, which makes the car more exclusive, e.g. alloy wheels, climate control

feed 26
1. to give food; 2. food given to animals

feed supplement 26
See animal feed supplement

feedback 4
the information that tells you how well you have performed

feeder 16
a set of conductors that starts at a main distribution centre and supplies power to one or more secondary or branch distribution centres

feldspar 22
a group of rock-forming minerals that make up 60% of the earth's crust

fell 27
to cut down a tree

felting 30
a method for creating fabric by using heat, moisture, and pressure

ferment 13
to change chemically as the result of the addition of an organic compound, e.g. yeast

fermentation 26
a chemical change such as when a carbohydrate is transformed to carbon dioxide and alcohol

fertilizer 26, 12, 24
a substance which makes soil more fertile

fibre 12, 30
a long thin thread of maerial used to make textiles

fibre optic cable 28
a high-bandwidth transmission wire that uses light to carry digital information. See also optic cable.

fibre optics 16
glass fibres that are used for data transmission

fibre processing 30
the treatment of fibres into finished products – cloth, fabric or textile

fibreglass 11
a mixture of glass fibres and resin that produces a very light and strong material; it is used to build car bodies and to repair damaged areas

fidelity 17
the extent to which a signal (sound or picture) is close to the original, as in hi-fi (high fidelity)

file 5, 29
a program, document, utility, in fact anything that isn't hardware on a computer

file a patent 3
to apply for an exclusive right by law to make use of and exploit an invention for a limited period of time

findings 3
a written statement of facts and conclusions based on the evidence presented

finished design 21
the final design stage in which the drawings for the construction are prepared

finished product 1
a product sold as completed: finished products are products ready for sale

fire 19
a device in a house that produces heat

firmware 18
software that is stored in a hardware device and that controls the device

fixture 16
a piece of equipment that cannot (easily) be moved, e.g. a junction box

fixtures 1
machines or equipment which are attached to the land or factory building, and are therefore classified as real property

flame resistant 12
describes a substance that can prevent burning

flame-retardant 12
describes a substance that can reduce, or delay burning

flammable 9, 23
describing a material that burns easily

flavour 12
the characteristics of a food that cause a simultaneous reaction of taste on the tongue and odour in the nose

flexible 25
that can be easily bent

floor 15
a level of a building, e.g. the first floor in a block of flats

flour milling 26
the process of grinding wheat into flour

flow 1, 2, 7
to move smoothly and without stopping

flow rate 23
the rate at which oil flows out of a well

fluid mechanics 20
a branch of mechanics that deals with the properties of liquids and gases

flume 20
a sloping passage or pipe to carry water, e.g. to a power plant

fluoride 12
a compound which occurs naturally in both groundwater and surface water; it is added to toothpaste to provide protection against tooth decay

Food and Drug Administration 13
the U.S. Agency responsible for overseeing food and pharmaceutical products. See also Medicines Control Authority.

food hygiene 26
the practice of keeping food clean in order to avoid illness

food packing 26
the process of putting food into packaging for sale

food poisoning 26
illness caused by bacteria or unwanted chemicals in food

food preservation 26
the activity of keeping food safe for eating

footbridge 20
a bridge for pedestrians

footwear 26
shoes

forecast 2
1. to say in advance how many items will need to be produced; 2. the number of items which will need to be produced

foreign matter 30
something that should not be there

forge 10, 11
to shape metals by heating and then hammering, e.g. horse shoes

forklift truck 7
a machine which picks up and moves
goods

formation 23
the rock around the borehole
forward 7
to send on
fossil fuel 19
conbustible material which comes from
ancient living things
found 10
to melt metal and then pour it into a
form, e.g. iron components
foundation 15
the supporting part of a structure below
the first floor construction
fraction 24
either a pure chemical compound or
a mixture which is distilled from
petroleum
fractional distillation 24
the process to distill either a pure chemical
compound or a mixture from petroleum
freeze 26
to make something, e.g. food, very cold
freight 7
either the cargo carried or the charges for
the carriage of the cargo
frequency 4
the number of times an event happens
frequency modulation 28
where voltage levels change the frequency
of a carrier wave
friction 9
the rubbing together of surfaces, often
causing pain or injury
friction pile 15
a pile calculated to carry all of its load by
skin friction
fuel 19, 24
material, e.g. coal, wood, petrol, that is
burned to produce energy
fuel line 11
the pipes through which the fuel passes
from the fuel tank to the fuel pump and to
the carburettor
fuel system 11
a system that stores, cleans, and delivers
the fuel to the engine
fuel tank 11
the storage compartment that holds the
fuel for the vehicle
full-motion 29
used to describe video that plays on the
computer at between 24 and 30 frames
per second
fumes 9
strong-smelling air given off by smoke,
gas, paint, etc., that can cause pain or
injury if breathed in
fumigation 9
the act of clearing an infected building or
room by chemical smoke or gas
fungicide 12, 26
a chemical that kills or destroys fungi

fuse 16
a piece of wire used in an electric system
which breaks if too much electrical power
passes through

galvanize 10
to protect from rusting by coating in zinc,
e.g. food cans
gas 9, 19
a substance, like air, which is neither solid
nor liquid
gas engine 10
an engine in which the motion of the
piston is produced by the combustion or
sudden production or expansion of gas
gas field 23
a place where gas can be extracted
gas fired central heating 19
a home heating system powered by gas
gas power 19
the power produced by gas in gasworks
gas station 19
See gasworks
gasoline (AmE) 24
See petrol
gasworks 19
a place where gas for use in the home is
made from coal
gateway 6
a gateway transfers information between
physically separate networks that are
based on differing protocols. It performs
high-level information translation (while
routers provide low-level).
gauze 30
a loosely woven, thin, sheer, plain weave
fabric usually cotton
General Packet Radio Service (GPRS) 29
a system of transferring data over the
GSM network, allowing wireless
communications at speeds up to 150
kilobits per second. GPRS permits faster
internet access and improved mobile
technology through continuous
connectivity.
generate 17
to produce (a signal)
generating station 19
a place where energy, usually electrical,
is produced
generation 17, 19
the process of converting mechanical
energy into electrical energy
generative 17
having the ability to produce or reproduce
generator 17, 19, 16
a machine that converts mechanical
energy into electrical energy
genetic damage 9
harm passed on to a child from its
parents' genes
geochemist 22
a person who studies the chemistry of
earth materials
geologist 22
a person who is trained in and works in
any of the geological sciences

geology 21
a science that deals with the composition
of the earth's soil, rocks, etc.
geophysicist 22
a person who studies seismic,
gravitational, electrical, thermal,
radiometric, and/or magnetic
phenomena to investigate geological
phenomena
geothermal energy 19
energy produced by the internal heat of
the earth.
germanium 17
a hard element similar to silicon, used as
a semi-conductor in transistors
girder 15
a large beam

gloss 27
a highly reflective, shiny surface
glossy 12
shiny; describes a surface from which
much more light is specularly reflected
than is diffusely reflected
goggles 9
large glasses which some workers wear to
protect their eyes
gold 22
a soft, yellow, valuable metal. It is used for
coins, jewelry, decoration, dental work,
plating, and for coating certain space
satellites. It is a standard for monetary
systems in many countries.
grade 27
paper is classified into different grades
according to the end use, the pulp used
and the treatment of the paper
graphic software 5
a program that allows the user to see text
and images on a computer screen
granite 22
a rock in which quartz constitutes 10% to
50%
greenhouse effect 19
the warming of the earth caused by the
presence of certain gases in the
atmosphere
grind 10
1. to polish or sharpen by rubbing on a
rough surface, e.g. stone; 2. to crush into
particles
ground 16, 27
(the use of) the earth as a common return
for an electric circuit
ground fault 16
circuit failure where current
unintentionally flows to ground
groundwood 27
a heavier, more absorbent paper that
folds easily without cracking
grow 26
to make plants and crops increase in size
growth 26
the act or rate of increasing in size
growth regulator 26
plant substance that controls how plants
or crops grow

hack 6
to gain illegal access to a computer or network

haemorrhage 14
an uncontrollable flow of blood

handle 9
to touch with one's hands

harbour (AmE harbor) 20
a protected place where boats can stop

hard 12
describes a material that is compact, solid, and difficult to deform

hard hat 9
hard hat which some workers wear to protect their head (from falling objects)

harden 10, 25
to make a material strong, e.g. steel

hardware 5
computer machinery, such as the CPU, disk drives, monitor, and printer. Contrast with software.

harmful 9, 13
causing damage or injury to a person

harvest 13
to gather in the crops when they are fully grown; the crops which are ready to be gathered in

haul 7
to carry, especially heavy goods

hazard 9
danger

hazardous 25
dangerous

headframe 22
the steel or timber frame at the top of a mine shaft

healthy 13
not having any illness

heart attack 14
a medical condition caused by irregular beating of the heart

heat 24, 25
1. to make hot; 2. a high temperature

heat exchanger 19
equipment or process to control the flow of heat at a desired rate

heat resistant 12
relating to the ability of a material to prevent heat from flowing through it

heating 15, 19
the system needed to keep a building at a required temperature, especially during the winter

herbicide 12, 26
a substance that destroys unwanted plants, e.g. weeds

hereditary 14
to describe a disease which is passed on from parent to child

high bandwidth 28
the bandwidth determines the rate at which information can be transmitted through the circuit: high bandwidth allows more information to be sent in a given amount of time

high speed 17
very fast

high voltage 19
See voltage

highway 10
a wide main road

home computer 18
a computer (an electronic device that can store and recall information, and make calculations very quickly) that is normally used at home rather than in a company

hospital 13
a place where ill people are treated

hub 6
a device which handles data arriving from one or more directions and forwards it in one or more other directions

hydraulic 10
concerning the pressure of water or other liquid

hydraulic power 19
the energy produced by the movement of water

hydraulics 20, 21
a branch of science that deals with practical applications of water in motion

hydrocarbon 23
a naturally occurring organic compound made up of hydrogen and carbon

hydroelectric energy 19
the eletrical energy produced by the power of falling water

hydroelectric scheme 19
a system for producing eletrical energy by the power of falling water

hydrogeologist 22
a person who studies and works with groundwater

hygiene 26
practices which keep a place, e.g. a kitchen, clean

hygienic 25
good for health, not causing disease

identify 4
to find out the identity of something

idle 2
not working, especially for a piece of equipment

illness 13
mental or physical problem

image 17, 29
a two-dimensional representation of a scene, a picture

imaging equipment 18
a piece of equipment, e.g. a scanner, that can produce a visual representation of an object, such as a body part, for the purpose of medical diagnosis or data collection

immobilizer 11
a device that makes a car immobile (unable to move)

impair fertility 9
to damage the ability to have normal children

impairment 14
reduced ability

import 7
to receive goods from a foreign country

improve 4, 3
1. to make better; 2. to become better

improvement 8
the situation where something is better

impurity 24
a substance which is mixed with the oil so that it is not pure

in transit 7
in passage

incineration 25
the process of burning a material to dispose of it

increased reliability 17
describing the ability to work for a long(er) time without breaking down

inductor 17
a passive electronic component that stores energy in the form of a magnetic field

industrial 10
concerning factories

industrial automation 18
the practice of using equipment in a factory which does not need (much) human control

industrial gas 12
a gas used in an industrial process, e.g. the production of steel, plastics, chemicals, pulp and paper, microchips, auto parts, rubber, textile, glass, etc.

infectious 14
describing a disease that can be spread, especially in the air or water

influenza (flu) 14
a disease in which the patient has a usually mild fever

information extraction 17
technology which takes the meaningful message from the electronic signal

infra-red computer connection 29
a type of connection that allows data to be wirelessly transmitted from one device, e.g. a computer directly to another device, e.g. a computer, when the infrared window on one device is lined up with an infrared sensor on the other device

inject 23
to put in a liquid

injection moulding 25
a process in which molten plastic is squeezed into a mould to make lots of identical objects. They can be very small like a washer or quite large, like a bowl or a clothes basket.

inkjet printer 5
a printer that places extremely small droplets of ink onto paper to create an image

innovate 3, 4
to begin or introduce (something new) for or as if for the first time

innovation 3
a new technique or idea

innovative 3
being or producing something new

innovator 3
someone who helps to open up a new line of research or technology

inorganic elements and compounds 13
substances made with the use of chemicals

input 1
work or materials which go into production

insecticide 12, 26
a substance that kills or destroys insects

inspect 8, 13
to check carefully

inspection 8, 22
the process of checking carefully,
especially to identify faults

install 6
to prepare a piece of equipment or an
electronic device so that it is ready for use

instrument 29
an electrical or mechanical device

insulator 25
a material, e.g. plastic, which does not
allow heat or electricity to pass through

intake manifold 11
the tubes that connect the base of the
carburettor to the intake ports

integrate 17
to put together so that the resulting
product can work more efficiently

integrated circuit 5, 17
a small electronic device that contains
many transistors. For example, the
central processing unit in a computer is
usually built on a single integrated
circuit, called a chip.

integration 17
the process of putting together so that the
resulting product can work more
efficiently

integrative 17
having the tendency to put together so
that the resulting product can work more
efficiently

interactive 6
describing data communications, where a
user enters data and then waits for a
response from the destination before
continuing

interconnect 6
to connect a telecommunications device
or service to the public switched
telephone network

interference 28
undesirable signals caused by two or more
signals combining together; interference
can be constructive or destructive

interference immunity 28
the ability of equipment to receive signals
without the loss of accuracy

interior partition 15
an inside wall that separates two rooms

internet 6
a worldwide collection of interconnected
networks, providing a wide variety of
services

internet service provider (ISP) 6
a company that provides businesses and
consumers with access to the internet.

interview 4
1. to ask a person asks questions in order
to collect information; 2. the meeting at
which a person asks questions in order to
collect information

intranet 6
a network internal to an organization
that uses the same methodology and
techniques as the internet

inventory 1
items held in stock, work in progress and

finished items

inventory control 8
all the activities and procedures used to
control and maintain the right amount
of each item in stock or to provide the
required level of service at minimum
cost

investigate 4, 13
to search or inquire into

iron 22
the fourth most common element, by
weight, making up the crust of the earth.
Its symbol is Fe

irradiation 26
the application of X rays or ultraviolet
light to make food last longer

irreversible effects 9
a result that cannot be changed back to
its original state

irrigation 20
the sytem of supplying land with water by
artificial means

ISP 6
See internet service provider

jack 29
a socket which is used to complete an
electrical connection. A plug is inserted
into a jack to connect switches to
electronic devices.

jelly 24
a material that is between liquid and solid

join 25
1. to bring together, to connect; 2. the
place where two or more materials are
connected

junction (electrical) box 16
a connection point where several cables
are connected

**keep...dry, clean, away from children,
etc.** 9
to cause something to continue to be...
dry, clean, away from children, etc.

kelly 23
a long square steel bar
with a hole drilled through
the middle through which
fluids flow

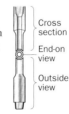
Cross
section

End-on
view

Outside
view

kerb (AmE curb) 20
a line of raised stones between the
pavement and the road

kerosene (AmE) = paraffin (BrE) 24
an oil made from petroleum which can be
burned to give heat and light

keyboard 5
the device, consisting of letters, numbers
and symbols, that a user types on to input
information to a computer

kinetic energy 19
the power of something moving, e.g.
running water

knit 30
to construct a fabric by looping yarns
together either by hand or by machine

knitting mill 30
a factory where knitted fabrics are made

kraft 27
a high-strength paper made almost
entirely of unbleached kraft pulp. Kraft
paper is suitable for the production of
paper sacks and paper bags.

lab technician 3
a technical specialist who works on
scientific experimentation or research.

laboratory (lab) 3, 13
a place where experiments are carried out

lace-making 30
the activity of making lace (a decorative
fabric made by knotting or twisting
threads)

lading 7
the freight shipped; the contents of a
shipment

LAN (local area network) 6
a group of personal computers linked
together in order to share resources, such
as programs, data, and peripherals

laptop (lap top) 5
a type of computer that is easily portable.
See also desk top.

laser 28, 16
a narrow beam of light that can be used
to read barcodes in a supermarket, play
compact discs, etc.

laser printer 5
a printer that uses a laser beam to
produce fast, high-quality output

launder 30
to wash clothes

layer 23
a thickness of rock laid over oil or gas

layout 1
the arrangement of equipment and
tools

LCD screen 29
a liquid crystal display consisting of two
plates of glass with liquid crystal material
between them

lead 22
a bluish-white shiny metal; it is very soft,
highly malleable, ductile, and a poor
conductor of electricity; it is very resistant
to corrosion; its symbol is Pb

lead time 2
the time between two events, e.g. between
an order being placed and its delivery

LED (light-emitting diode) 28
a semiconductor that produces light
when activated

licence 13, 23
(the written document that gives)
permission to do something, usually in
return for payment

lift (bridge) 20
a bridge that can be lifted to allow boats
to pass through

light 16
the electric system that produces artificial
light

light-emitting diode 28
See LED

lighting 15
the electrical system that lights a room or
building

135

lighting system 16
See light

lightweight 25, 28
not heavy, light

lignite 22
the lowest rank of coal, often referred to as brown coal or young coal; it is used almost exclusively for electric power generation

limestone 22
a general term used commercially (in the manufacture of lime) for rocks containing at least 80% of the carbonates of calcium or magnesium

line 1
See assembly line

linen 27, 30
a type of heavy cloth made from a plant called flax

link 6
1. to join together; 2. a physical circuit between two points

livestock 26
animals kept on a farm

load 7
1. to put goods into the vehicle in which it will be transported; 2. the amount of freight to be carried

load-bearing 21
the ability to support the weight of a construction. The support can be provided by the earth or by a wall.

load-bearing wall 15
a wall that supports any vertical load in addition to its own weight

local area network 6
See LAN

location-based service 29
an information service that tracks a cellular phone user's location within the mobile network and provides a variety of additional services. An example is Global Positioning System and cellular technologies that enable a new generation of electronic devices to know where they are, and are capable of modifying the information they collect and present based on that knowledge.

lock 20
the section of a canal where the water level changes to raise boats from one level to the next

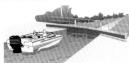

log 27
a thick piece of wood which has been cut down

logistics 1
the control of the movement of materials in a factory

lorry 7, 11
a large vehicle for transporting goods by road

lot 1, 2
a group of items, often finished goods

low attenuation 28
a low level loss in power of a signal between transmission and reception points. See also attenuation.

lubricant 24
a substance, often oil, which makes solid surfaces move more easily together

lubricate 24
to put a substance, often oil, onto a solid surface to make it move more easily against another solid surface

lubricating oil 24
an oil which makes a solid surface move more easily against another solid surface

lubrication 24
the process of putting a substance, often oil, onto a solid surface to make it move more easily against another solid surface

luxury 11
top-of-the-range cars, offering speed, comfort and lots of features, at a high cost

macadam 20
road surface material made from small stones and tar (after MacAdam 19th century British engineer)

machine operator 11
a worker who works on one of the machines used in car assembly

machine part 10
a part of a machine

machine tool 10
a machine for cutting or shaping wood, metal, etc., by means of a tool

machinery 1, 2, 9, 16
machines used in production

magnetic energy 19
the power produced by a a piece of metal, especially iron, which can draw other objects to it naturally or because an electric current is passed through it

main 20
a chief pipe which supplies gas or water

mainframe 5
a large computer

maintain 1, 5
to keep in good working order

maintenance 21
activities carried out after the project to ensure that the structure is kept in good working order

make-to-order 2
to produce goods after an order has been received

make-to-stock 2
to produce goods which will be stored until an order is received

malaria 14
a tropical disease transmitted by the mosquito

manganese 22
a gray-white, hard, brittle metallic element; its symbol is Mn

manhole 20
a hole near a road through which a man may go down, especially to gain access to an underground or enclosed structure

manipulate 5
to use for one's own purpose, e.g. to extract data from a database and then create a special report using that data

manufacture 18
to make, using machinery, often in a factory

manufacturing 1
making a product, usually in a factory

manufacturing cost 17
includes quality-related costs, direct and indirect labour, equipment repair and maintenance, other manufacturing support and overheads, and other costs directly associated with manufacturing operations. It typically does not include purchased materials or costs related to sales and other non-production functions.

manufacturing process 10
the production of goods using manual labour or machinery

mapping 23
the activity of drawing a map

marble 22
a type of hard limestone, usually white and streaked or mottled, which can be polished; it is often used in sculpture and architecture

mason 15
a craft worker who works with brick, stone, concrete or similar materials

master brake cylinder 11
the part of the hydraulic brake system which stores the brake fluid

mat 15
1. a large footing or foundation slab used to support an entire structure; 2. a grid of reinforcing bars

matchbox 27
a small box for matches

material 2, 7
anything used in production to make the finished product

materials handling 1
the efficient movement of materials from one part of the factory to another

materials management 7
the movement and management of materials and products from procurement through production

mathematics 10
the science of numbers

matt 12
describes the appearance of a surface which is dull; not shiny

maximize 1
to get the greatest benefit or use of something, e.g. a machine

MCA 13
See Medicines Control Authority

mean 4
the arithmetic average of a set of data

measure 1
to calculate the amount, weight or size of something

measurement scale 4
the complete range of possible values for a measurement

mechanical 10
describing something that is moved or produced by a machine

mechanical loader 22
a mechanical shovel or other machine for loading coal, ore, mineral, or rock

mechanics 10, 20
the science of the action of forces on objects

median 4
the middle value in a distribution

medical instrumentation 18
objects used in the field of medicine, also medical instruments

medicinal drug 13
a drug that is taken for healing, rather than recreational, purposes

Medicines Control Authority 13
the U.K. Agency responsible for overseeing food and pharmaceutical products. See also Food and Drugs Administration.

medium 11
a range of medium-size cars sold at a moderate cost

meet 8
to reach the expected level

melting point 13
the temperature at which a solid turns into a liquid

memo 29
a short communication that reminds someone of something

message 29
a communication sent from a person or program to another person or program

metal 20
small, broken stones used to make the surface of roads

metallic-pair circuit 28
a pair of wires which connect the subscriber's network termination to the fixed public phone network

metalliferous 22
containing metal or metals of the heavier type

methanol 12
a colourless, toxic, flammable alcohol with the formula CH_3OH, which boils at 64.5°C, and mixes with water, ether, alcohol; used in manufacture of formaldehyde, chemical synthesis, antifreeze for autos, and as a solvent

me-too product 3
a product that has been made using principles, practices, or designs copied from and closely similar to a competitor

microphone 29
a device which modulates an electric current so that it can transmit or record sound

microwave 28
1. the portion of the electromagnetic spectrum above about 760 megahertz (MHz); 2. high-frequency transmission signals and equipment that employ microwave frequencies, including line-of-sight open-air microwave transmission and, increasingly, satellite communications

midwife 14
a medical professional who delivers babies

mill 27
the factory where paper is made

mine 22
1. to get ore, metals, coal, or precious stones out of the earth; 2. an opening or excavation in the ground for the purpose of extracting minerals

mine car 22
a car that can be loaded at production points and hauled to the pit bottom or surface in a train

miner 22
a person engaged in the business or occupation of getting ore, coal, precious substances, or other natural substances out of the earth

mineral 22
a natural resource extracted from the earth for human use; e.g. ores, salts, coal, or petroleum

mini 11
a range of small cars, usually sold at a cheap price and offering good fuel economy

mining 10, 22
the process of removing soil and/or rock materials from one place and transporting them to another; the science, technique, and business of mineral discovery and exploitation

mining engineer 22
a specialist in one or more branches of work. Activities may include prospecting, surveying, sampling and valuation, technical underground management, ventilation control, geological examination, and company administration.

mint 10
to make a metal piece by stamping, e.g. coins

mitigation 13
steps taken to avoid or minimize negative environmental influences

mobile 29
able to move

mobility 29
the capacity or ability to move or be moved

mode 4
the single category among the categories in the distribution with the largest number of observations

model 11
a vehicle can be identified by features, e.g. manufacturer, make, engine size

modify 4
to change

modifying compound 25
chemical combinations of materials which make a finished plastic product

modulation 17, 28
the process of changing a signal for transmission by phone, radio or TV

molten 25
the liquid state that results when a solid, e.g. plastic, is heated to a very high temperature

monitor 5, 8
1. a piece of equipment, like a TV, on which the user can see text and graphics; 2. to check

monomer 25
the simple form of a chemical (derived from oil, coal or natural gas) from which plastic is made. See also polymer.

motor 19, 16
a machine that changes power, especially electrical power, into movement

mould (AmE mold) 11, 25
a hollow form into which very hot metal or plastic is poured to form a product in the desired shape

mouse 5
a small device with a ball on the bottom. As you move the mouse across a surface, the ball turns, turning receptors inside the mouse, which send signals to the computer.

movement 7
transportation

MPV 11
See multi-purpose vehicle

muffler (AmE) 11
See silencer

multipair cable 28
one of four basic types of wire found in telecommunications, a multiconductor cable with a single outer insulation and many internal balanced (twisted-pair) lines bundled into a common sheath. The other types are single-wire line, open-wire pairs, and coaxial cable.

single channel

multiple sclerosis 14
a disease which, over time, causes loss of movement and control of bodily actions

multi-purpose vehicle 11
a range of cars which combines comfort for 6–8 passengers and their luggage, style and performance

nap 30
1. to raise the surface of a fabric by brushing; 2. the soft, brushed surface of a fabric

natural gas 19
gas which is taken from under the earth or seabed

navigation 18
used to describe the equipment that keeps a vehicle, e.g. a car, ship or plane, on the right course

needs (usually pl) 8
what someone, usually the customer, needs. See also requirements.

net-making 30
the activity of making net (an openwork fabric made of threads or cords that are woven or knotted together at regular intervals)

network 6, 29
any number of computers (e.g. PCs and servers) and devices (e.g. printers and modems) joined together by a physical communications link

neurosis 14
a mental disorder in which the sufferer has unreasonable fears about the real world

newsprint 27
an inexpensive type of paper made from wood pulp or recycled paper, used mainly for newspapers

nitrate 12
a compound containing NO_3 and including nitrogen and oxygen with more oxygen than a nitrite

noise 9, 28
unwanted or unpleasant sound
noisy 9
loud
nonload-bearing wall 15
a wall that doesn't support a vertical load
nonmetalliferous 22
not containing metal. See also metalliferous.
non-rusting 25
the quality of plastic not to oxidize (rust)
norm 4
a standard
notebook (note book) 5
a small compact computer, smaller than a lap top
nozzle 25
the narrow end through which hot plastic is squeezed
nuclear energy 19
energy which is produced in a power station using the nucleus of an atom
nuclear physics 21
the study of an atom's nucleus, and the interactions of its parts
nuclear plant 19
a power station which produces nuclear energy
nuclear power plant 19
See nuclear plant
nuclear power station 20
a place where atomic energy is produced
nurse 14
a medical professional who looks after the sick, often in hospital
nutrient management 12
the use of a combination of fertilization techniques to ensure healthy growth of crops
nutritionist 14
a medical professional who specializes in food and food disorders
nylon 30
a synthetic fibre that is strong, silky, resistant to creases and stains, and washable

observe 13
to watch closely
obstetrician 14
a medical professional who specializes in the birth of children
occupational health 9
the area that deals with your health at work
occupational therapist 14
a medical professional who helps patients recover from their illness by helping them to start work again
octavo 27
the size of a piece of paper after it has been folded 3 times, i.e. there are 8 pieces
odour 13
smell
offshore 23
places in oceans, seas or large lakes. See also onshore.
oil 12, 19
a viscous, combustible liquid that does not mix with water

oil and gas 18
used to describe the industry which looks for, extracts and produces oil and gas for industrial or commercial use
oil field 23
a place where oil can be extracted
oily 23
covered with oil; having the feel of oil
olefin 12
a family of unsaturated, chemically active hydrocarbons with one carbon-carbon double bond, made by cracking alkanes and used to make plastics and antifreeze
omnidirectional antenna 29
an antenna that is equally effective in all directions
onshore 23
on the land. See also offshore.
opacity 27
the quality of paper to let the light through
open coal fire 19
a small open area (without doors) in a house where coal is burned to produce heat

open-pit 22
a type of mine where the minerals are extracted from the surface. See also strip mine.
open-wire pair 28
one of four basic types of wire found in telecommunications, this is a parallel copper wire for the forward and return current path. The parallel arrangement produces a balanced transmission circuit; however, cross talk is more difficult to eliminate. The other types are single-wire line, coaxial cable, and multipair cable.
operating system 5
the basic set of instructions that a computer uses to operate
operations 1
the production system in a service industry
optic cable (also optical cable) 28
a cable made of glass fibres through which signals are transmitted as pulses of light. It is a broadband medium that can easily provide capacity for a large number of channels.
optical communications 28
a technology which transmits signals in the form of light along fibres made of glass or plastic
optical fibre 6
a plastic or glass (silicon dioxide) fibre no thicker than a human hair that carries signals in the form of laser light pulses. An optical fibre pair can carry thousands of telephone calls at the same time, or a combination of video and voice. An optical fibre cable can contain tens or even hundreds of fibres.
optical transmission 28
a process which sends signals in the form of light along fibres made of glass or plastic

optimization 2
the process of using equipment in the best possible way
optimize 1
to get the best use of something, e.g. a machine
ore 22
the naturally occurring material from which a mineral or minerals of economic value can be extracted
organic compound 13
a compound (material made up of two or more elements) containing carbon
organize 5
to plan; to put together in an orderly way
ornamental 22
describing any stone of beauty and durability used for decoration
orthodontist 14
a medical professional who specializes in putting teeth straight
orthopaedist 14
a medical professional who specializes in straightening (children's) bones
osteopath 14
a medical professional who treats patients by by moving and applying pressure to muscles and bones
output 2
the volume of goods which are produced
overcurrent 16
a current higher than the rated current for a device or conductor. An overcurrent can result from an overload, short circuit, or ground fault.
overload 16
the result of too much electricity passing through the system
overtime 2
the working time in addition to normal working time
oxide 12
a compound of oxygen and another element; magnetic tape is coated with fine particles of manganese oxide

pack 7
1. to put into containers, e.g. boxes, cartons, packaging, ready for transportation; 2. the goods in a container
packaging 7, 27
materials, either paper or plastic, used to protect goods in transit
packet 6
a block of information; a collection of bits that contains both control information and data, and is the basic unit of transmission in a packet-switched network
packet-based 29
a method of transmitting messages through a communication network, in which long messages are subdivided into short packets and routed to their final destination
packing list 7
a document prepared by the shipper listing the kinds and quantities of goods in the shipment
paddle 20
a sluice that is raised and lowered to allow water in or out of a lock

paediatrician 14
a medical professional who specializes in children's diseases

paint 24
1. to put a liquid (a pigment plus oil or water) on a surface to change its colour; 2. a liquid (a pigment plus oil or water) that can be put on a surface to change its colour

paint finish 12
a paint's finish affects how shiny the finished paint surface will look

paint shop 11
the place in automobile manufacturing where the body of a car is painted

painter 15
a worker who uses pigments to decorate and protect coatings

paints and coatings 12
a group of emulsions generally consisting of pigments suspended in a liquid medium for use as decorative or protective coatings. Modern paints and coatings consist of very many compounds designed to fulfil the different requirements of hundreds of thousands of applications.

pallet 7
a platform with or without sides, on which a number of packages or pieces may be loaded so that they can be moved more easily, e.g. by forklift truck.

panelboard 16
electrical power distribution device in commercial and industrial applications which provide circuit control and overcurrent protection for light, heat or power circuits

paperboard 27
thicker paper

papermaking stock 27
a mixture of water and fibres

paraffin (BrE) = kerosene (AmE) 24
an oil made from petroleum which can be burned to give heat and light

paramedic 14
a medical professional who helps at the scene of an accident, but who does not have the same training as a doctor

Pareto chart 8
a graphical tool for showing causes from most significant to least significant. It is based on the suggestion that most effects come from relatively few causes; that is, 80% of the effects come from 20% of the possible causes. The Pareto chart is one of the "seven tools of quality".

part 11
a component of a vehicle

particle size 13
the size of a tiny mass of material

PAS 11
See power-assisted steering

passive 17
a passive device does not need a source of energy for its operation. See also active.

pasteurization 26
process to destroy dangerous organisms in liquids, e.g. milk, by heating

patent 3
an exclusive right by law for inventors to make use of their inventions for a limited period of time

patient 13
a person who goes to hospital for treatment

pavement 20
a special area where pedestrians can walk

PBX 29
See Private Branch Exchange

PDA (Personal Digital Assistant) 29
a handheld computer that serves as an organizer for personal information

peat 22
peat is formed in marshes and swamps from the dead and partly decomposed remains of the marsh vegetation

pedestrian crossing 20
a place where pedestrians can cross a busy road

people carrier 11
a range of large vehicles, which combine size and comfort

permit 23
a document which allows you to do something

personal organizer 29
See PDA

pest 26
an animal or insect which damages food

pest control 26
the activity of stopping animals or insects from damaging food, either by better hygience or by chemicals

pest management 12
the reduction of pest problems

pesticide 12, 26
a substance that kills or destroys small animals

petrochemical 12, 24
a chemical derived from petroleum or natural gas

petrol (BrE) 24
an oil made from petroleum used to power cars, planes, etc.

petroleum 19
mineral oil found under the earth or seabed which is used to produce petrol and other chemicals

petroleum production 10
the process which takes crude oil and turns it into petrol

pharmaceutical 18
relating to the production of medicine

pharmaceuticals 12
describing drugs or medicines in general

pharmacist 14
a medical professional who sells medicines

phone line 29
includes all wires, cables, instruments, etc., to make a phone call

phosphate rock 22
a mineral containing the element phosphorus, a basic plant nutrient; it is essential to all forms of life and is used in the manufacture of fertilizer

physical 10
concerning material things

physical connection 6
a link made with cables

physics 10
the science which deals with matter and natural forces

physiotherapist 14
a medical professional who uses exercise to help patients to use their bodies again

picking list 7
the list of products to be taken to fulfill an order

pickup 11
a truck with a closed cab and an open box

pie chart 8
a graphical tool, drawn like a cake, that helps you to visualize the relative importance of several categories of a variable

pier 20
a structure built out into the water, usually a sea or a lake, which can be used as a landing place for boats, as a walking area for pedestrians or to protect a harbour

pile 15
a long substantial pole of wood, concrete or metal, driven into the earth or sea bed to secure a firm foundation, on which the foundation footing is laid

pill 14
a tablet

pilot 3
a small-scale experiment

pipeline (in the pipeline) 3, 24
undergoing preparation, production, or completion

placebo 13
a substance which is given in place of a real medicine

planning 1
the stage in a process when you say what you are going to do (see also controlling)

plant 1, 13
a factory

plasterer 15
a craft worker who covers walls and ceilings with a material, usually made of portland cement mixed with sand and water

plastic 12, 24
a carbon-based substance consisting of long chains (polymers) of simple molecules

plastics and fibres 12
man-made polymers, made by the chemical industry, using raw materials obtained from crude oil

plate 10
1. to cover one metal with a thin layer of another, e.g. silver plate; 2. the metal covering

plate girder 20
a horizontal iron or steel place in a building or bridge that supports vertical loads

platform 23
an offshore structure from which wells are drilled

plumber 15
a craft worker skilled in the installation, repair, and maintenance of water and waste systems in buildings

plutonium 19
a manmade substance widely used in the production of nuclear power

pneumonia 14
a serious disease of the lungs which causes difficulty in breathing

poison 9, 14
a substance which is harmful if eaten or drunk

polish 30
1. to smooth the surface of a fabric; 2. material used to smooth the surface of a fabric

pollutant 24
something that makes the air, water or soil dirty

pollute 24
to make the air, water or soil dirty

pollution 24
the effect caused by making the air, water or soil dirty.

polyester 30
a synthetic fibre that is crease resistant, quick drying and strong, used in clothing and carpets

polyethylene 12
a polymer made from ethylene; it is a tough, sturdy plastic film having very good, low temperature characteristics

polymer 25
the compound form of a chemical made from a number of monomers. See also monomer.

polypropylene 12
a derivative of propylene used to make plastics and fibres, with a wide range of applications, e.g. kitchen tools and carpets

porosity 27
the porosity describes the extent to which a paper's surface allows air to pass through and ink to penetrate. Generally, coated papers have low porosity and hold ink on the surface well.

portable 29
describing something that can be easily carried

poster 27
a type of highly mechanical, highly filled, mostly coloured paper that has been made weather resistant by sizing

post-harvest handling 26
activities in the food and fibre sector that occur after agricultural products are sold from, or leave, the farm

pothole 20
a hole in the surface of a road caused by traffic or bad weather

power 15, 16, 18, 24
the force generated by electricity or other energy

power assisted steering 11
a steering system in which a hydraulic pump helps the driver to turn the steering wheel

power plant 19
a place where energy is produced, e.g. nuclear power plant, gas power plant

power station 19
see power plant

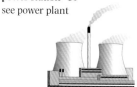

power train 11
an engine and transmission combination

powerhouse 19
See power plant

practical application 3
the action of using something for a particular purpose

precautionary 9
describing action taken to stop loss, damage or injury

preliminary design 21
the development stage in which dimensions, materials and costs are estimated

preliminary feasibility study 21
an investigation to assess both financial and engineering aspects of a number of proposals in order to choose one or more for more detailed examination

preservative 13
a substance, usually a chemical, that helps to keep something good for a longer time

press 26, 27, 30
to squeeze out liquid by pressure; to squeeze out water between rollers (in papermaking)

press shop 11
the production stage in automobile manufacturing when the bodywork panels are pressed into shape

pressure 23
the natural force of the oil underground which can push it naturally out of the well

prevent 8
to stop something happening

prevention 8
the action of stopping something from happening

prioritize 8
to organize activities according to their importance

Private Branch Exchange (PBX) 29
a private telephone network used within an organization. Users of the PBX share a certain number of outside lines for making external calls.

process 5, 8, 21, 1, 12, 24
1. to examine data; 2. a system(s) used to manufacture products; 3. to change a raw material into a finished product

process control 8
methods to keep a process within boundaries and minimize the variation of the process

processing 26
the treatment of agricultural outputs into finished (food) products

produce 1
to make

product approval 18
the process which gets permission for a product to be used

product development 3
changing and improving a product to achieve the best possible result

product labelling 13
the use of written, printed, or graphic materials with a product or its container or wrapper, giving information about the product and its use

production 10
1. the department of a company concerned with making something, often in a factory; 2. the activity of making something in a factory

productivity 1, 2
the output rate per worker or per machine

program 5
this gives a computer instructions which provide the user with tools to perform a task, e.g. word processing

proposal 21
a suggested plan for a structure, usually giving technical and price information

propylene 12
a petroleum derivative used to make plastics; it is a colourless unsaturated hydrocarbon gas, with boiling point of −47°C; used to manufacture plastics and as a chemical intermediate

prospect 22
to examine a territory for its mineral wealth

prospector 22
a person who looks for valuable minerals

protect 9
to keep safe from loss, damage or injury

protection 9
the act or material to keep someone or something safe from loss, damage or injury

protective 9
describing something that keeps someone or something safe from loss, damage or injury, e.g. clothing

protocol 6
rules for communicating, particularly for the format and transmission of data

prototype 2, 3, 11
the first version of a product

psychosis 14
a serious disease of the mind, where the patient loses touch with reality

pulp 27
1. to convert wood into a fibrous material by a mechanical or a chemical process; 2. a cellulose plant fibre cleaned and beaten into a wet mixture used to form sheets of paper

pulp and paper 18
the industry which converts wood into paper

pump 10, 22, 23
1. to force a liquid, air or gas out of or into something; 2. a machine to force a liquid, air or gas out of or into something

pure basic research 3
the study of pure scientific principles

pure research 3
research carried out to increase knowledge about an area with little concern for any immediate or practical benefits that might result.

purity standards 13
the extent to which a substance is free from harmful or damaging matter

pylon 20
a tall tower to support the ends of a number of power wires over a long span

qualitative research 4
this type of research gives an in-depth understanding of why people hold particular views. It is used to identify not only *what* people think but also, more importantly, the reasons *why* they hold such views.

quality 1
the level of goodness: the concept of quality concerns how well and for how long a product or service meets the requirements of the customer

quantity surveyor 15
a person who measures and prices building work

quarry 22
an open or surface mineral working, usually to extract building stone, such as slate and limestone

quartz 22
a mineral which includes amethyst, rock crystal and tigereye

query 5
a question which allows a computer user to extract data from a database

quick-freezing 26
process which keeps flavours in food by reducing the temperature of the food very quickly

quire 27
24 identical pieces of paper

radar 16, 18
a device that uses electromagnetic waves to calculate the distance of an object

radiation 9, 14
the (harmful) effects of heat, light or other energy in the form of energy

radiator 11
equipment which keeps the engine cool

radio 18
a device to receive wireless audio signals

radio transmission 28
the process and technology of sending signals as radio waves through the atmosphere

radio wave 17, 28
a sound wave which is sent or received through the air

radioactive dosage form 14
a medical preparation based on X-rays

radiographer 14
a medical professional who takes X-rays for medical purposes

radiologist 14
a medical professional who uses X-rays to treat patients

rag 27
the two main rag fibres used in papermaking are cotton and linen. Rag paper consists of 25–60% rag fibre and the rest is chemical wood pulp.

railway line 20
the metal tracks along which trains run

rainproof 16
describing the ability to stay dry in spite of the rain

raintight 16
describing the ability to keep rain out

raise 22, 26
1. to keep animals and help them to grow; 2. a vertical or inclined opening in a mine driven upward from a level to connect with the level above, or to explore the ground for a limited distance above one level

RAM (Random Access Memory) 5
the memory that can be used by applications to perform necessary tasks while the computer is on

random 4
having no specific pattern

rate process 10
the speed at which a manufacturing step is carried out

raw materials 1
items which are used in the conversion process from input to output

rayon 30
an early synthetic textile like silk, made from fibres produced chemically from cellulose. It is similar to polyester but more elastic.

react 25
to change when mixed with another chemical

reaction 12
the recombination of two substances using parts of each substance to produce new substances

reaction injection moulding 25
a process in which two chemicals are mixed together and squirted into a mould. The chemicals react together. This is how they make car bumpers, some disposable cups and plates, and the meat trays in supermarkets.

ream 27
500 identical sheets of paper

receive 6, 17, 29
to obtain a signal; to turn electrical waves into sound and pictures

receiver 28
a device that captures a broadcast over the air, or a transmission by satellite or cable or microwave, and then presents it for listening, data processing, or viewing

reception 17, 29
the ability of a radio or television to turn electrical waves into sound and pictures

receptive 17
being willing to take in new ideas (usually of a person)

record 4, 5
1. to set down in writing; 2. all documentary material set down in writing; data which can be stored in an electronic form, e.g. as a file or in a database

recover 17, 23
to return something, e.g. a radio or TV signal, to its former or normal state so that the information in the signal can be heard or seen

recovery 17
the process of returning something, e.g. a radio or TV signal, to its former or normal state so that the information in the signal can be heard or seen

rectify 8
to correct a problem

recurrent 14
something that happens again and again

recycle 9, 25
to prepare a material so that it can be used again, e.g. paper, glass

redundant 28
describing that part of the total information contained in a message that can be taken away without loss of essential information

refine 24, 27
to make pure or clean; to break down into fibres for pulp making

refiner 27
a machine containing rotating disks between which wood chips are broken down into fibres for pulp making

refinery 24
a plant or equipment to clean petroleum

reflected propagation 28
the movement of energy in the form of waves which have contact with a very large object when compared to the wavelength of the propagating wave. Reflection occurs from the surface of the earth and from buildings and walls. See also surface propagation.

refrigeration 26
the keeping of food cool to preserve it

register a patent 3
to record an exclusive right in law to make use of an invention for a limited period of time

regulated 9
controlled

regulator 26
something which controls, e.g. a plant growth regulator controls the speed at which plants grow

regulatory authority 13
the organization that checks whether rules and regulations are being followed

reinforced-concrete 15
a combination of steel and concrete

relay station 29
an intermediate station that passes information between terminals or other relay stations

release 18
a (new version of a) product that is offered to users

reliability 4, 17
the extent to which different experiments using the same data produce consistent results.

reliable 17
the quality that an item has when it can perform a required function under stated conditions for a specified period of time

rely 17
to trust someone or something to perform a required function under stated conditions for a specified period of time

removal 22
the process of taking out minerals

repair 1, 8, 18
to mend

repeater 28
a device inserted at intervals along a circuit to boost, and amplify an analogue signal

report 4
1. to make or present often official, formal, information; 2. the official, formal, information collected

requirement 2
something that is needed for a particular process

requirements (usually pl) 8
what someone, usually the customer, needs (see also needs)

research 4, 11
1. to investigate the causes and effects of a subject of interest; 2. an investigation into the causes and effects of a subject of interest

research assistant 3
a person who helps with research

reserves (normally pl) 23
the total quantity of oil or gas which can still be extracted

reservoir 23
rock formation containing oil and/or natural gas

resistor 17
an electrical component that limits or regulates the flow of electrical current in an electronic circuit

response 4
a reply, an answer

restore 28
to return a signal to its previous state

retransmit 28
to transmit again

retrieve 5, 29
to get back, e.g. data which has been stored on a disk

reverse osmosis 26
filtration process to remove particles from a solution. It is used to purify water and remove salts and other impurities in order to improve the colour, taste or properties of the fluid.

reversible fabric 30
a fabric that can be worn in two different ways by simply reversing it to the other side

rework 8
to correct a fault in a product

rice milling 26
the process of crushing rice into small grains

rig 23
a structure that contains all the necessary equipment for drilling

rigid connection 15
a connection between two structural members that prevents end rotation of one relative to the other

rinse 9
to wash in clean water

risk 9
danger

road 20
a general word for open ways along which vehicles, persons, and animals can move

road roller 20
a machine with heavy wide smooth rollers used in road making to make the surface smooth

robot 18
computer software that runs continuously and responds automatically to a user's activity; machine that is programmed to do some of the work of man

robotics 16
the study of how robots are made and used

rock 22
in geology, the material that forms the essential part of the earth's solid crust; a combination of one or more minerals

rock formation 23
the particular location and type of rock

rock mapping 23
the activity of drawing a map to show the location and type of rock

rocket 24
a vehicle for space travel

roll 10, 25, 27
1. to turn over; 2. to make flat by pressure applied by a roller, e.g. to make thin sheets of steel by passing it between large rollers; 3. a mass of material in cylindrical or rounded form; a quantity of paper formed into a large cylinder or ball

roof 15
the top cover of a building or structure

roofer 15
a craft worker who constructs or repairs roofs

roofing felt 15
a fibrous material saturated with asphalt used under the roof

rotary table 23
the revolving or spinning section of the drillfloor that provides power to turn the drill string in a clockwise direction (also called turntable)

rubber 12
a natural, synthetic, or modified high polymer with elastic properties; it is a good insulator

rubbery 25
flexible, easy to bend, like rubber

rug 30
small carpet

run 2
1. to operate equipment; 2. the time when equipment operates; 3. the output from the operation of equipment

safety engineer 22
an employee who inspects all dangerous places in a mine or plant

safety risk 13
a danger; something that can cause injury or damage

safety standard 13
rules or models to ensure freedom from danger

salt 12
the chemical sodium chloride (NaCl), which is used in baking and cooking to add or improve the flavour of food

sampling 4, 8
the process of choosing cases or elements for a study

sanitary 27
a type of paper made from waste paper and/or chemical pulp. These grades are used to make toilet paper and other sanitary products, such as handkerchiefs, kitchen wipes, towels and cosmetic tissues.

sanitary engineering 26
the treatment of animal waste with machines

satellite 28
a man-made object that is sent into orbit around the earth, the moon, etc., for some purpose

satellite communications 18
the use of a man-made object that is sent into orbit around the earth, the moon, etc., to send and receive electronic signals

satin 30
a very shiny, soft fabric made of silk, rayon or polyester. It is often used for formal dresses and men's evening wear.

satisfy 2
to give customers what they want, need or expect

scanner 5
a device which analyses an image, and then captures and processes it so that it can be saved to a file on your computer

schedule 2
1. to timetable (a part of) production; 2. a production timetable

scheme 21
a plan

scientific 3
describing knowledge obtained by the collection of evidence or data.

scientist 3
a person who collects evidence or data in order to convert it into knowledge

scrap 8
a product which cannot be used, usually because it has a defect

screen 5
a monitor on which the user can see text and graphics

seal 9
to fasten or close tightly so that air or water cannot get in

search 3
1. to make a thorough examination of;
2. the act of making a thorough
examination of or exploration for

search engine 5
a special site on the web that is designed
to help you find information stored on
other sites. A search engine searches the
internet, based on important words, keeps
an index of the words it finds, and where
they find them, and allows you to look for
words or combinations of words found in
that index.

secondary feasibility study 21
an investigation to choose the best
scheme from those that have been
shortlisted

sediment 22
solid broken material that comes from
weathering of rocks and is carried or
deposited by air, water, or ice

seize 13
to take, usually by force

semiconductor 18, 17
a special type of material with more
resistance than a conductor, but less than
that of an insulator.

Transistor   Diode

separate 24
to divide into parts

separation 24
the process of dividing into parts

sequence 2
the order of steps in which production
will be carried out

server 5
a networked computer that provides
services to client computers. Servers
include file servers, disk servers, print
servers, etc.

service panel 16
main power cabinet through which
electricity is brought into a building

serviette 27
soft paper for wiping one's mouth when
eating

set up 2, 11
1. to put in place ready for use; 2. the
physical organization of equipment in a
workshop or factory

set-up time 2
the time needed to change the physical
organization of equipment

severe 14
serious

sewer 20
an underground structure to carry off
waste and surface water

shallow 15
not going far down, usually into the
ground. See also deep.

share files 6
when two or more users give each other
access to electronic information

shear 30
to cut off the wool from sheep

sheet 27
a cut piece of paper

shelter 15
a place which provides protection against
the elements

shift 2
the period of time worked by a group of
workers

ship 7, 24
1. to transport, especially by sea; 2. a
vehicle for transporting goods by sea

shipment 7
goods for tansportation

shipper 7
a company which transports goods

shock 9
violent force, often of electricity passing
through a body

shock absorber 11
an oil filled device used to control the
movement of the springs in the
suspension system

shoe sole 25
the underside of the front part of a
shoe

short circuit 16
a situation where the electrical current
takes an easier path than the one
intended

shovel 20, 22
a long-handled tool with a broad blade
used to lift and throw material

showroom 11
a large room where customers can look at
cars for sale

shrinkage 30
the amount of loss due to contraction of
the fibres, especially during washing

sign 25
a notice giving information

signal 6, 16, 28, 29
a pulse of light, current or sound that is
used to convey information

silencer (AmE muffler) 11
a unit through which exhaust gases pass
to reduce the noise of the running
engine

silicon 17
very common substance widely used to
make semiconductor material

silk 30
a fine, strong fibre produced by the larva
of silk worms and silk moths. It is strong,
resilient and takes colour very well.

single-wire line 28
one of four basic types of wire found in
telecommunications, a single wire is
strung between poles without shielding or
protection from noise interference (used
in early days of telegraphy). The other
types are open-wire pairs, multipair
cables, and coaxial cables.

Open wire

site 1
the place where a factory is built

site investigation 21
a survey of the area where a structure
will be built

skip 22
an open iron vehicle or car on four
wheels, running on rails and used
especially on inclines or in inclined shafts

slack 2
the period of time when there is low
demand for products and for production

slate 22
a rock that can be split into slabs and thin
plates

slippery 25
difficult to hold or stand on, especially
when wet

sluice 20
a structure that allows water to flow in or
out in order to change the water level in a
canal

slurry 27
a liquid mixture consisting of fibres in
water used in the papermaking process

small family 11
a range of cars intended for a small family

smoking 9
the habit of taking in the smoke from
cigarette, cigar or pipe tobacco, which
is often prohibited or is a risk in
factories

soap 12, 24
a material with which you can wash

soft shoulder 20
the edge of a motorway or other road
where cars can stop in an emergency

soften 10, 25
to make something softer, e.g. fibres

software (program) 5
the set of instructions that make
computer hardware perform tasks
Programs and operating systems are
examples of software.

soil 26, 20
top layer of the earth where plants grow

soil makeup 26
the elements that you can find in soil

soil management 12
soil management can improve soils in
terms of their fertility

soil mechanics 21
a branch of mechanics that evaluates the
load-bearing qualities and stability of the
ground

solar cell 19
a device for producing electricity from
sunlight

solar energy 19
energy which is produced by the sun

solar panel 19
a collection of solar cells fitted into a
board

solid dosage form 14
a medical preparation based on solid, e.g.
a tablet, rather than a liquid

solid-state electronics 16
describing equipment that contains
semiconductor devices in an electronic
circuit

solubility 13
the ability of a solid or powder to dissolve in water

solution 14
something in the form of a liquid

solvent 24
a chemical substance that dissolves other substances

sort 25
to arrange things into different groups

sound-deadening material 15
a material which prevents the passage of sound

source encoder 28
a device which maps the source into a set of binary strings

space technology 18
practical science which deals with what is outside the earth's air

span 20
the stretch between two supports on a bridge

speaker (= loudspeaker) 29
a device that converts electrical signals into sound waves

specialty chemicals 12
a group of chemicals that improve the performance of paints and coatings, computers and electronic devices, household goods, adhesives, personal care products, etc.

specification 8, 18, 21
detailed plan which states, e.g. the size, weight, functionality of a product

spill 24
to allow a liquid to pour or fall out

spillage 24
the act of allowing a liquid to pour or fall out; the quantity that pours or falls out

spin 26, 30
to draw out and twist fibre into thread

spoilage 26
the action or waste that results when something, e.g. food goes bad

sports 11
a range of small and fast cars

spray drying 26
process to change a liquid into a dry powder or particles

spray gun 11
equipment shaped like a gun which delivers an atomized mist of liquid for painting

spraying 9
the act of scattering liquid in very small drops usually under pressure, e.g. spraying water on a fire

spread footing 15
a type of foundation with a large base, which distributes the weight over a large area, rather than concentrating it

spreadsheet 5
the computer equivalent of a paper ledger sheet, it consists of a grid made from columns and rows, which can make number manipulation easy

squeeze 25
to press a liquid through a narrow hole or space

stability 15, 21
ability to restore to original condition after being disturbed by some force

stamp 11
to form or cut out

standard 4
1. an accepted measure which can be used for comparison; 2. serving as an accepted measure

statistics 4
techniques and procedures for analysing, interpreting and displaying data

steam cracking 24
a process in which hydrocarbon molecules are broken into small fragments by steam at very high temperatures

steam power 19
energy which is produced by the vapour (steam) given off by very hot water

steel 11
hard, shiny metal made from iron

steering system 11
the equipment (steering wheel, steering column, steering gear, linkages, and the front wheel supports) that allows the driver to guide the car and turn the wheels as he wishes

steering wheel 11
the wheel which controls the car's movement

step 21
a part of an activity

stereo 18
a hi-fi or other sound system which gives out sound from 2 places, creating a three-dimensional sound effect

sterile medicament 14
a medicine that is free from germs

stiff 12
describes a material that does not bend easily

stiffness 27
the ability of paper not to bend too easily

still-frame 29
a single image transmitted over a communications link

stock 1, 2
products or materials which are stored and ready to sell or use

stock-out 2
the situation where there is no product for delivery to customers

stope 22
an excavation from which ore has been removed in a series of steps

storage 1, 7, 17
see store

storage capacity 17
the maximum quanitity of data that a device can keep (store) in any form, usually for the purpose of orderly retrieval and documentation

storage device 5
a piece of equipment, e.g. a floppy disk, hard disk or CD, on which you can record your data for later retrieval

storage system 17
a physical or electronic method to store items so that they can be easily retrieved at a later date

store 1, 5, 17, 24
1. to put something into a system so that it can easily been found again; 2. the place where materials are kept, e.g. a warehouse storage

strand 20
one of the wires twisted together to form the cable which supports a bridge

strategic basic research 3
studies that are carried out with the expectation that they will produce a broad base of knowledge likely to form the background to the solution (compare with pure research)

string 25
a long thin piece of material

stringent conditions 13
demanding strict attention to rules and regulations practices that set hard standards

strip mining 22
the mining of coal by surface mining methods as distinguished from the mining of metalliferous ores by surface mining methods

stripping machine 22
a machine used in strip mining to cut the rock

stroke 14
a sudden and serious disorder in the brain which can lead to paralysis of the body

structural 10
concerning the main part of a building

structural works 20
any building work

structure 15, 10, 20
a building

study 4
1. to investigate; 2. the results of an investigation

substance 9, 13
a material; it can be a liquid, a solid or a gas

subsurface 23
the area under the surface

suffer 13
to be ill or in pain

sump 22
an excavation made underground to collect water, from where it is pumped to the surface

sun 19
burning star in the sky

sunroof 11
a panel in the roof of a car which can tilt or slide open, either manually or electrically, to provide extra light and/or ventilation

supercomputer 17
a very powerful computer

superconductor 16
a material that allows electricity to pass through freely at the lowest possible temperature

supermini 11
a range of cars between mini and small family

supplement 26
something that is added, e.g. to animal food, to make it better

support 15
the structural foundation for essential building elements

surface 22
the top of the ground

surface propagation 28
the movement of energy in the form of waves through the lowest portion of the atmosphere close to the earth

surgeon 14
a medical professional who specializes in operations

survey 4, 20
1. to carry out a well-planned research study; to collect data for measurement; 2. a well planned research study

suspender 20
a structure on which a part of a bridge can be hung

suspension (bridge) 20
a bridge that has its roadway hanging from two or more cables

sustainable production systems 12
a sustainable production system benefits society, the manufacturer and the customer

swamp 22
land which is very wet

sweetener 12
a substance used instead of sugar to make food or drink sweet

swing (bridge) 20
a bridge that moves through 90 degrees to open and allow boats to pass along the river

switch 6, 16
1. to select the paths or circuits to be used for transmission of information; 2. a device that selects the paths or circuits to be used for transmission of information and establishes a connection

switchboard 16
a large panel or assembly of panels containing switches, overcurrent protective devices, buses, and associated instruments

switching machine 29
a device that opens or closes circuits or selects the paths or circuits to be used for transmission of information

switching system 28
a set of one or more systems that act together to route data from its source to its destination

symptom 14
a change in the mind or body that shows that someone is ill

synthesize 24
to make or put together

synthetic 12, 30
artificial

synthetic fibre 12
a fibre made from materials such as glass, rayon, or nylon

synthetic rubber and fibre 24
products which are used in place of rubber and fibre, typically derived from petroleum

synthetics 24
man-made materials that are made by putting together various chemicals

system 16
a group of related (electrical) parts

system failure analysis 8
an investigation into why (a part of) the production system has not worked as intended

systems analysis 10
a study carried out to help a person or organization to take a better course of action and make a better decision than they might otherwise have made

tablet 14
a medicine in a small round form

tail pipe 11
exhaust pipe which runs from the silencer to the rear of the vehicle

talc 22
a mineral which has a greasy or soapy feel, easily cut with a knife

tan 26
to convert animal skin to leather

tanker 7, 24
1. a vehicle for carrying liquid goods by road; 2. a large ship for carrying liquids, especially oil

tarmac 20
a mixture of tar and very small stones used to make the surface of roads

technical drawings 21
specialist designs and plans

technical know-how (TKH) 3
techical specialist knowledge

technical support 18
scientific help

technician 3, 18
a person who is skilled in carrying out operations in a specific field; usually someone who understands and can work in fields using modern technology

technique 6
the systematic procedure by which a complex or scientific task is accomplished

telecommunications 18
the use of different technologies to send and receive messages

telephony 29
the science behind telephones

television 18
the method of sending electrical signals (audio and visual) which can then be received (viewed and heard)

television station 29
the organization or business that produces and/or broadcasts television content

temper 10
to heat and then cool metals to obtain the required hardness and elasticity, e.g. steel

tender 21
1. to make an offer to carry out works, e.g. an engineering contract; 2. an offer to carry out works

terminal 5, 24
a computer work station which is usually part of a network

test 4, 13, 18
1. to put to test or proof; 2. a critical examination, observation, or evaluation

test 11
to put the car through a series of tests under hard working conditions

textile 30
any cloth or fabric produced by weaving, knitting, or felting

therapeutic practice 13
actions that treat medical conditions

thermal cracking 24
the process by which petroleum is heated to a high temperature and the heavier parts of the oil are cracked (converted) into petrol (gasoline)

thermal processing 26
process to treat food with heat to make it safe

thermodynamics 10, 21
the science which deals with the relationship between and the power that works and drives machines

thermoplastics 25
a type of plastic which softens with heat and hardens with cooling

thermoset 25
a type of plastic which is cured or hardened by heat

throughput 2
the volume of products that can be made within a certain period of time

tidal barrage 19
a manmade bar built in a shallow part of the sea to change the energy of the water into electrical power

tidal power 19
the electricity produced by the sea

tide mill 19
a power plant where tidal power is converted into electricity

tightly 9
closed so that neither air nor water can get in

tin 22
a soft, bluish white mineral, used as a coating to protect iron and copper

tinplate 10
to cover a metal with a thin layer of tin, e.g. food cans. See also plate.

tissue 27
a type of light paper mainly used to wrap delicate items and for hygienic purposes

tough 12
describes a material that is hard; difficult to break

tower 24, 20
a large tower (cylindrical column) used to separate the different liquids in crude oil

town-gas 19
gas produced from coal which is used in homes and in industry

toxic 9, 12
poisonous

toy 25
something that children play with

track 11
area where cars are put through a series of tests under hard working conditions

tractor 24
a machine that pulls farming machines

transducer 17
a device which coverts energy from one form into another, e.g. microphone, loudspeaker

transfer 6, 29
to move (data)

transfer process 10
a manufacturing process which takes laboratory tests and applies them to a practical application

transformer 16
a piece of electrical equipment to convert electric power from one voltage to another

transistor 17
a tiny electrical device that can amplify an electrical signal and switch a device on and off

transmission 11, 17, 29
a device that changes the ratio between engine rpm (revolutions per minute) and driving wheel rpm

transmission line 16
a power line to carry large quantities of high-voltage electricity between regions

transmission network 19
the system of pipes and wires that is used to carry electricity from the power plant to the users (homes and industry)

transmission speed 6
the rate at which information is passed through communications lines, generally measured in bits per second (bps)

transmit 6, 17, 18, 28
to send information from one location to another

transmittable 17
describing the ability of a signal to be sent

transmitter 28
a piece of radio equipment capable of transmitting electromagnetic signals but not capable of receiving them

transparent 12
describes a material that allows light to pass through

transponder 28
a combined receiver and transmitter whose function is to transmit signals automatically

transport 24
to move from one place to another by a vehicle

transport fuel 19
petrol used in vehicles, e.g. cars and trucks

transportation 7, 18, 24
the movement of goods from one place to another

trap 23
a configuration of rocks that may contain hydrocarbons

traprock 22
any dark-coloured fine-grained nongranitic rock, such as a basalt

travertine 22
a dense, finely crystalline, limestone; generally white, tan, or cream

treatment 13
the process or substances given to an ill person to make them better (healthier)

trial 4
the act of trying and testing

trial pit 21
a shallow hole, usually dug by an excavator, to assess the ground and what is under it

trona 22
a mineral, $Na_3(CO_3)(HCO_3).2(H_2O)$; soft; vitreous; colourless to white; alkaline tasting; found in saline lake deposits and desert soils

truck 7, 11, 24
a large vehicle for transporting goods by road

truss 15
a prefabricated framework of girders, struts and other items which support a roof or other load-bearing elements

tuberculosis 14
a serious disease, especially of the lungs

tumble dry 30
to make or become dry by turning about in the heated drum of a clothes dryer

tumour 14
when diseased cells grow too quickly and cause swelling and sickness

tunnel 20
an underground passage, often for a road or a railway, through a mountain or under a river

turbine 10, 19, 16
an engine or motor in which the pressure of a liquid or gas turns a wheel, usually to produce energy

turnkey 21
a building or installation which is built, supplied, or installed complete and ready for use

turntable 23
See rotary table

twill 30
one of the three basic weaves – Plain, Satin and Twill. Twill has diagonal patterns throughout the fabric

twisted pair 6
two insulated wires twisted together, which can be shielded (STP) or unshielded (UTP).

ulcer 14
a break in the skin (inside or outside the body) which may bleed and cause poisonous matter

ultrahigh image definition 17
an image which is very clear on a TV or other visual device

uncertainty 2
the situation when the future is not clearly known

underdrain 20
a drain below the surface of the road

underground 22
below the earth's surface

unit 1
an item of production

unload 7
to remove a shipment from a vehicle, e.g. boat, truck, etc.

update 2
1. to provide more precise information about the present situation; 2. more precise information about the present situation

upholstery 30
the cloth covering on padded furniture such as sofas and armchairs

upload 6
to transfer data or code from a client to a larger server (see also download)

upstream 23
exploration and production activities for oil and natural gas. See also downstream.

uranium 19
heavy radioactive metal used to produce nuclear power

vacuum tube (AmE) 17
a sealed glass tube with no air in it, used to control the flow of electricity, e.g., in radio or TV

validate 13
to ensure that something is legitimate or correct

validity 4
the extent to which a test measures what it is intended to measure.

valve (BrE) 17
See vacuum tube

van 7, 11
a small vehicle for carrying goods by road

vaporize 24
to turn into gas

vaporous 24
like gas

vapour 9, 24
a mixture of liquid and gas, e.g. steam

vapour barrier 15
a building product installed on exterior walls and ceilings under the drywall and on the warm side of the insulation

variability 8
the extent to which the results of production are different from their specifications

variable 4, 8
any characteristic in a study that is not fixed and can change in numerical value

variance 4
a measure of how spread out, or scattered, a distribution is

velvet 30
a soft fabric made of silk rayon or nylon

vendor 18
a seller

ventilating 15
a system through which vapour or dirty air is removed from a room or fixture

ventilation shaft 22
a channel in a mine that delivers air to miners underground

viaduct 20
a structure which carries a road or railway across water

vibration 9
a continuous shaking movement, for example when using a power drill

video camera 29
a hand-held camera used for taking moving pictures. A video camera can record data on magnetic tape or it can be uploaded to a computer.

video game 18
an electronic game which the player can control with a keyboard and view on a television screen

video signal 17
a signal intended to be seen

videophone 29
a telephone-like service with a picture as well as sound

viscosity 13
the measurement of a fluid's resistance to flow, often used to describe its thickness

visible 29
describing something that can be seen

visual 29
producing something that can be seen

voice 29
speech

(high) voltage 19
electrical force measured in volts; a volt is the standard measure of force

vomiting 9
the act of being sick

wall 15
a member, usually vertical, used to enclose or separate spaces

wallpaper 27, 29
a type of paper that is suitable to cover the walls inside a house.

WAN (wide area network) 6
a network linking computers, terminals, and other equipment over a large area

WAP (Wireless Application Protocol) 29
a global standard which enables WAP devices such as mobile phones or Personal Digital Assistants (PDAs) to access internet services and information (like email and news bulletins)

warehouse 7
a place for the reception, delivery, distribution, and storage of goods

wash 9
to make clean in water

wash and wear 30
describing clothes that do not need ironing after washing

washer 25
a ring of plastic which is put between two surfaces to make a better joint

waste 27
what is thrown away

waste disposal 15
the process of permanently isolating waste

water 19
one of the renewable sources of energy used in hydroelectric schemes and wave power

water desalination 20
the process of removing salt and other unwanted matter from groundwater to make it drinkable

water main 20
a chief pipe which supplies water

water power 19
the energy produced by water in hydroelectric schemes and wave power

water resistance 27
the quality of paper not to absorb water (see also absorbance)

water supply 15
the system in a building which is composed of the water service pipe, the water distributing pipes and the various connecting pipes, control valves and fittings

watercourse 20
a natural or manmade channel through which water flows

waterfall 19
water falling from a great height sometimes used to produce energy

water-proof 11
to cover the outer materials so that rain does not go through

water-supply system 20
the network of reservoirs, tunnels, and pipelines that supplies water to users in a community

watertight 16
describing the ability to stay dry

waterway 20
a way or channel for water

waterworks 19
network of buildings, pipes and water supplies within a public water system

wave 19, 28
1. movement of the sea; 2. an electric, electromagnetic, acoustic, mechanical or other form whose physical activity rises and falls as it travels through a medium

wave power 19
the energy produced by the sea

wavelength 28
the distance travelled by a wave in one period (the period is the time required to complete one cycle)

wax 24
a solid or semi-solid material derived from petroleum, which is resistant to water and scratches

weapons system 17
the collection of instruments used for attack or defence

weatherproof 16
describing the ability to stay in good condition in spite of bad weather

weave 26, 30
to make cloth with thread

weaving mill 30
a factory where fabric is made by weaving (by interlacing yarns on a loom)

web page 6
a World Wide Web document, usually based on Hypertext Markup Language (HTML), that may contain text, graphics, online audio, video, Java or ActiveX objects

website 6
a collection of files that covers a particular theme or subject and managed by a particular person or organization. Its opening page is called a home page. A website is accessed through a web address known as a uniform resource locator (URL).

weir 20
a dam in a stream or river to raise the water level or change its flow

well 20, 23
1. a deep hole in ground where people can get water; 2. a hole drilled into the earth to recover oil or gas

wellbore (= borehole) 23
well

well-ventilated 9
allowing fresh air to enter and circulate in a room

wide area network 6
See WAN

wildcat (wildcat well) 23
an exploration well

wildcat well 23
See wildcat

wind 19
one of the renewable sources of energy produced by the air moving at a high speed

wind (wound – wound) 27
to turn around so as to form a roll

wind farm 19
a place where the energy produced by the wind is changed into electrical energy

wind power 19
the energy produced by the wind

wind tunnel 11
a test area where vehicles are tested to check their aerodynamic properties and the effects of wind pressure

windmill 19
a device consisting of large sails that are driven by the wind to produce electrical power

wire 28
a thin piece of metal for conducting electrical current

wire transmission 28
the process and technology of sending signals along metal wire

wood pulp 27
wood reduced to a pulp for papermaking

woodchip 27
small pieces of wood which have been cut from logs in chippers before conversion into pulp in a digester

wool 30
the soft, curly hair of a sheep which is spun into yarn

word processing 5
a program which provides the user with the tools necessary to create, edit and format text

work in progress 2
goods that are not yet finished

work plan 21
a document which lists all planned activities, the date of completion, the resources that will be needed, and the people responsible for carrying out the activities

work station (workstation) 5
a desktop machine, usually considered more powerful than a personal computer

workforce 2
all the people who work in a particular company

workload 2
the amount of work that has to be done

workshop 1, 2
a part of a factory where an item is made or a product is assembled

World Wide Web 6
a collection of internet sites offering text, graphics, sound, and animation resources in an easy to use way

wrap 27
to cover with paper

wrapper 27
paper that is used to cover a product, e.g. a chocolate bar

wrapping paper 27
a type of paper that is used to cover products, e.g. presents. This type of paper is often attractively designed.

yarn 30
continuous strand of textile fibres

zero defects 8
the policy and practice of making products which meet specifications

zinc 22
a bluish-white metal used in alloys with other metals including brass, nickel silver, and commercial bronze; it is used extensively by the automotive, electrical, and hardware industries

Notes

Notes